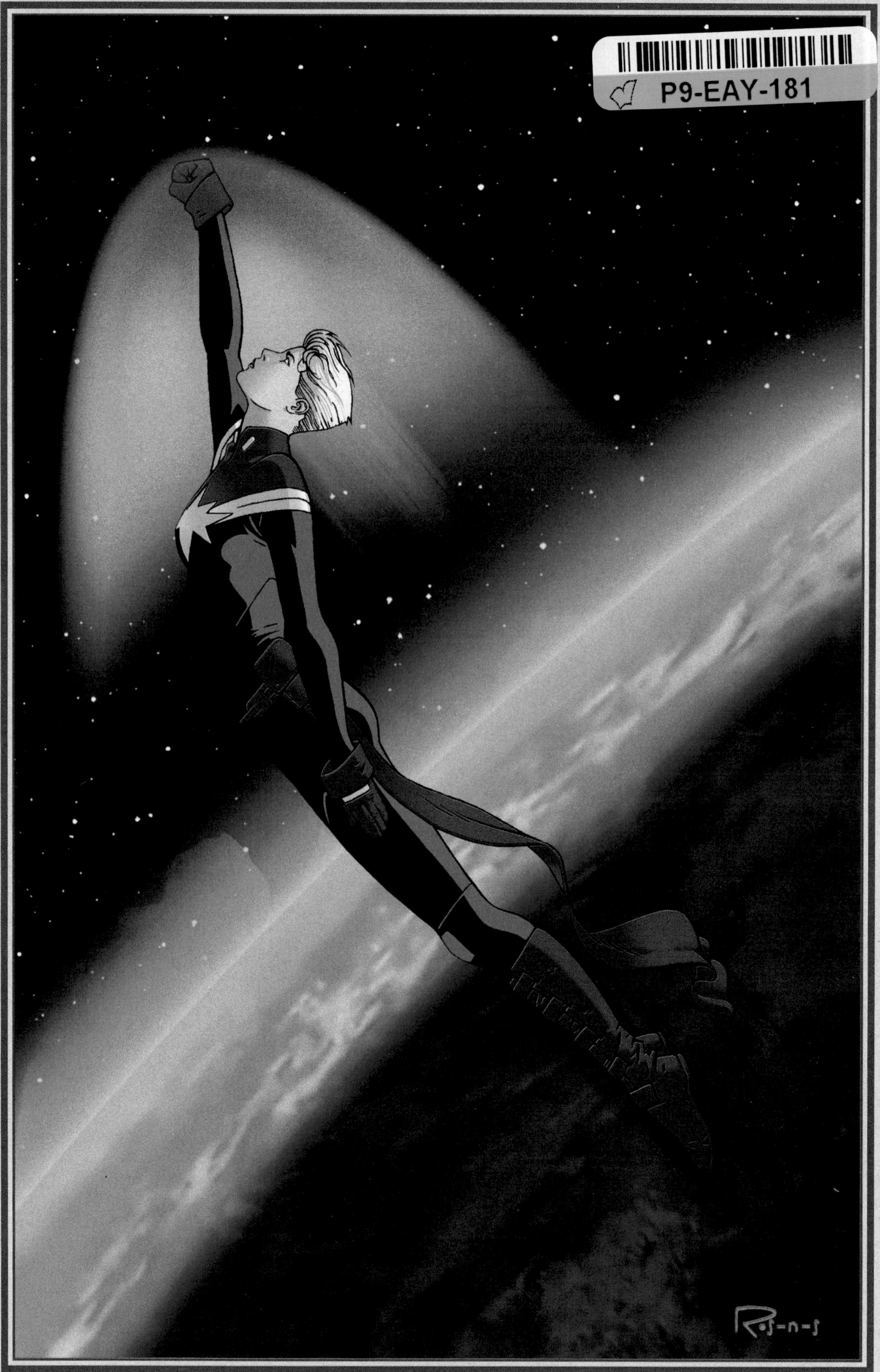

#0 VARIANT BY
RAMON ROSANAS

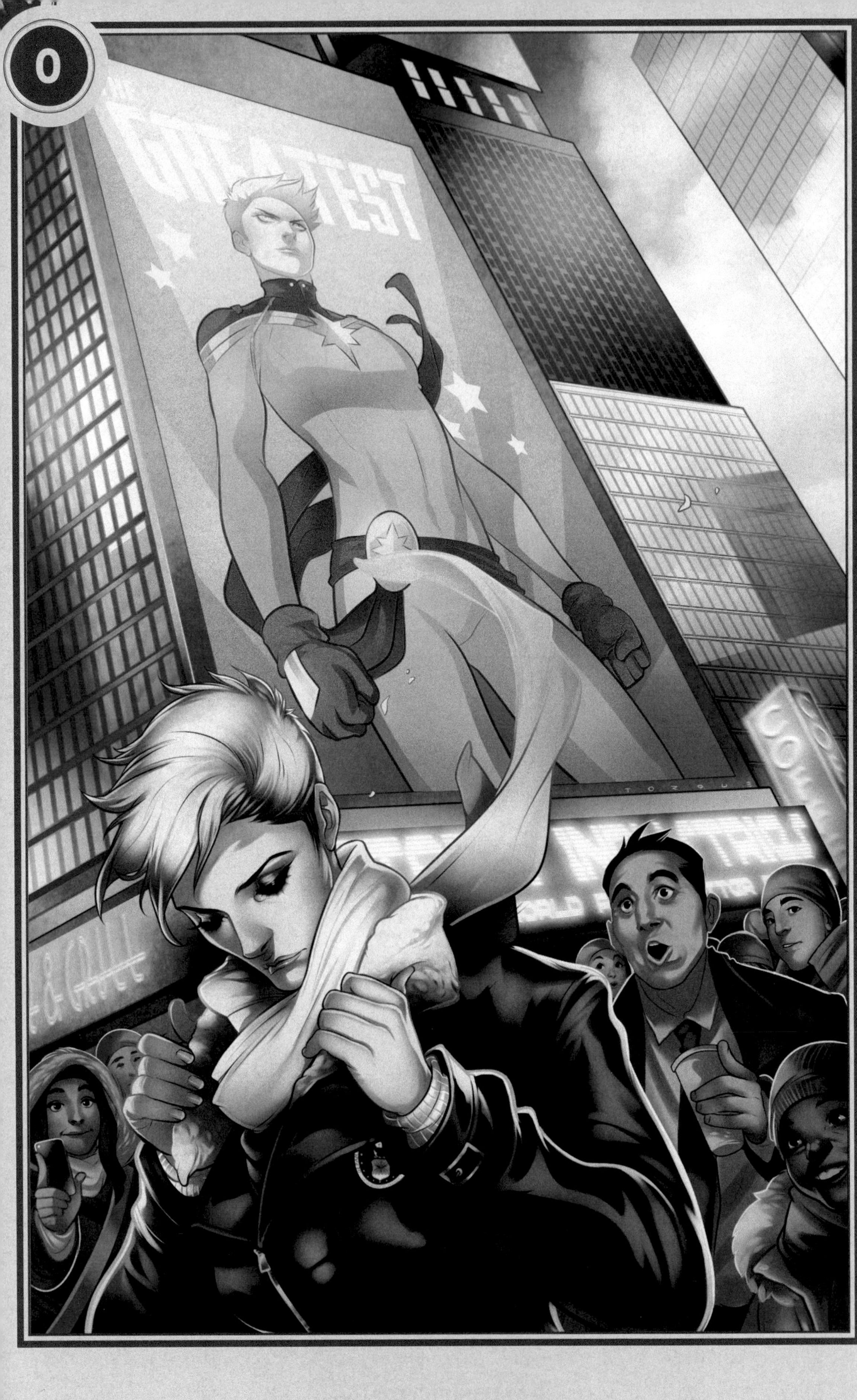

NO CHALLENGE IS TOO GREAT FOR THE FORMER AIR FORCE PILOT TURNED SUPER HERO. CAROL DANVERS HAS COME A LONG WAY SINCE AN INCIDENT WITH ALIEN TECHNOLOGY LEFT HER WITH AMAZING POWERS. PART KREE, PART HUMAN, CAROL IS NOW THE MOST POWERFUL AND POPULAR SUPER HERO ON EARTH.

THE MIGHTY
CAPTAIN MARVEL

ALIEN NATION

IR

WESTMINSTER PUBLIC LIBRARY

3 3020 01090 2418

Westminster Public Library
3705 W. 112th Avenue
Westminster, CO 80031
www.westminsterlibrary.org

DISCARD

THE MIGHTY CAPTAIN MARVEL
ALIEN NATION

CAROL KNEW THAT ACCEPTING THE POSITION AS COMMANDER OF ALPHA FLIGHT SPACE STATION WAS GOING TO TEST HER AS A SOLDIER AND AS A LEADER — HEADING UP AN INTERPLANETARY DEFENSE INITIATIVE IS NO SMALL TASK, AFTER ALL. THOUGH SHE FACED THE CHALLENGE HEAD-ON, A RECENT CONFLICT AMONG MEMBERS OF THE SUPER-HERO COMMUNITY PUSHED CAPTAIN MARVEL TO THE BRINK. AND WHILE THE WORLD STILL LOOKS TO HER AS A HERO, CAROL MUST FIND A WAY TO DEAL WITH THE LOSS OF HER ALLIES, FRIENDS AND LOVED ONES.

MARGARET STOHL
WRITER

ISSUE #0

EMILIO LAISO & RAMON ROSANAS
ARTISTS

RACHELLE ROSENBERG
COLOR ARTIST

ISSUES #1-3

RAMON ROSANAS
ARTIST

MICHAEL GARLAND
WITH **MARCIO MENYZ** (#3)
COLOR ARTISTS

ISSUE #4

BRENT SCHOONOVER, RO STEIN & TED BRANDT
ARTISTS

MICHAEL GARLAND
COLOR ARTIST

VC'S JOE CARAMAGNA
LETTERER

CHARLES BEACHAM
ASSISTANT EDITOR

ELIZABETH TORQUE
COVER ART

SANA AMANAT
EDITOR

COLLECTION EDITOR **JENNIFER GRÜNWALD** ASSISTANT EDITOR **CAITLIN O'CONNELL**
ASSOCIATE MANAGING EDITOR **KATERI WOODY** EDITOR, SPECIAL PROJECTS **MARK D. BEAZLEY**
VP PRODUCTION & SPECIAL PROJECTS **JEFF YOUNGQUIST** SVP PRINT, SALES & MARKETING **DAVID GABRIEL**
SPECIAL THANKS TO **ANTHONY GAMBINO**

EDITOR IN CHIEF **AXEL ALONSO** CHIEF CREATIVE OFFICER **JOE QUESADA**
PRESIDENT **DAN BUCKLEY** EXECUTIVE PRODUCER **ALAN FINE**

THE MIGHTY CAPTAIN MARVEL VOL. 1: ALIEN NATION. Contains material originally published in magazine form as THE MIGHTY CAPTAIN MARVEL #0-4. First printing 2017. ISBN# 978-1-302-90605-4. Published by MARVEL WORLDWIDE, INC., a subsidiary of MARVEL ENTERTAINMENT, LLC. OFFICE OF PUBLICATION: 135 West 50th Street, New York, NY 10020. Copyright © 2017 MARVEL No similarity between any of the names, characters, persons, and/or institutions in this magazine with those of any living or dead person or institution is intended, and any such similarity which may exist is purely coincidental. **Printed in the U.S.A.** DAN BUCKLEY, President, Marvel Entertainment; JOE QUESADA, Chief Creative Officer; TOM BREVOORT, SVP of Publishing; DAVID BOGART, SVP of Business Affairs & Operations, Publishing & Partnership; C.B. CEBULSKI, VP of Brand Management & Development, Asia; DAVID GABRIEL, SVP of Sales & Marketing, Publishing; JEFF YOUNGQUIST, VP of Production & Special Projects; DAN CARR, Executive Director of Publishing Technology; ALEX MORALES, Director of Publishing Operations; SUSAN CRESPI, Production Manager; STAN LEE, Chairman Emeritus. For information regarding advertising in Marvel Comics or on Marvel.com, please contact Vit DeBellis, Integrated Sales Manager, at vdebellis@marvel.com. For Marvel subscription inquiries, please call 888-511-5480. **Manufactured between 6/30/2017 and 7/31/2017 by QUAD/GRAPHICS WASECA, WASECA, MN, USA.**

10 9 8 7 6 5 4 3 2 1

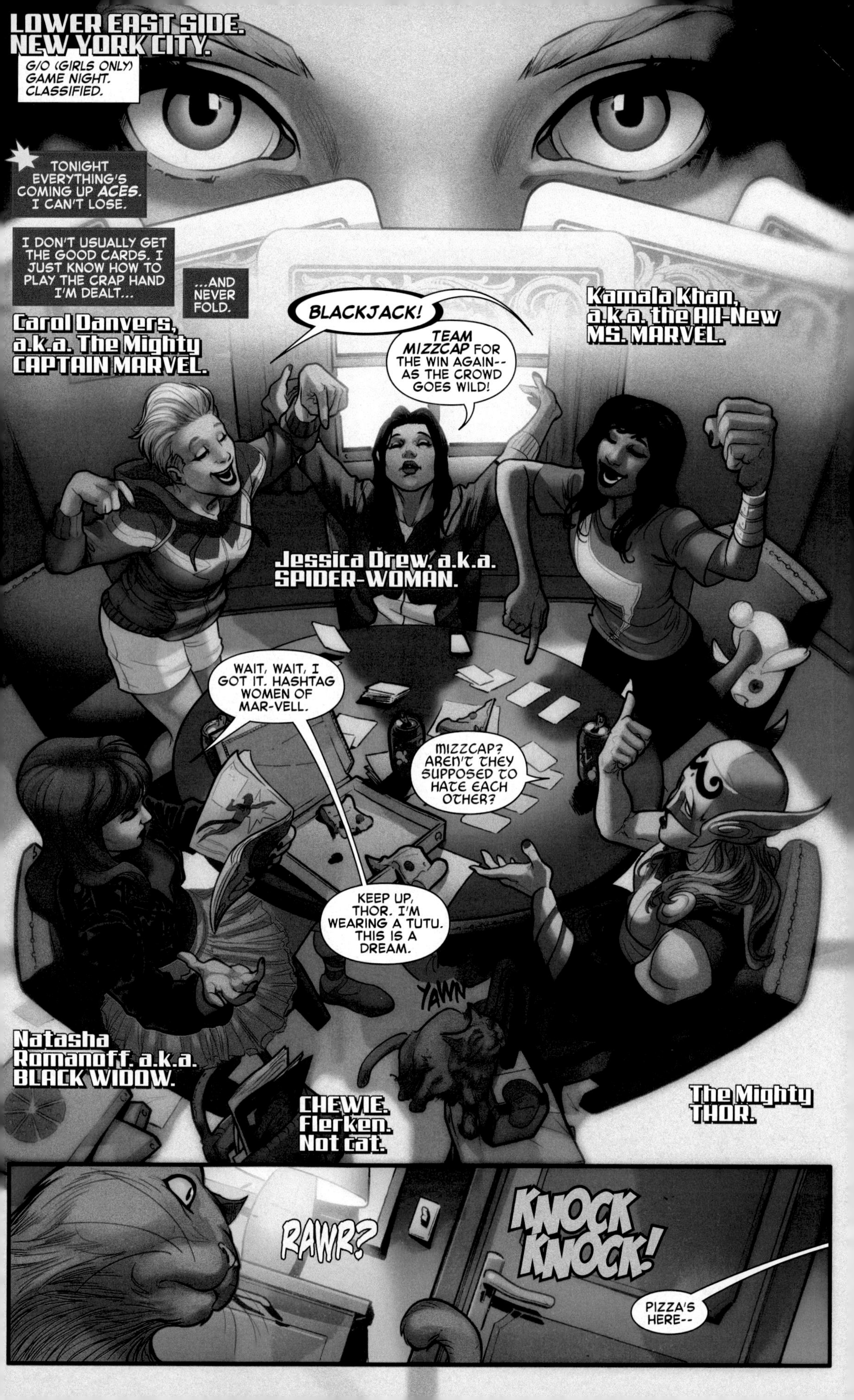
LOWER EAST SIDE. NEW YORK CITY.
G/O (GIRLS ONLY) GAME NIGHT. CLASSIFIED.
TONIGHT EVERYTHING'S COMING UP ACES. I CAN'T LOSE.
I DON'T USUALLY GET THE GOOD CARDS. I JUST KNOW HOW TO PLAY THE CRAP HAND I'M DEALT...
...AND NEVER FOLD.
Carol Danvers, a.k.a. The Mighty CAPTAIN MARVEL.
BLACKJACK!
TEAM MIZZCAP FOR THE WIN AGAIN-- AS THE CROWD GOES WILD!
Kamala Khan, a.k.a. the All-New MS. MARVEL.
Jessica Drew, a.k.a. SPIDER-WOMAN.
WAIT, WAIT, I GOT IT. HASHTAG WOMEN OF MAR-VELL.
MIZZCAP? AREN'T THEY SUPPOSED TO HATE EACH OTHER?
KEEP UP, THOR. I'M WEARING A TUTU. THIS IS A DREAM.
YAWN
Natasha Romanoff, a.k.a. BLACK WIDOW.
CHEWIE. Flerken. Not cat.
The Mighty THOR.
RAWR?
KNOCK KNOCK!
PIZZA'S HERE--

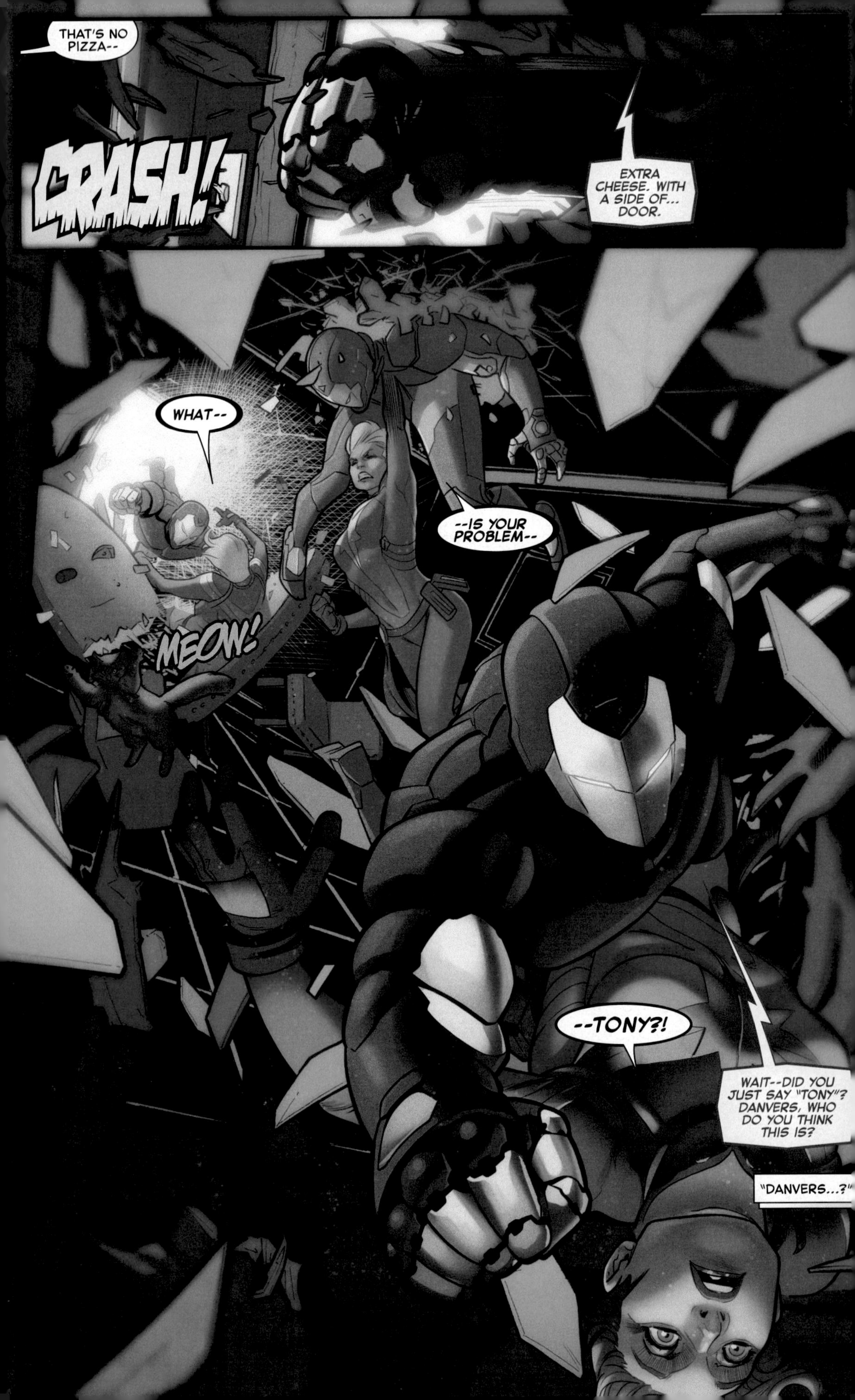
THAT'S NO PIZZA--
CRASH!
EXTRA CHEESE. WITH A SIDE OF... DOOR.
WHAT--
--IS YOUR PROBLEM--
MEOW!
--TONY?!
WAIT--DID YOU JUST SAY "TONY"? DANVERS, WHO DO YOU THINK THIS IS?
"DANVERS...?"

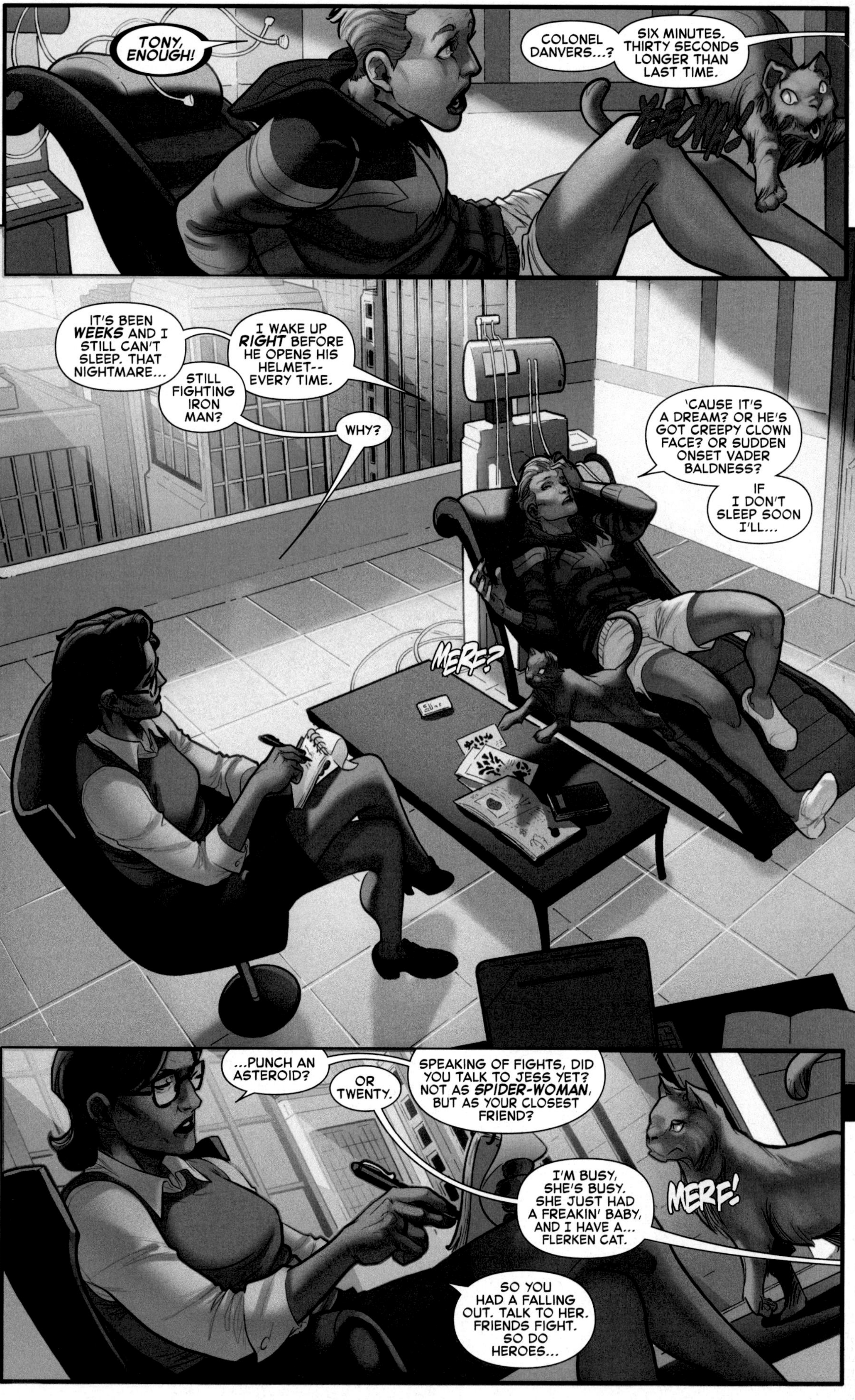
TONY, ENOUGH!
COLONEL DANVERS...?
SIX MINUTES. THIRTY SECONDS LONGER THAN LAST TIME.
YEEOWW!
IT'S BEEN WEEKS AND I STILL CAN'T SLEEP. THAT NIGHTMARE...
I WAKE UP RIGHT BEFORE HE OPENS HIS HELMET-- EVERY TIME.
STILL FIGHTING IRON MAN?
WHY?
'CAUSE IT'S A DREAM? OR HE'S GOT CREEPY CLOWN FACE? OR SUDDEN ONSET VADER BALDNESS?
IF I DON'T SLEEP SOON I'LL...
MERF?
...PUNCH AN ASTEROID?
OR TWENTY.
SPEAKING OF FIGHTS, DID YOU TALK TO JESS YET? NOT AS SPIDER-WOMAN, BUT AS YOUR CLOSEST FRIEND?
I'M BUSY, SHE'S BUSY. SHE JUST HAD A FREAKIN' BABY, AND I HAVE A... FLERKEN CAT.
MERF!
SO YOU HAD A FALLING OUT. TALK TO HER. FRIENDS FIGHT. SO DO HEROES...

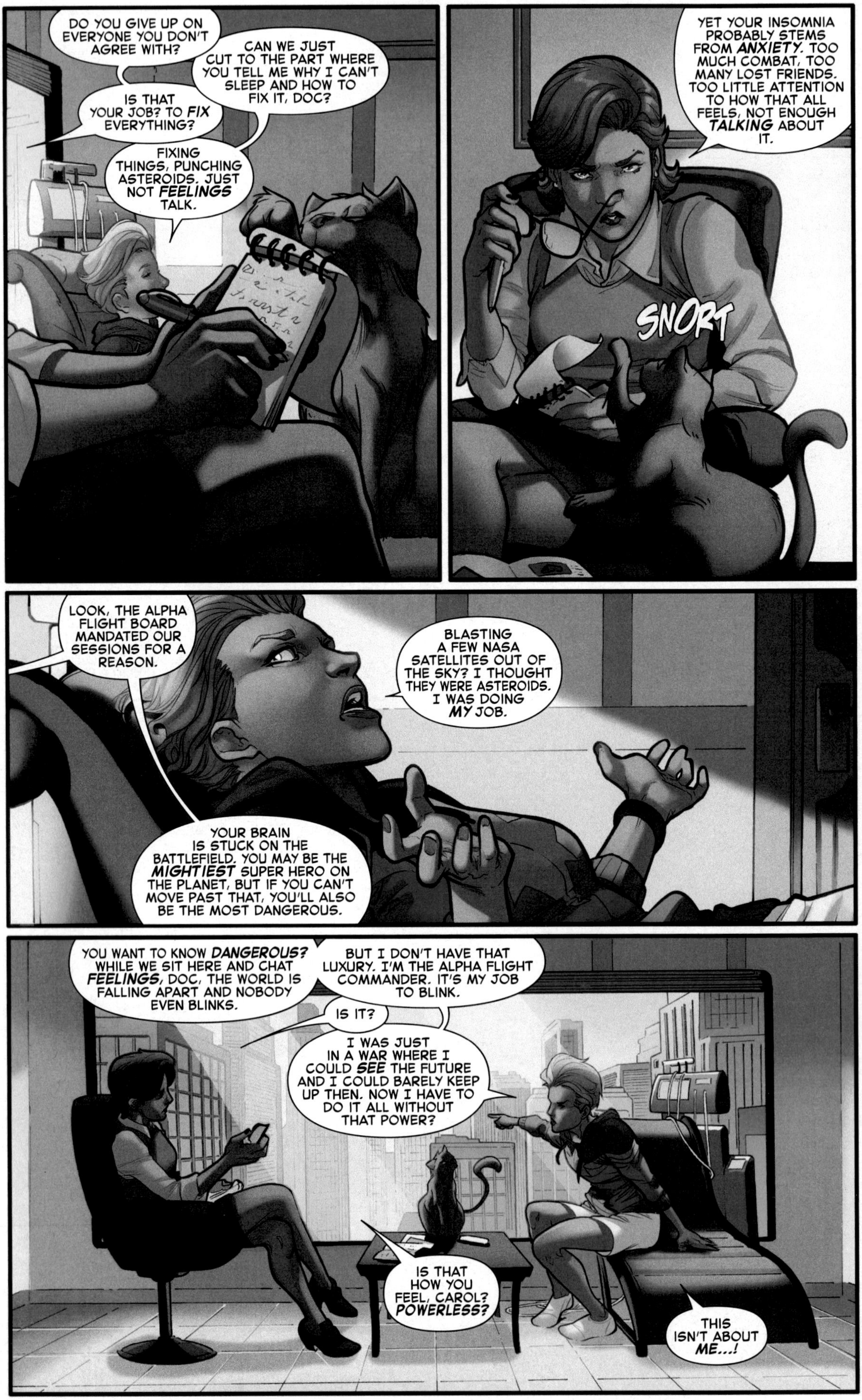
DO YOU GIVE UP ON EVERYONE YOU DON'T AGREE WITH?
CAN WE JUST CUT TO THE PART WHERE YOU TELL ME WHY I CAN'T SLEEP AND HOW TO FIX IT, DOC?
IS THAT YOUR JOB? TO *FIX* EVERYTHING?
FIXING THINGS, PUNCHING ASTEROIDS. JUST NOT *FEELINGS* TALK.
SNORT
YET YOUR INSOMNIA PROBABLY STEMS FROM *ANXIETY.* TOO MUCH COMBAT, TOO MANY LOST FRIENDS. TOO LITTLE ATTENTION TO HOW THAT ALL FEELS, NOT ENOUGH *TALKING* ABOUT IT.
LOOK, THE ALPHA FLIGHT BOARD MANDATED OUR SESSIONS FOR A REASON.
BLASTING A FEW NASA SATELLITES OUT OF THE SKY? I THOUGHT THEY WERE ASTEROIDS. I WAS DOING *MY* JOB.
YOUR BRAIN IS STUCK ON THE BATTLEFIELD. YOU MAY BE THE *MIGHTIEST* SUPER HERO ON THE PLANET, BUT IF YOU CAN'T MOVE PAST THAT, YOU'LL ALSO BE THE MOST DANGEROUS.
YOU WANT TO KNOW *DANGEROUS?* WHILE WE SIT HERE AND CHAT *FEELINGS,* DOC, THE WORLD IS FALLING APART AND NOBODY EVEN BLINKS.
BUT I DON'T HAVE THAT LUXURY. I'M THE ALPHA FLIGHT COMMANDER. IT'S MY JOB TO BLINK.
IS IT?
I WAS JUST IN A WAR WHERE I COULD *SEE* THE FUTURE AND I COULD BARELY KEEP UP THEN. NOW I HAVE TO DO IT ALL WITHOUT THAT POWER?
IS THAT HOW YOU FEEL, CAROL? *POWERLESS?*
THIS ISN'T ABOUT *ME...!*

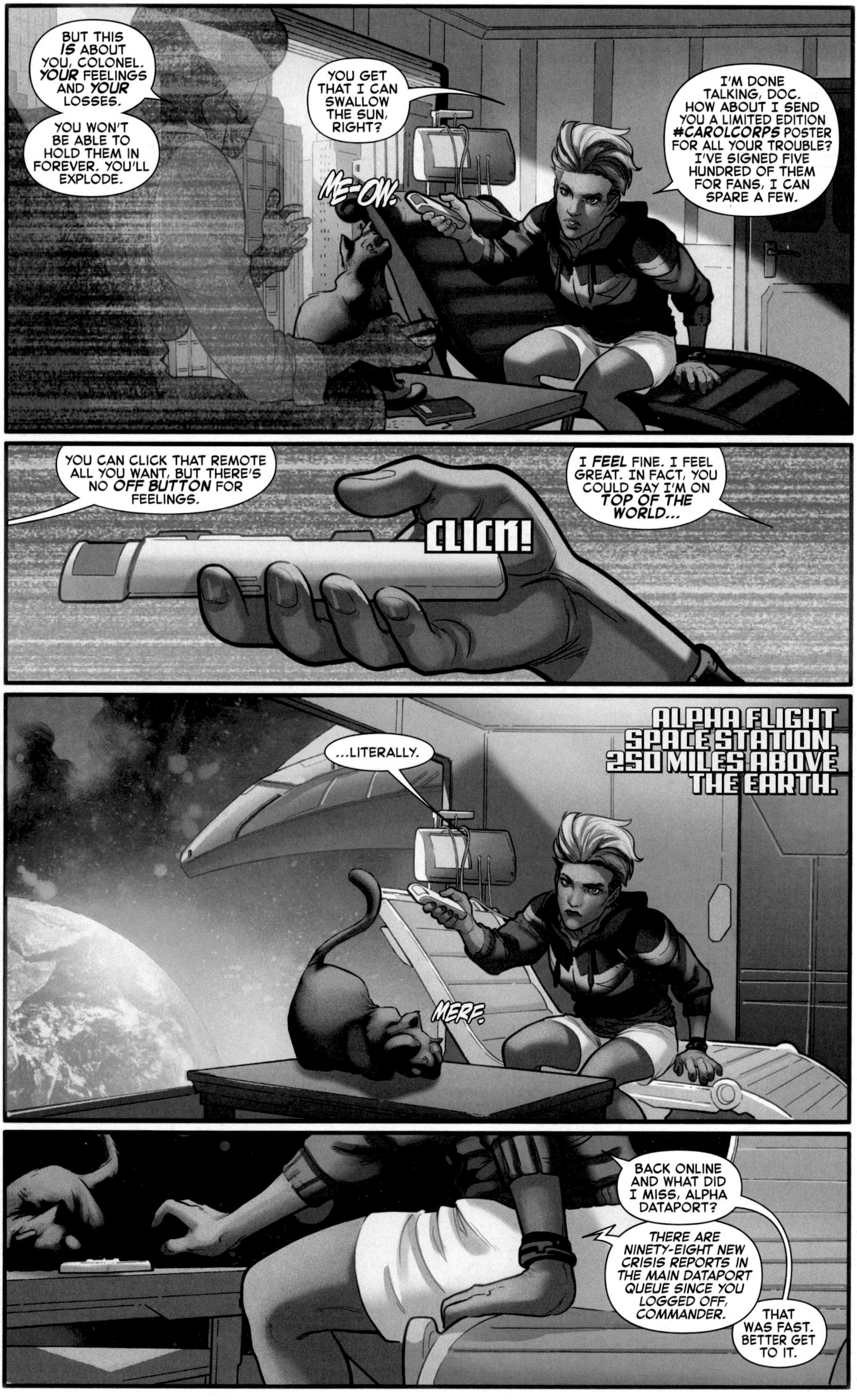
BUT THIS IS ABOUT YOU, COLONEL. YOUR FEELINGS AND YOUR LOSSES.
YOU WON'T BE ABLE TO HOLD THEM IN FOREVER. YOU'LL EXPLODE.
YOU GET THAT I CAN SWALLOW THE SUN, RIGHT?
ME-OW.
I'M DONE TALKING, DOC. HOW ABOUT I SEND YOU A LIMITED EDITION #CAROLCORPS POSTER FOR ALL YOUR TROUBLE? I'VE SIGNED FIVE HUNDRED OF THEM FOR FANS, I CAN SPARE A FEW.
YOU CAN CLICK THAT REMOTE ALL YOU WANT, BUT THERE'S NO OFF BUTTON FOR FEELINGS.
I FEEL FINE. I FEEL GREAT. IN FACT, YOU COULD SAY I'M ON TOP OF THE WORLD...
CLICK!
ALPHA FLIGHT SPACE STATION. 250 MILES ABOVE THE EARTH.
...LITERALLY.
MERF.
BACK ONLINE AND WHAT DID I MISS, ALPHA DATAPORT?
THERE ARE NINETY-EIGHT NEW CRISIS REPORTS IN THE MAIN DATAPORT QUEUE SINCE YOU LOGGED OFF, COMMANDER.
THAT WAS FAST. BETTER GET TO IT.

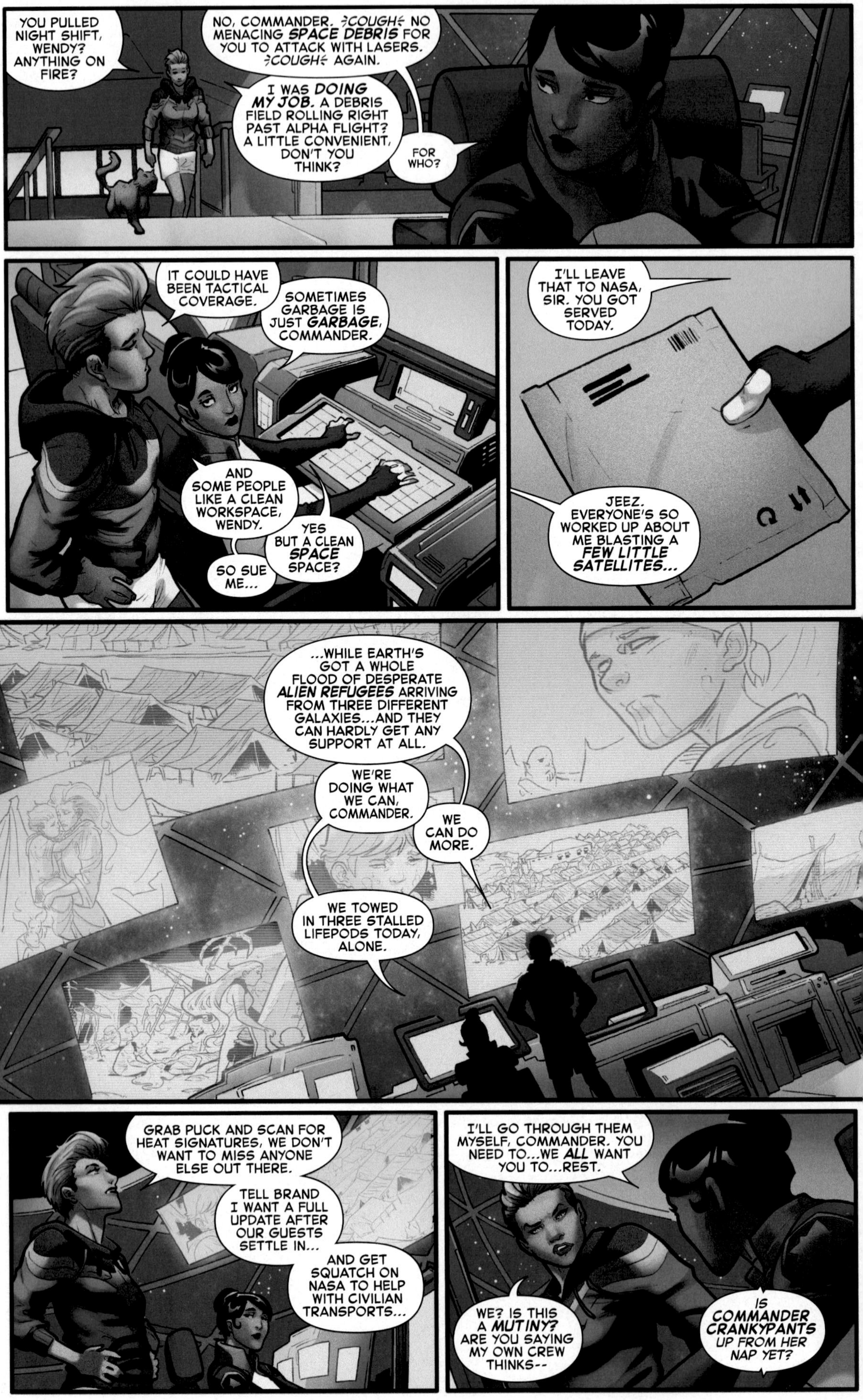
YOU PULLED NIGHT SHIFT, WENDY? ANYTHING ON FIRE?
NO, COMMANDER. *COUGH* NO MENACING SPACE DEBRIS FOR YOU TO ATTACK WITH LASERS. *COUGH* AGAIN.
I WAS DOING MY JOB. A DEBRIS FIELD ROLLING RIGHT PAST ALPHA FLIGHT? A LITTLE CONVENIENT, DON'T YOU THINK?
FOR WHO?
IT COULD HAVE BEEN TACTICAL COVERAGE.
SOMETIMES GARBAGE IS JUST GARBAGE, COMMANDER.
AND SOME PEOPLE LIKE A CLEAN WORKSPACE, WENDY.
YES BUT A CLEAN SPACE SPACE?
SO SUE ME...
I'LL LEAVE THAT TO NASA, SIR. YOU GOT SERVED TODAY.
JEEZ. EVERYONE'S SO WORKED UP ABOUT ME BLASTING A FEW LITTLE SATELLITES...
...WHILE EARTH'S GOT A WHOLE FLOOD OF DESPERATE ALIEN REFUGEES ARRIVING FROM THREE DIFFERENT GALAXIES...AND THEY CAN HARDLY GET ANY SUPPORT AT ALL.
WE'RE DOING WHAT WE CAN, COMMANDER.
WE CAN DO MORE.
WE TOWED IN THREE STALLED LIFEPODS TODAY, ALONE.
GRAB PUCK AND SCAN FOR HEAT SIGNATURES, WE DON'T WANT TO MISS ANYONE ELSE OUT THERE.
TELL BRAND I WANT A FULL UPDATE AFTER OUR GUESTS SETTLE IN...
AND GET SQUATCH ON NASA TO HELP WITH CIVILIAN TRANSPORTS...
I'LL GO THROUGH THEM MYSELF, COMMANDER. YOU NEED TO...WE ALL WANT YOU TO...REST.
WE? IS THIS A MUTINY? ARE YOU SAYING MY OWN CREW THINKS--
IS COMMANDER CRANKYPANTS UP FROM HER NAP YET?

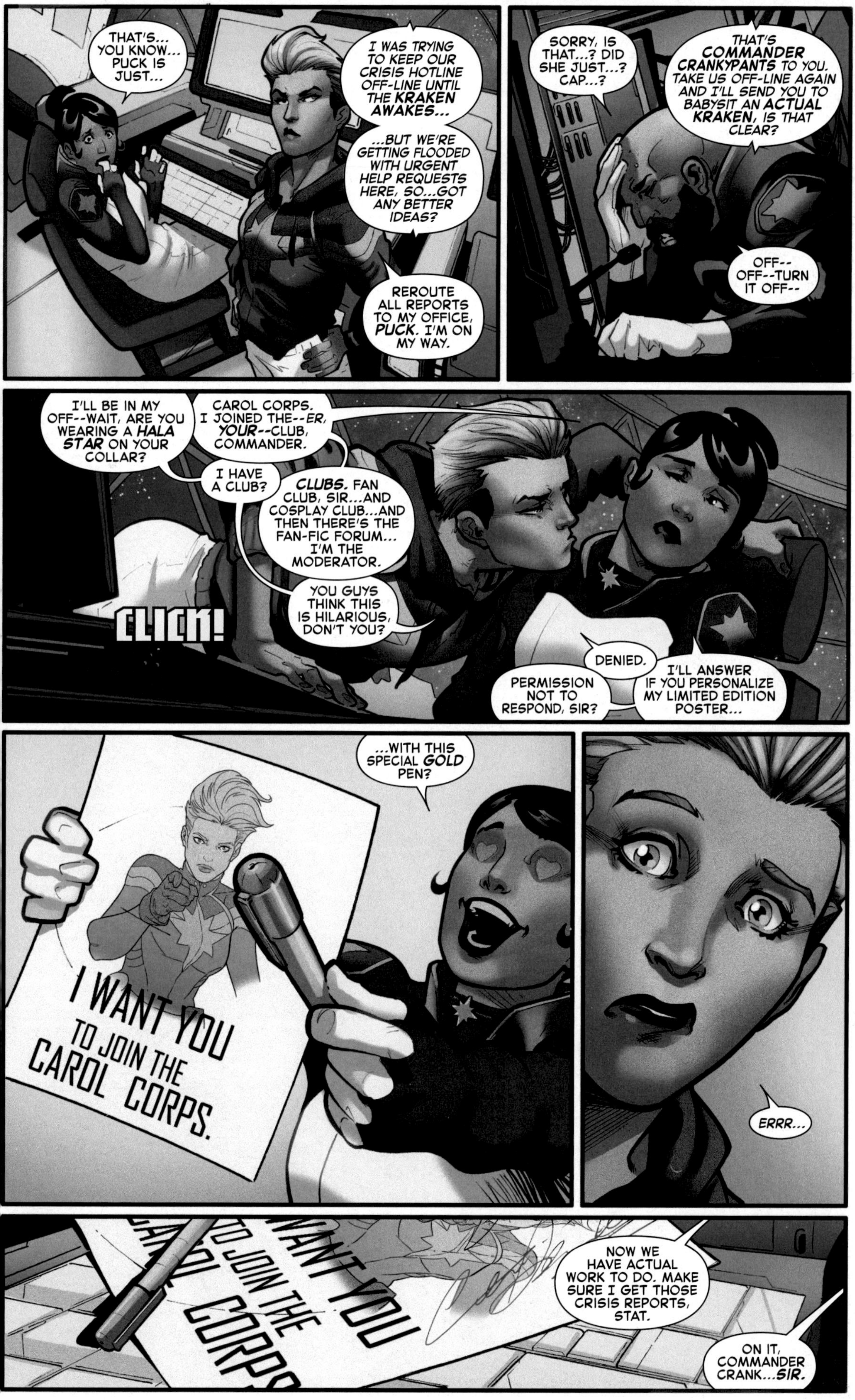
THAT'S... YOU KNOW... PUCK IS JUST...
I WAS TRYING TO KEEP OUR CRISIS HOTLINE OFF-LINE UNTIL THE KRAKEN AWAKES...
...BUT WE'RE GETTING FLOODED WITH URGENT HELP REQUESTS HERE, SO...GOT ANY BETTER IDEAS?
REROUTE ALL REPORTS TO MY OFFICE, PUCK. I'M ON MY WAY.
SORRY, IS THAT...? DID SHE JUST...? CAP...?
THAT'S COMMANDER CRANKYPANTS TO YOU. TAKE US OFF-LINE AGAIN AND I'LL SEND YOU TO BABYSIT AN ACTUAL KRAKEN, IS THAT CLEAR?
OFF-- OFF--TURN IT OFF--
I'LL BE IN MY OFF--WAIT, ARE YOU WEARING A HALA STAR ON YOUR COLLAR?
CAROL CORPS. I JOINED THE--ER, YOUR--CLUB, COMMANDER.
I HAVE A CLUB?
CLUBS. FAN CLUB, SIR...AND COSPLAY CLUB...AND THEN THERE'S THE FAN-FIC FORUM... I'M THE MODERATOR.
YOU GUYS THINK THIS IS HILARIOUS, DON'T YOU?
CLICK!
PERMISSION NOT TO RESPOND, SIR?
DENIED.
I'LL ANSWER IF YOU PERSONALIZE MY LIMITED EDITION POSTER...
...WITH THIS SPECIAL GOLD PEN?
I WANT YOU TO JOIN THE CAROL CORPS.
ERRR...
NOW WE HAVE ACTUAL WORK TO DO. MAKE SURE I GET THOSE CRISIS REPORTS, STAT.
ON IT, COMMANDER CRANK...SIR.

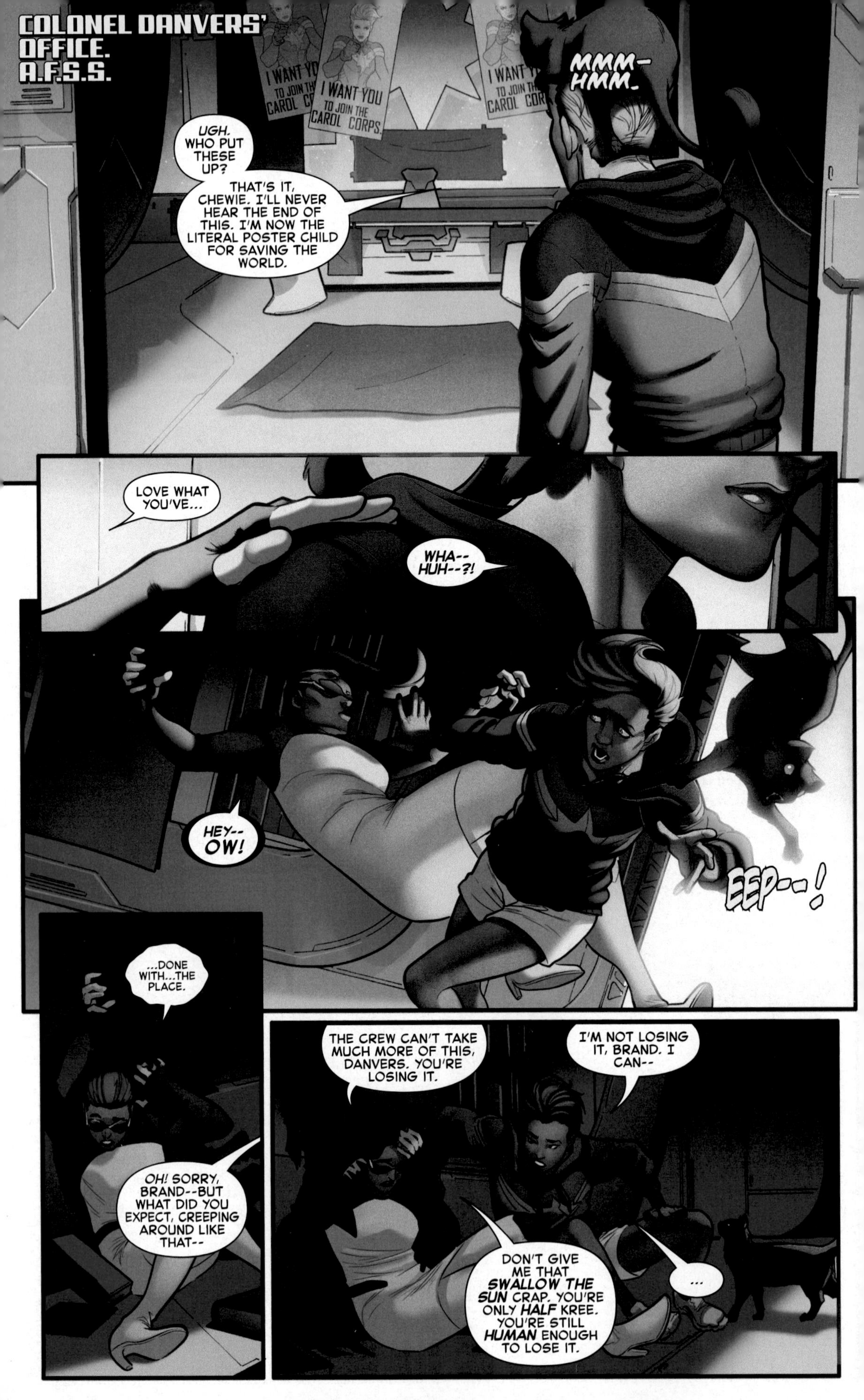
COLONEL DANVERS' OFFICE. A.F.S.S.
I WANT YOU TO JOIN THE CAROL CORPS
MMM-HMM.
UGH. WHO PUT THESE UP?
THAT'S IT, CHEWIE. I'LL NEVER HEAR THE END OF THIS. I'M NOW THE LITERAL POSTER CHILD FOR SAVING THE WORLD.
LOVE WHAT YOU'VE...
WHA--HUH--?!
HEY--OW!
EEP--!
...DONE WITH...THE PLACE.
OH! SORRY, BRAND--BUT WHAT DID YOU EXPECT, CREEPING AROUND LIKE THAT--
THE CREW CAN'T TAKE MUCH MORE OF THIS, DANVERS. YOU'RE LOSING IT.
I'M NOT LOSING IT, BRAND. I CAN--
DON'T GIVE ME THAT SWALLOW THE SUN CRAP. YOU'RE ONLY HALF KREE. YOU'RE STILL HUMAN ENOUGH TO LOSE IT.
...

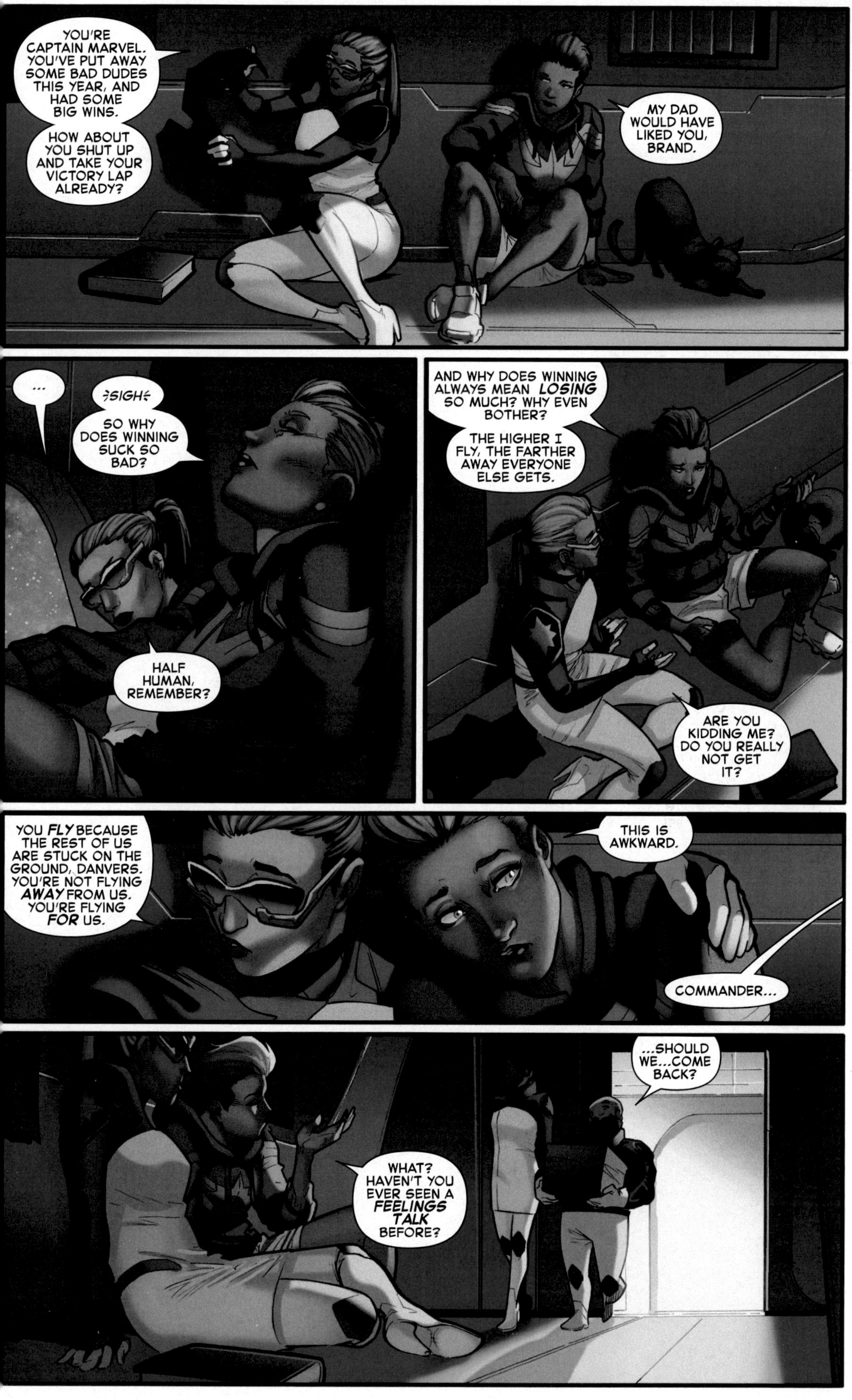
YOU'RE CAPTAIN MARVEL. YOU'VE PUT AWAY SOME BAD DUDES THIS YEAR, AND HAD SOME BIG WINS.
HOW ABOUT YOU SHUT UP AND TAKE YOUR VICTORY LAP ALREADY?
MY DAD WOULD HAVE LIKED YOU, BRAND.
...
⁂SIGH⁂
SO WHY DOES WINNING SUCK SO BAD?
HALF HUMAN, REMEMBER?
AND WHY DOES WINNING ALWAYS MEAN LOSING SO MUCH? WHY EVEN BOTHER?
THE HIGHER I FLY, THE FARTHER AWAY EVERYONE ELSE GETS.
ARE YOU KIDDING ME? DO YOU REALLY NOT GET IT?
YOU FLY BECAUSE THE REST OF US ARE STUCK ON THE GROUND, DANVERS. YOU'RE NOT FLYING AWAY FROM US. YOU'RE FLYING FOR US.
THIS IS AWKWARD.
COMMANDER...
...SHOULD WE...COME BACK?
WHAT? HAVEN'T YOU EVER SEEN A FEELINGS TALK BEFORE?

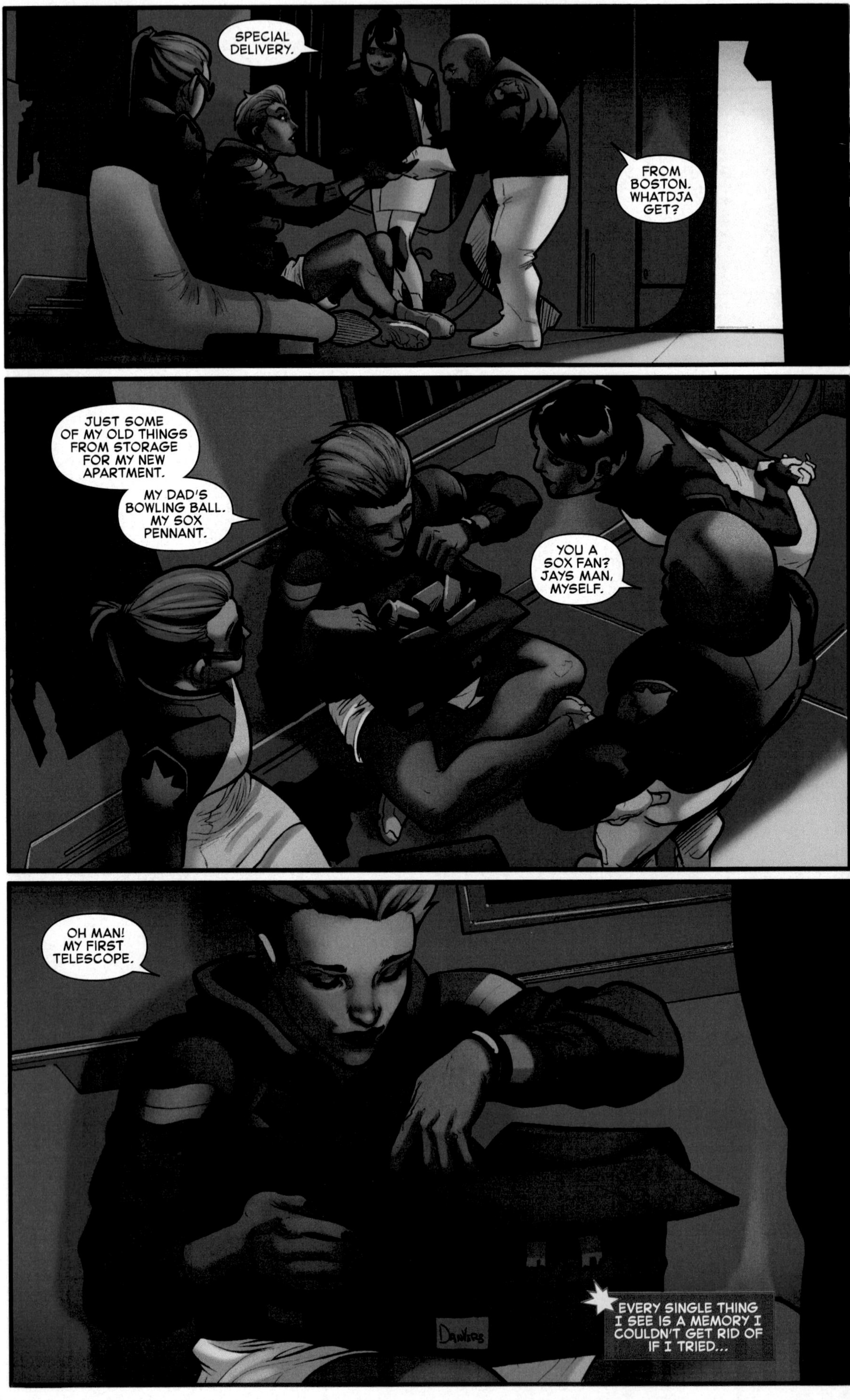
SPECIAL DELIVERY.
FROM BOSTON. WHATDJA GET?
JUST SOME OF MY OLD THINGS FROM STORAGE FOR MY NEW APARTMENT.
MY DAD'S BOWLING BALL. MY SOX PENNANT.
YOU A SOX FAN? JAYS MAN, MYSELF.
OH MAN! MY FIRST TELESCOPE.
EVERY SINGLE THING I SEE IS A MEMORY I COULDN'T GET RID OF IF I TRIED...

BOSTON'S BACK BAY.

BY FIRST GRADE I KNEW THE NAMES OF THE STARS BETTER THAN THE SOX'S OUTFIELD.

SACRILEGE.

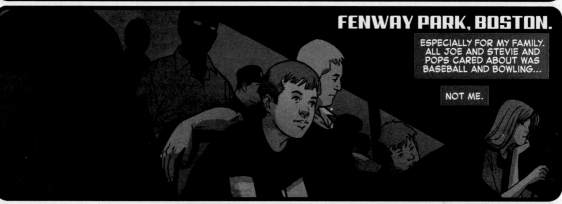

FENWAY PARK, BOSTON.

ESPECIALLY FOR MY FAMILY. ALL JOE AND STEVIE AND POPS CARED ABOUT WAS BASEBALL AND BOWLING...

NOT ME.

SOUTH BOSTON CANDLEPIN.

THE LAST TIME WE ALL WENT BOWLING WAS THE WORST NIGHT OF MY LIFE.

I SHOULD HAVE GOTTEN THAT STRIKE, POPS. BOWLING IS JUST PHYSICS--AND I GOT AN "A" IN PHYSICS.

GAME'S OVER, BEAN. BETTER HIT THE SKEE-BALL BEFORE STEVIE AND JOE PLAY YOUR DIME.

I'M STUDYING ASTROPHYSICS WHEN I GET TO U MASS. THAT'S THE BEST MAJOR FOR ASTRONAUTS.

HOW DO YOU KNOW?

I CALLED.

WHO?

NASA.

AH, BEAN...

SINCE MY TOUR OF DUTY ENDED, THINGS HAVE BEEN *TIGHT*. COLLEGE TUITION...

I'LL GET A JOB PART-TIME.

YOU START IN GIFT WRAPPING AT FILENE'S ON TUESDAY. FULL-TIME.

WHAT?! WAIT, ARE YOU *JOKING*--?

I CAN PAY *ONE* TUITION, BEAN. FOR STEVIE. JOE HAS MY HANDS, HE CAN FRAME HOUSES WITH ME.

I'LL NEVER FORGET THE GUT PUNCH OF THOSE WORDS...

THAT'S NOT FAIR! WHAT ABOUT ME? WHAT AM I SUPPOSED TO DO?

FIND YOURSELF A NICE BOY-- HECK, A *NICE ASTRONAUT*-- AND SETTLE DOWN.

POPS, *NO!* THERE'S *NO WAY*--

OF COURSE THERE'S A WAY; PUT ON A SKIRT ONCE IN A WHILE, COMB THAT CRAZY HAIR. ALL THAT *GIRL STUFF*...

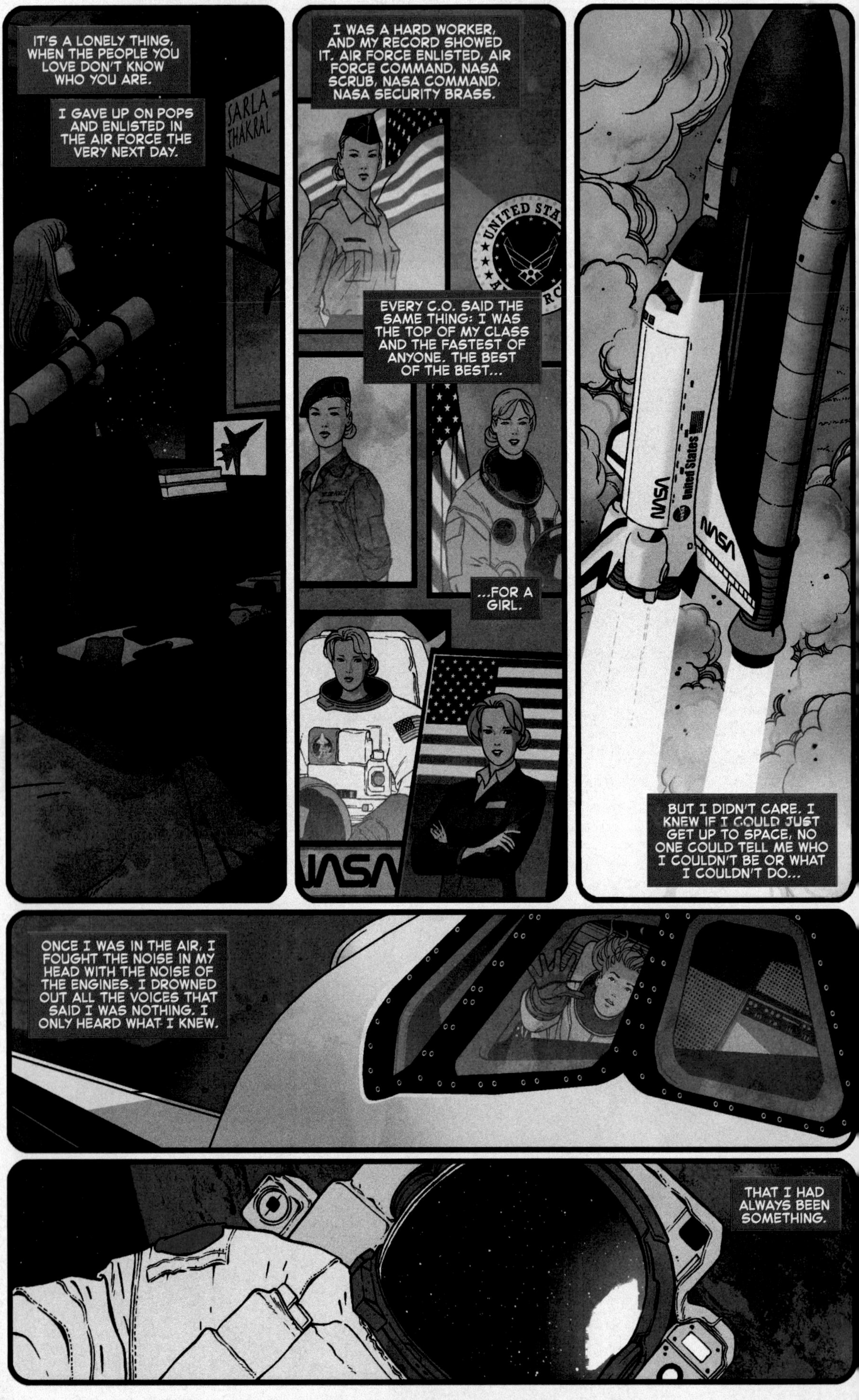
IT'S A LONELY THING, WHEN THE PEOPLE YOU LOVE DON'T KNOW WHO YOU ARE.
I GAVE UP ON POPS AND ENLISTED IN THE AIR FORCE THE VERY NEXT DAY.
SARLA THAKRAL
I WAS A HARD WORKER, AND MY RECORD SHOWED IT. AIR FORCE ENLISTED, AIR FORCE COMMAND, NASA SCRUB, NASA COMMAND, NASA SECURITY BRASS.
EVERY C.O. SAID THE SAME THING: I WAS THE TOP OF MY CLASS AND THE FASTEST OF ANYONE. THE BEST OF THE BEST...
...FOR A GIRL.
NASA
NASA
United States
NASA
BUT I DIDN'T CARE. I KNEW IF I COULD JUST GET UP TO SPACE, NO ONE COULD TELL ME WHO I COULDN'T BE OR WHAT I COULDN'T DO...
ONCE I WAS IN THE AIR, I FOUGHT THE NOISE IN MY HEAD WITH THE NOISE OF THE ENGINES. I DROWNED OUT ALL THE VOICES THAT SAID I WAS NOTHING. I ONLY HEARD WHAT I KNEW.
THAT I HAD ALWAYS BEEN SOMETHING.

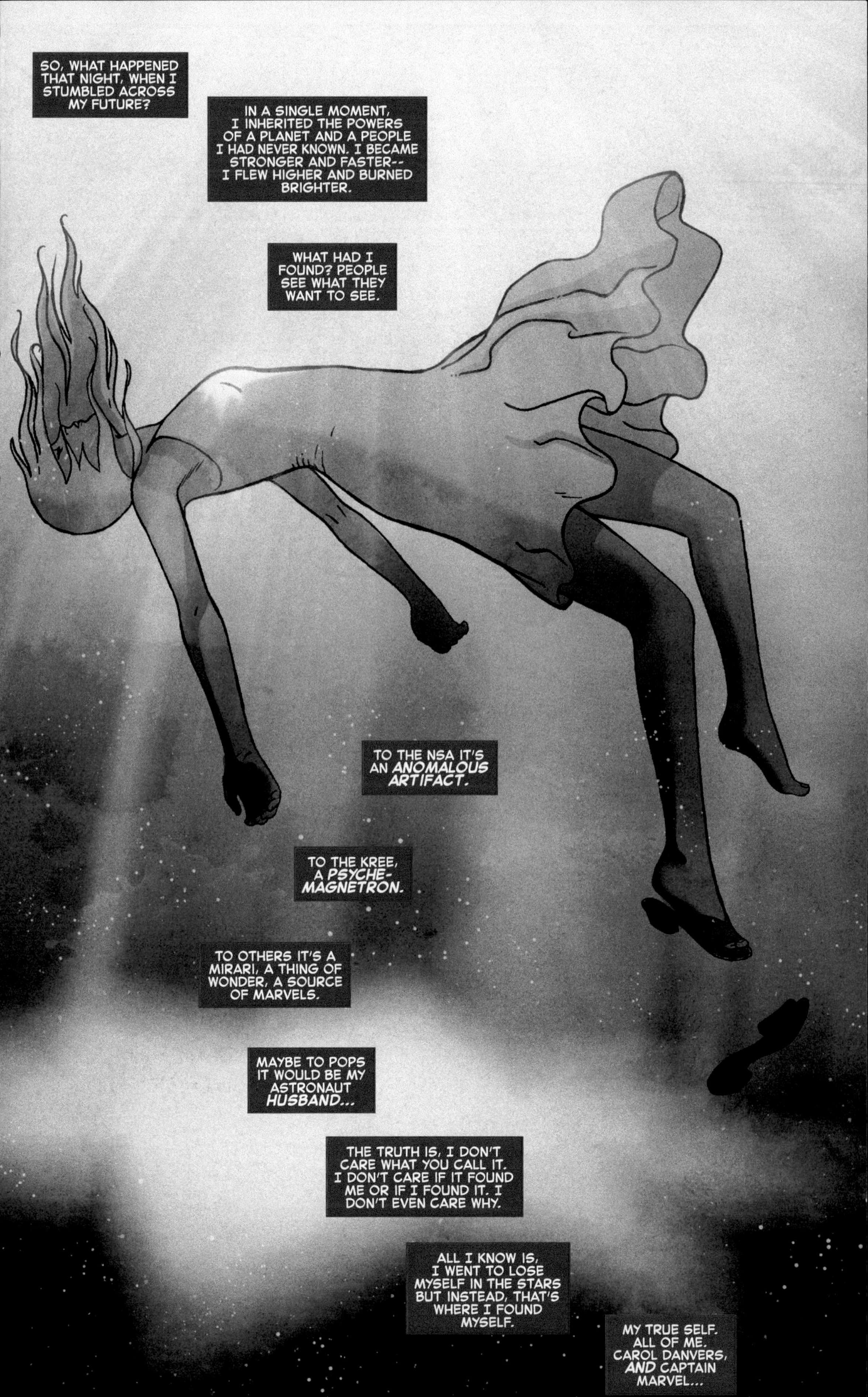
SO, WHAT HAPPENED THAT NIGHT, WHEN I STUMBLED ACROSS MY FUTURE?
IN A SINGLE MOMENT, I INHERITED THE POWERS OF A PLANET AND A PEOPLE I HAD NEVER KNOWN. I BECAME STRONGER AND FASTER-- I FLEW HIGHER AND BURNED BRIGHTER.
WHAT HAD I FOUND? PEOPLE SEE WHAT THEY WANT TO SEE.
TO THE NSA IT'S AN *ANOMALOUS ARTIFACT*.
TO THE KREE, A *PSYCHE-MAGNETRON*.
TO OTHERS IT'S A MIRARI, A THING OF WONDER, A SOURCE OF MARVELS.
MAYBE TO POPS IT WOULD BE MY ASTRONAUT *HUSBAND*...
THE TRUTH IS, I DON'T CARE WHAT YOU CALL IT. I DON'T CARE IF IT FOUND ME OR IF I FOUND IT. I DON'T EVEN CARE WHY.
ALL I KNOW IS, I WENT TO LOSE MYSELF IN THE STARS BUT INSTEAD, THAT'S WHERE I FOUND MYSELF.
MY TRUE SELF. ALL OF ME. CAROL DANVERS, *AND* CAPTAIN MARVEL...

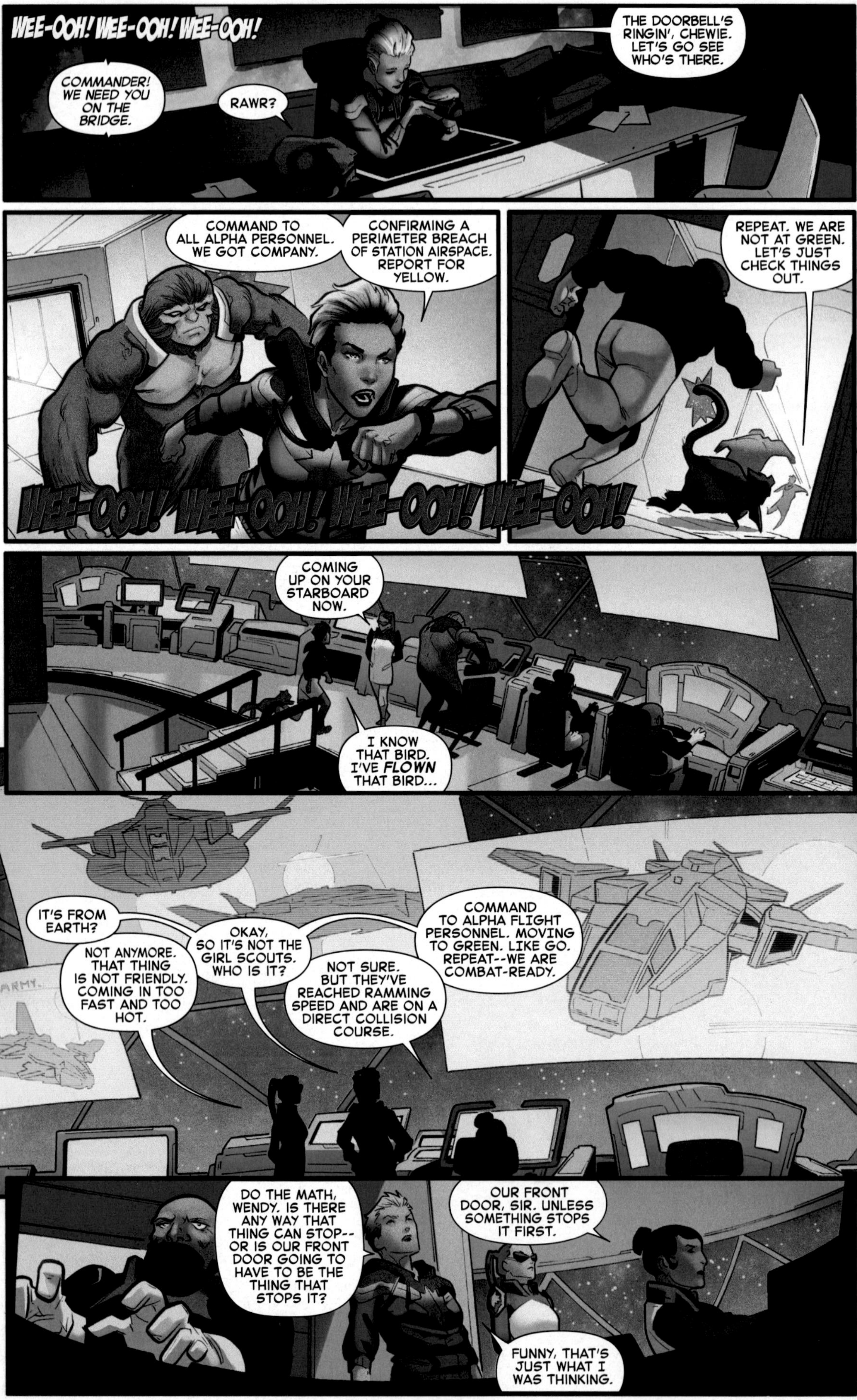
WEE-OOH! WEE-OOH! WEE-OOH!
COMMANDER! WE NEED YOU ON THE BRIDGE.
RAWR?
THE DOORBELL'S RINGIN', CHEWIE. LET'S GO SEE WHO'S THERE.
COMMAND TO ALL ALPHA PERSONNEL. WE GOT COMPANY.
CONFIRMING A PERIMETER BREACH OF STATION AIRSPACE. REPORT FOR YELLOW.
WEE-OOH! WEE-OOH! WEE-OOH! WEE-OOH!
REPEAT. WE ARE NOT AT GREEN. LET'S JUST CHECK THINGS OUT.
COMING UP ON YOUR STARBOARD NOW.
I KNOW THAT BIRD. I'VE FLOWN THAT BIRD...
IT'S FROM EARTH?
NOT ANYMORE. THAT THING IS NOT FRIENDLY. COMING IN TOO FAST AND TOO HOT.
OKAY, SO IT'S NOT THE GIRL SCOUTS. WHO IS IT?
NOT SURE. BUT THEY'VE REACHED RAMMING SPEED AND ARE ON A DIRECT COLLISION COURSE.
COMMAND TO ALPHA FLIGHT PERSONNEL. MOVING TO GREEN. LIKE GO. REPEAT--WE ARE COMBAT-READY.
DO THE MATH, WENDY. IS THERE ANY WAY THAT THING CAN STOP--OR IS OUR FRONT DOOR GOING TO HAVE TO BE THE THING THAT STOPS IT?
OUR FRONT DOOR, SIR. UNLESS SOMETHING STOPS IT FIRST.
FUNNY, THAT'S JUST WHAT I WAS THINKING.

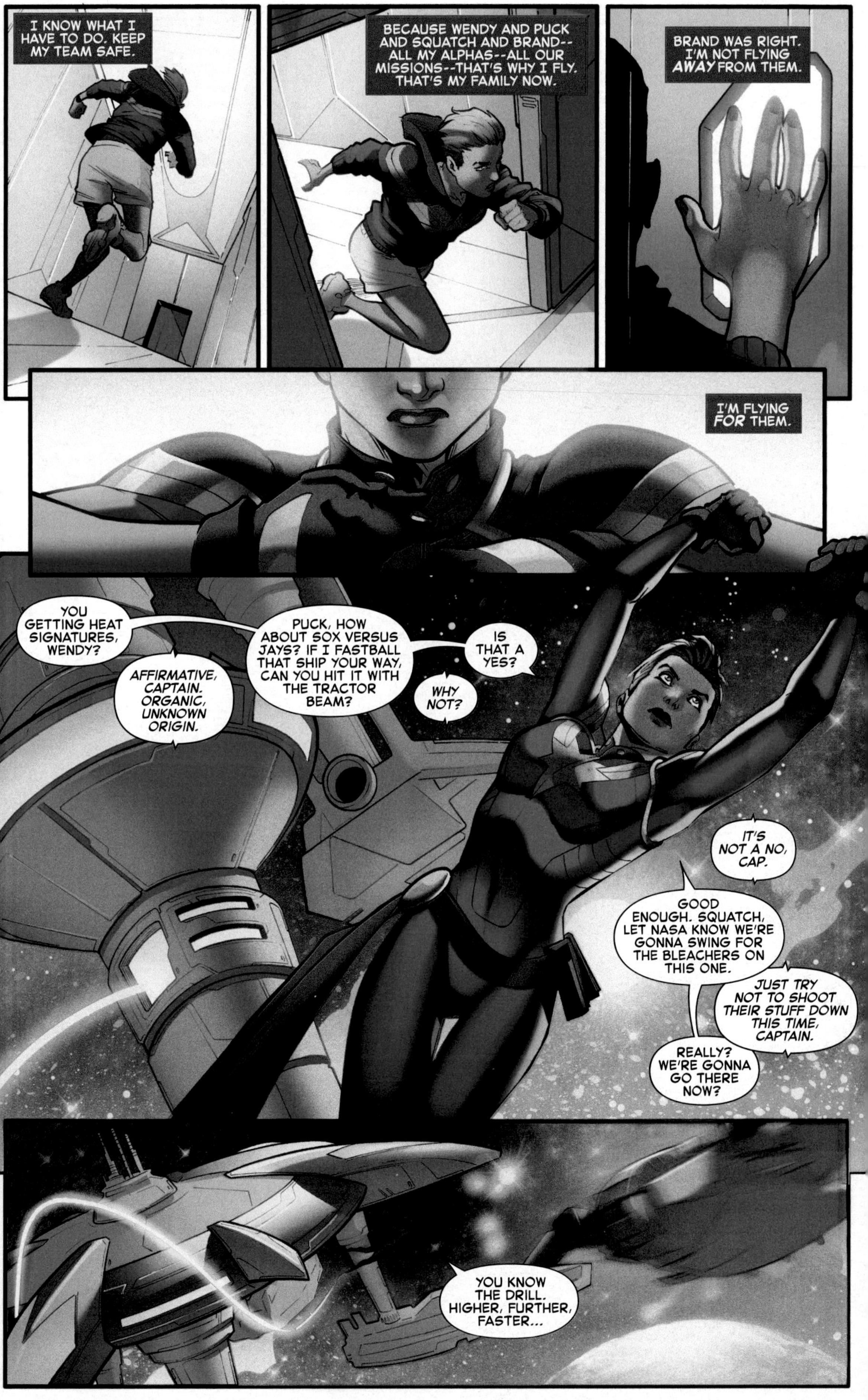

I KNOW WHAT I HAVE TO DO. KEEP MY TEAM SAFE.
BECAUSE WENDY AND PUCK AND SQUATCH AND BRAND--ALL MY ALPHAS--ALL OUR MISSIONS--THAT'S WHY I FLY. THAT'S MY FAMILY NOW.
BRAND WAS RIGHT. I'M NOT FLYING AWAY FROM THEM.
I'M FLYING FOR THEM.
YOU GETTING HEAT SIGNATURES, WENDY?
AFFIRMATIVE, CAPTAIN. ORGANIC, UNKNOWN ORIGIN.
PUCK, HOW ABOUT SOX VERSUS JAYS? IF I FASTBALL THAT SHIP YOUR WAY, CAN YOU HIT IT WITH THE TRACTOR BEAM?
WHY NOT?
IS THAT A YES?
IT'S NOT A NO, CAP.
GOOD ENOUGH. SQUATCH, LET NASA KNOW WE'RE GONNA SWING FOR THE BLEACHERS ON THIS ONE.
JUST TRY NOT TO SHOOT THEIR STUFF DOWN THIS TIME, CAPTAIN.
REALLY? WE'RE GONNA GO THERE NOW?
YOU KNOW THE DRILL. HIGHER, FURTHER, FASTER...

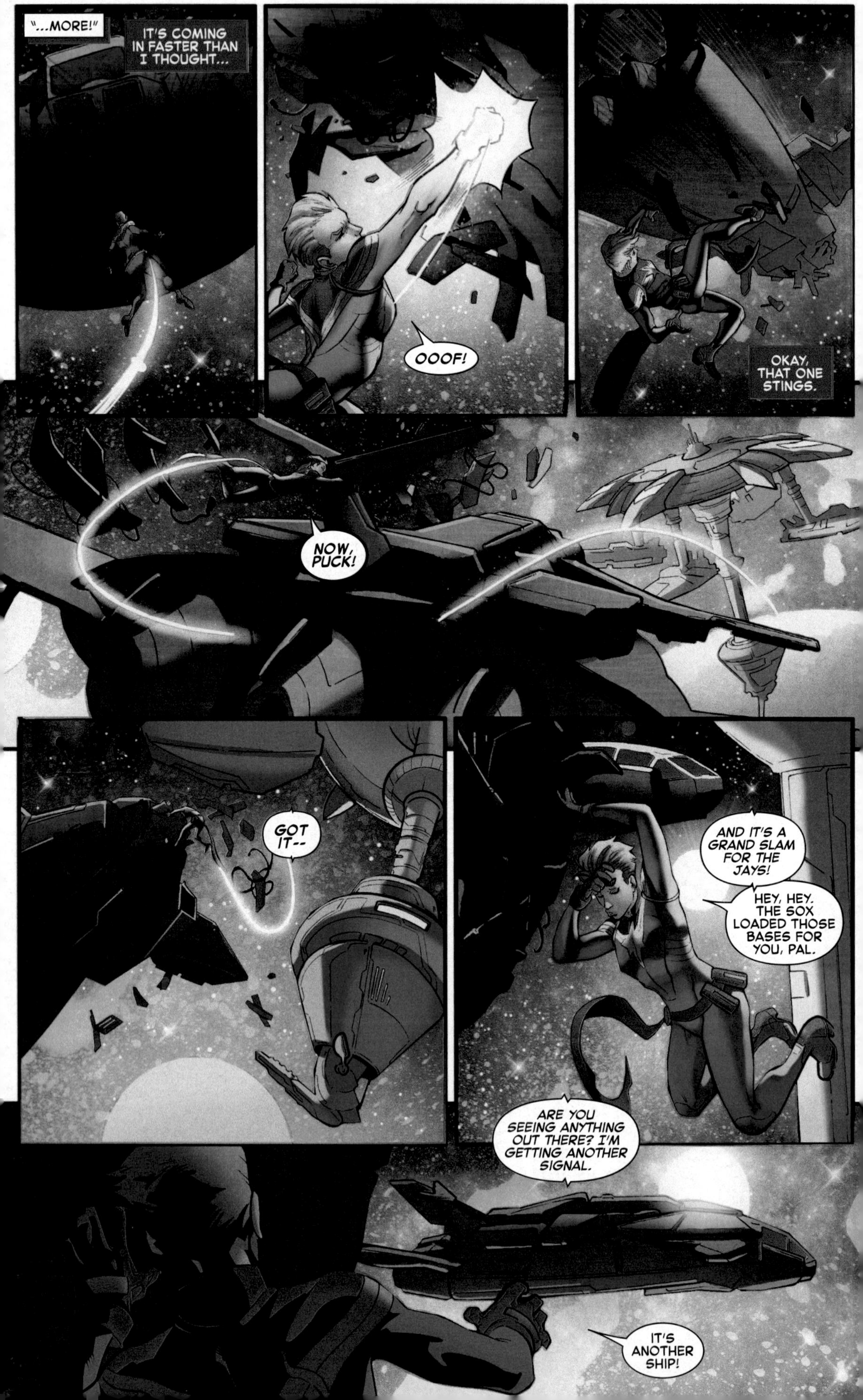
"...MORE!"
IT'S COMING IN FASTER THAN I THOUGHT...
OOOF!
OKAY, THAT ONE STINGS.
NOW, PUCK!
GOT IT--
AND IT'S A GRAND SLAM FOR THE JAYS!
HEY, HEY. THE SOX LOADED THOSE BASES FOR YOU, PAL.
ARE YOU SEEING ANYTHING OUT THERE? I'M GETTING ANOTHER SIGNAL.
IT'S ANOTHER SHIP!

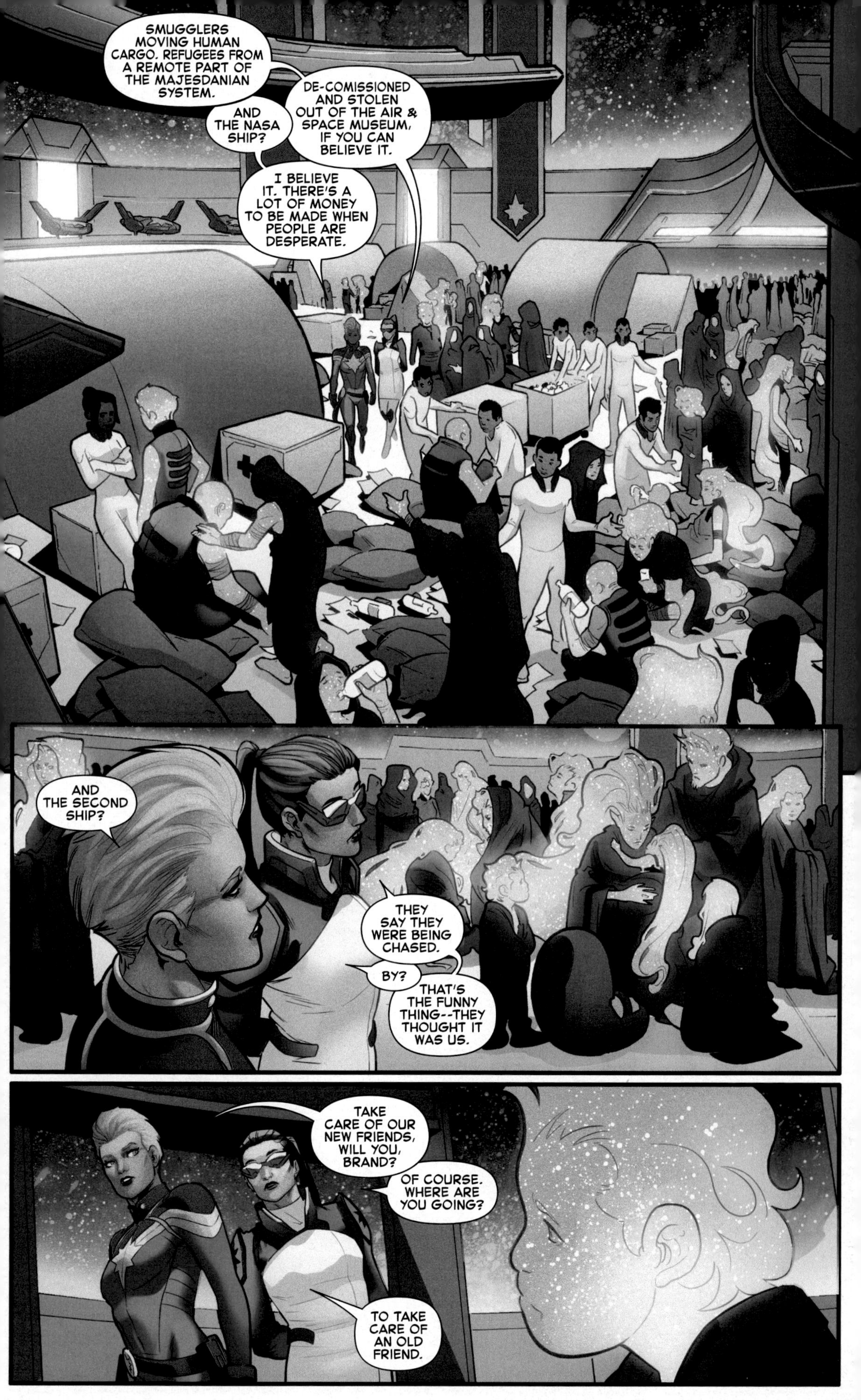
SMUGGLERS MOVING HUMAN CARGO. REFUGEES FROM A REMOTE PART OF THE MAJESDANIAN SYSTEM.
AND THE NASA SHIP?
DE-COMISSIONED AND STOLEN OUT OF THE AIR & SPACE MUSEUM, IF YOU CAN BELIEVE IT.
I BELIEVE IT. THERE'S A LOT OF MONEY TO BE MADE WHEN PEOPLE ARE DESPERATE.
AND THE SECOND SHIP?
THEY SAY THEY WERE BEING CHASED.
BY?
THAT'S THE FUNNY THING--THEY THOUGHT IT WAS US.
TAKE CARE OF OUR NEW FRIENDS, WILL YOU, BRAND?
OF COURSE. WHERE ARE YOU GOING?
TO TAKE CARE OF AN OLD FRIEND.

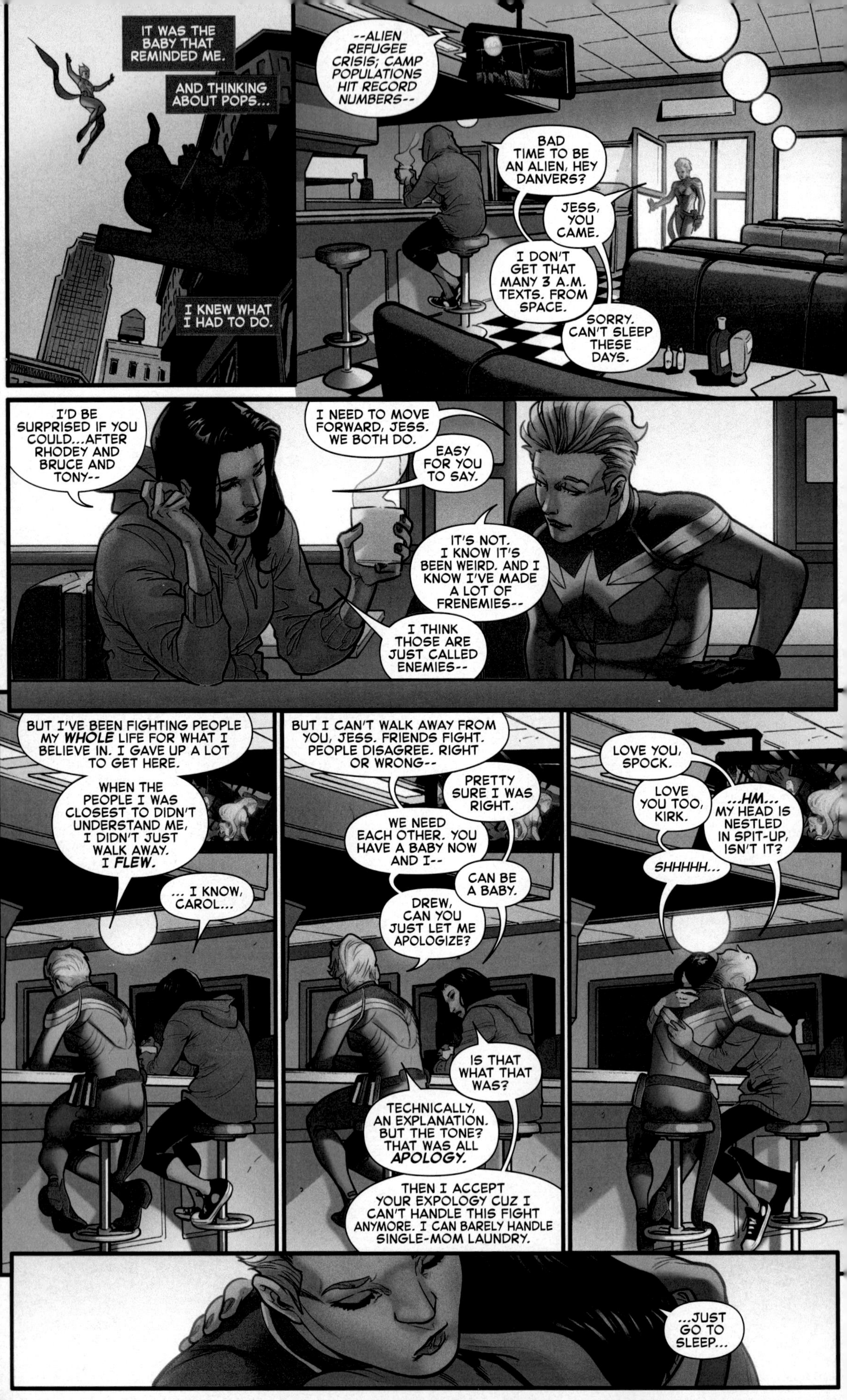
IT WAS THE BABY THAT REMINDED ME.
AND THINKING ABOUT POPS...
I KNEW WHAT I HAD TO DO.
--ALIEN REFUGEE CRISIS; CAMP POPULATIONS HIT RECORD NUMBERS--
BAD TIME TO BE AN ALIEN, HEY DANVERS?
JESS, YOU CAME.
I DON'T GET THAT MANY 3 A.M. TEXTS. FROM SPACE.
SORRY. CAN'T SLEEP THESE DAYS.
I'D BE SURPRISED IF YOU COULD...AFTER RHODEY AND BRUCE AND TONY--
I NEED TO MOVE FORWARD, JESS. WE BOTH DO.
EASY FOR YOU TO SAY.
IT'S NOT. I KNOW IT'S BEEN WEIRD. AND I KNOW I'VE MADE A LOT OF FRENEMIES--
I THINK THOSE ARE JUST CALLED ENEMIES--
BUT I'VE BEEN FIGHTING PEOPLE MY *WHOLE* LIFE FOR WHAT I BELIEVE IN. I GAVE UP A LOT TO GET HERE.
WHEN THE PEOPLE I WAS CLOSEST TO DIDN'T UNDERSTAND ME, I DIDN'T JUST WALK AWAY. I *FLEW.*
... I KNOW, CAROL...
BUT I CAN'T WALK AWAY FROM YOU, JESS. FRIENDS FIGHT. PEOPLE DISAGREE. RIGHT OR WRONG--
PRETTY SURE I WAS RIGHT.
WE NEED EACH OTHER. YOU HAVE A BABY NOW AND I--
CAN BE A BABY.
DREW, CAN YOU JUST LET ME APOLOGIZE?
IS THAT WHAT THAT WAS?
TECHNICALLY, AN EXPLANATION. BUT THE TONE? THAT WAS ALL *APOLOGY.*
THEN I ACCEPT YOUR EXPOLOGY CUZ I CAN'T HANDLE THIS FIGHT ANYMORE. I CAN BARELY HANDLE SINGLE-MOM LAUNDRY.
LOVE YOU, SPOCK.
LOVE YOU TOO, KIRK.
SHHHHH...
...HM... MY HEAD IS NESTLED IN SPIT-UP, ISN'T IT?
...JUST GO TO SLEEP...

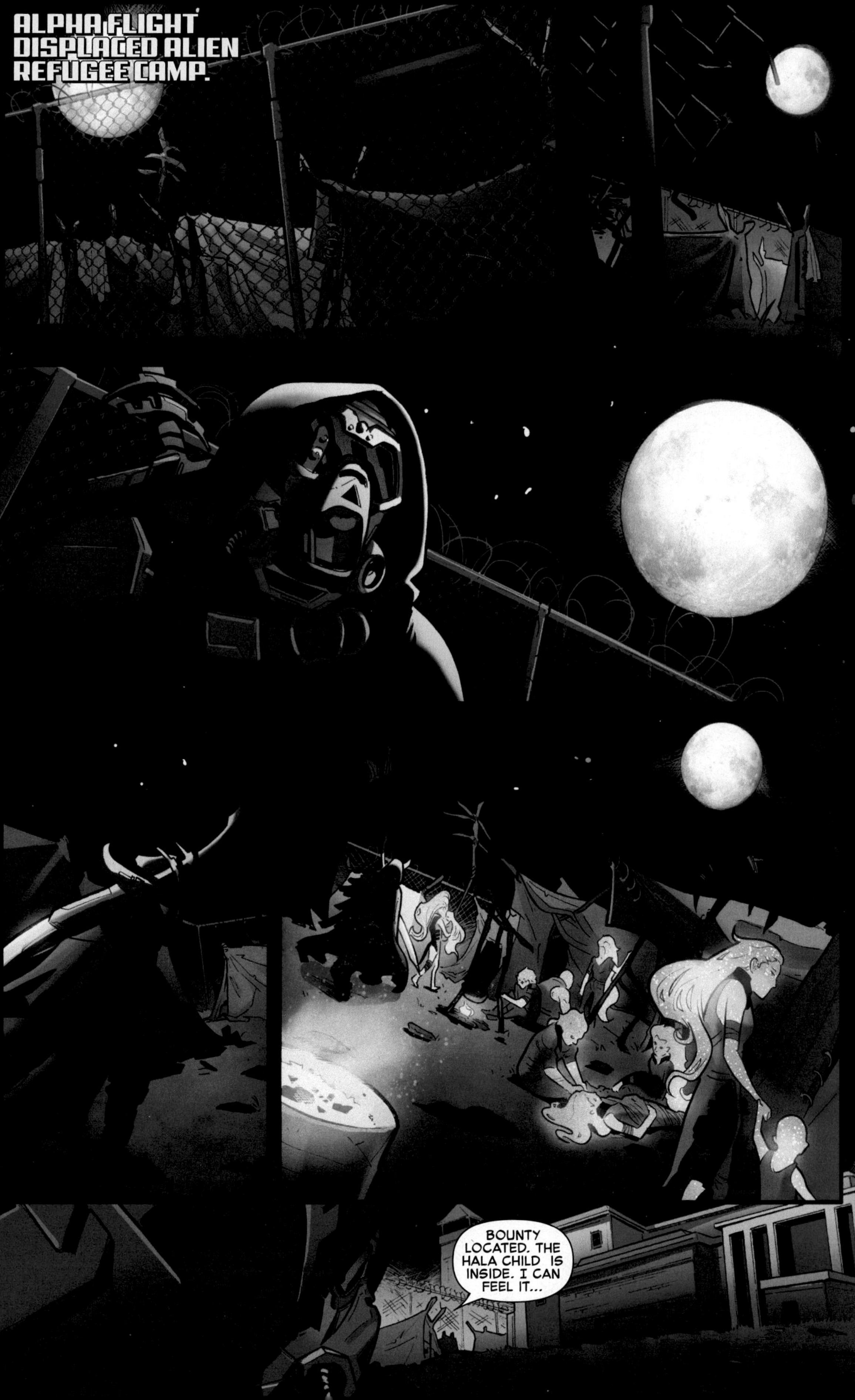
ALPHA FLIGHT DISPLACED ALIEN REFUGEE CAMP.
BOUNTY LOCATED. THE HALA CHILD IS INSIDE. I CAN FEEL IT...

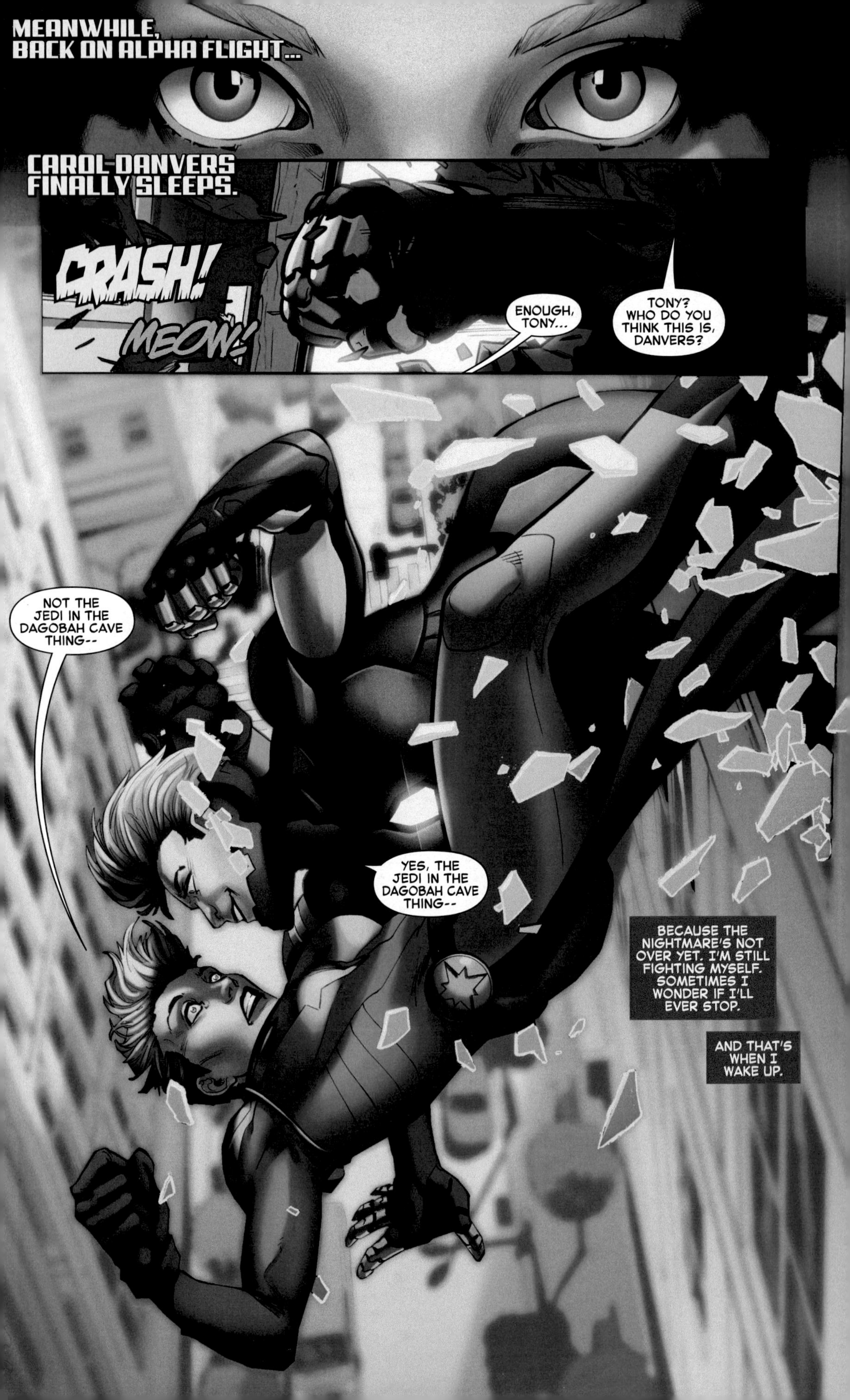
MEANWHILE, BACK ON ALPHA FLIGHT...
CAROL DANVERS FINALLY SLEEPS.
CRASH!
MEOW!
ENOUGH, TONY...
TONY? WHO DO YOU THINK THIS IS, DANVERS?
NOT THE JEDI IN THE DAGOBAH CAVE THING--
YES, THE JEDI IN THE DAGOBAH CAVE THING--
BECAUSE THE NIGHTMARE'S NOT OVER YET. I'M STILL FIGHTING MYSELF. SOMETIMES I WONDER IF I'LL EVER STOP.
AND THAT'S WHEN I WAKE UP.

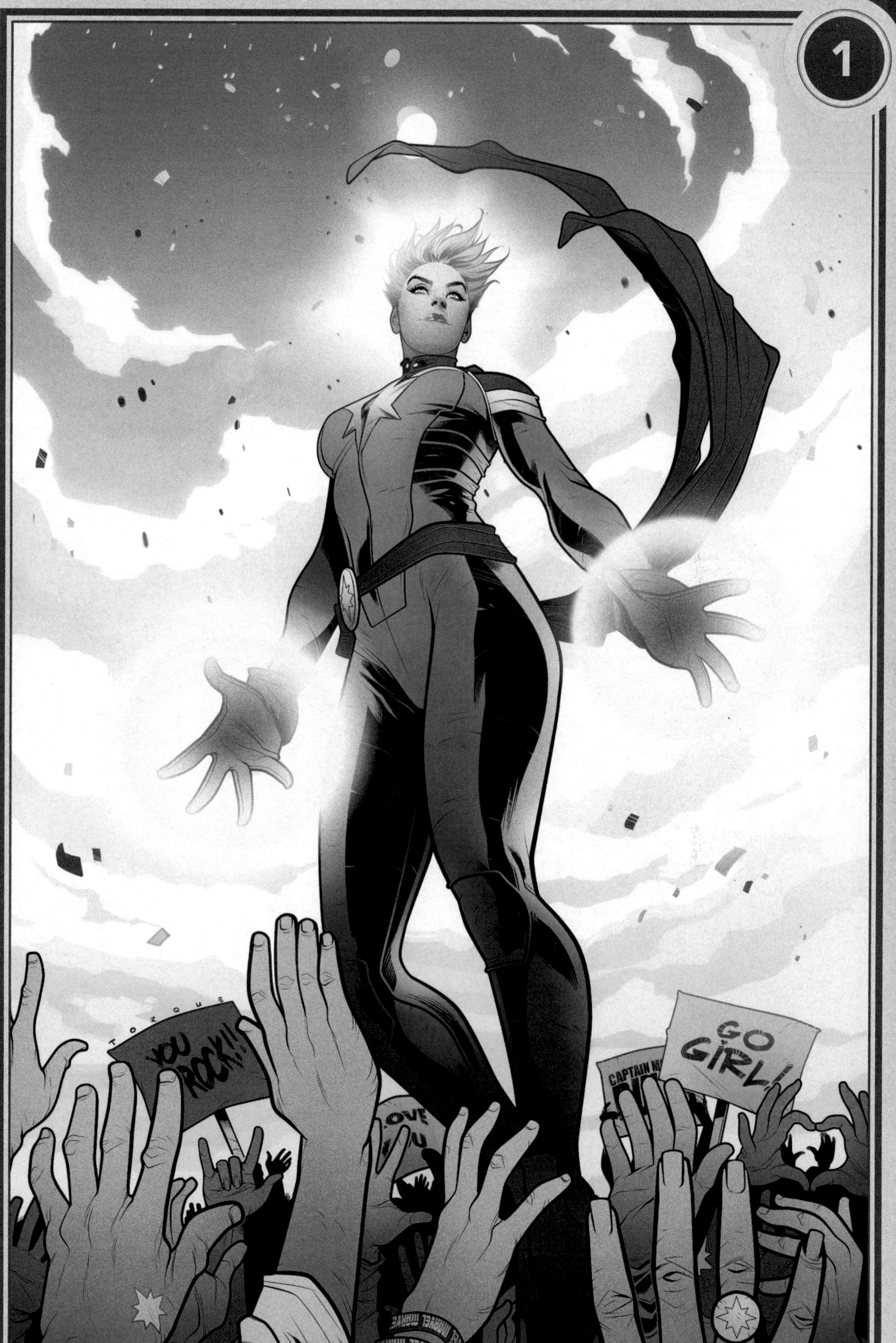
1
YOU ROCK!!
GO GIRL!

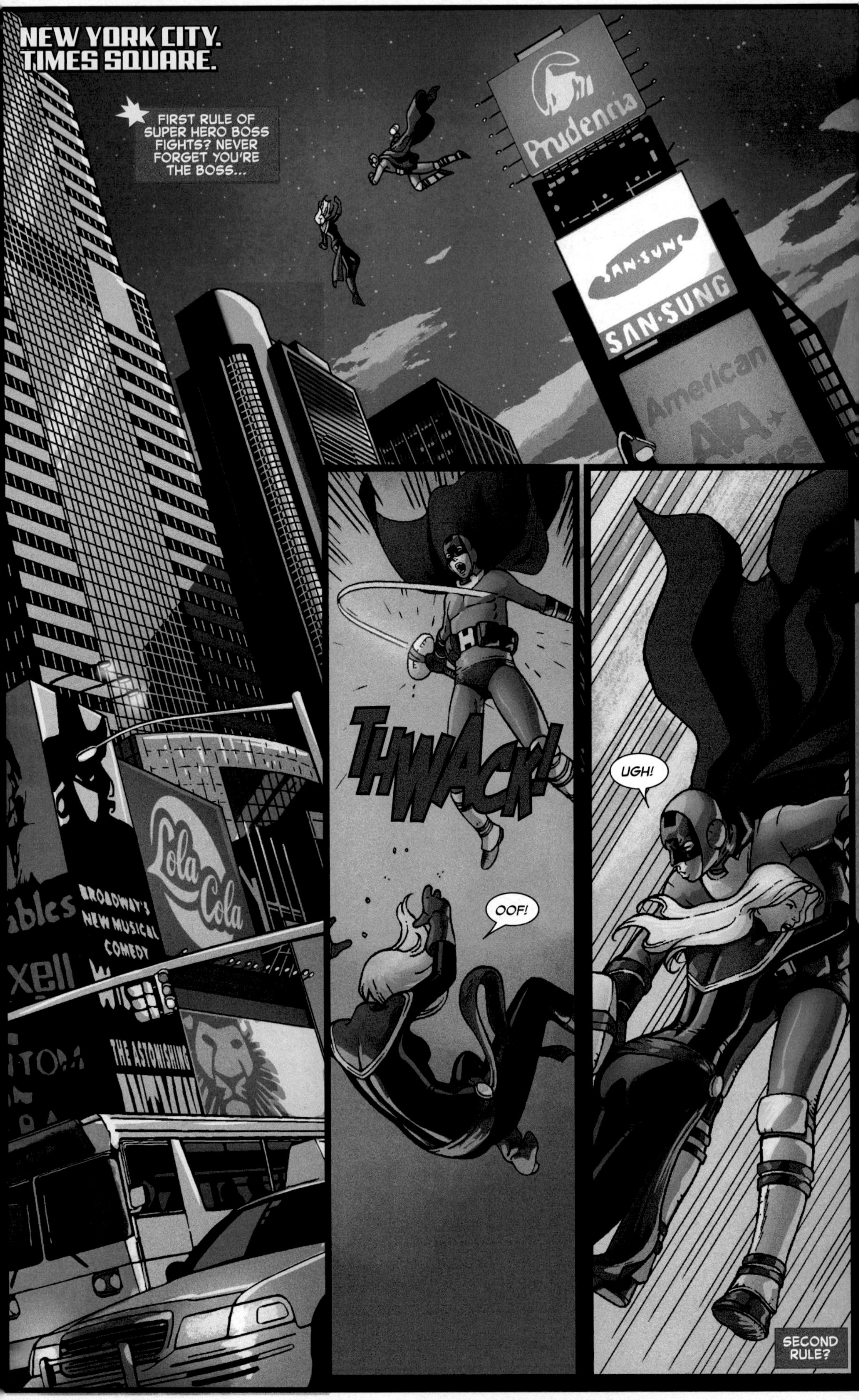
NEW YORK CITY. TIMES SQUARE.
FIRST RULE OF SUPER HERO BOSS FIGHTS? NEVER FORGET YOU'RE THE BOSS...
THWACK!
OOF!
UGH!
SECOND RULE?
Prudencia
SAN-SUNG
SAN-SUNG
American
Lola Cola
BROADWAY'S NEW MUSICAL COMEDY
THE ASTONISHING

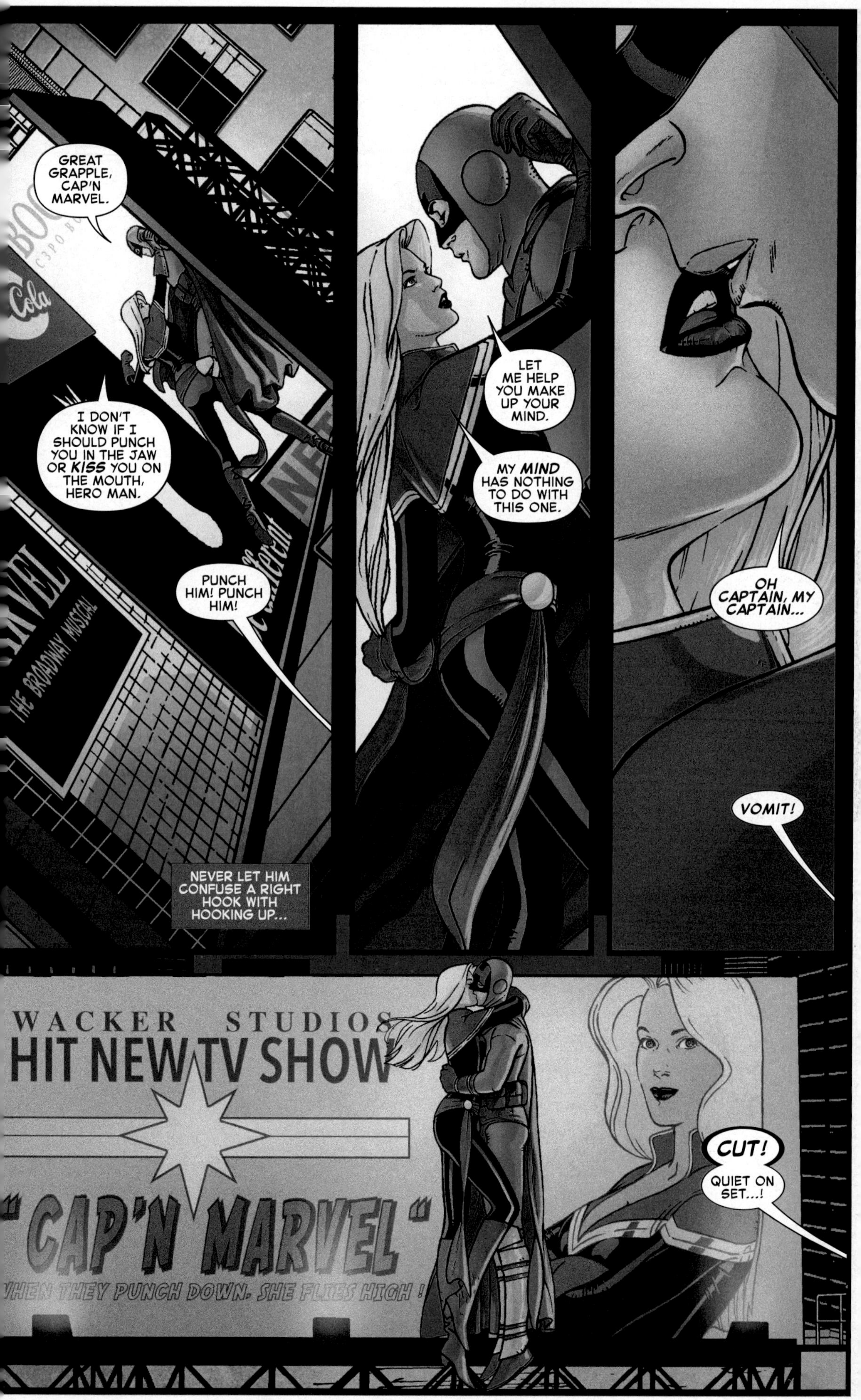
GREAT GRAPPLE, CAP'N MARVEL.
I DON'T KNOW IF I SHOULD PUNCH YOU IN THE JAW OR KISS YOU ON THE MOUTH, HERO MAN.
PUNCH HIM! PUNCH HIM!
LET ME HELP YOU MAKE UP YOUR MIND.
MY MIND HAS NOTHING TO DO WITH THIS ONE.
NEVER LET HIM CONFUSE A RIGHT HOOK WITH HOOKING UP...
OH CAPTAIN, MY CAPTAIN...
VOMIT!
WACKER STUDIOS
HIT NEW TV SHOW
"CAP'N MARVEL"
WHEN THEY PUNCH DOWN, SHE FLIES HIGH!
THE BROADWAY MUSICAL
Cola
CUT!
QUIET ON SET...!

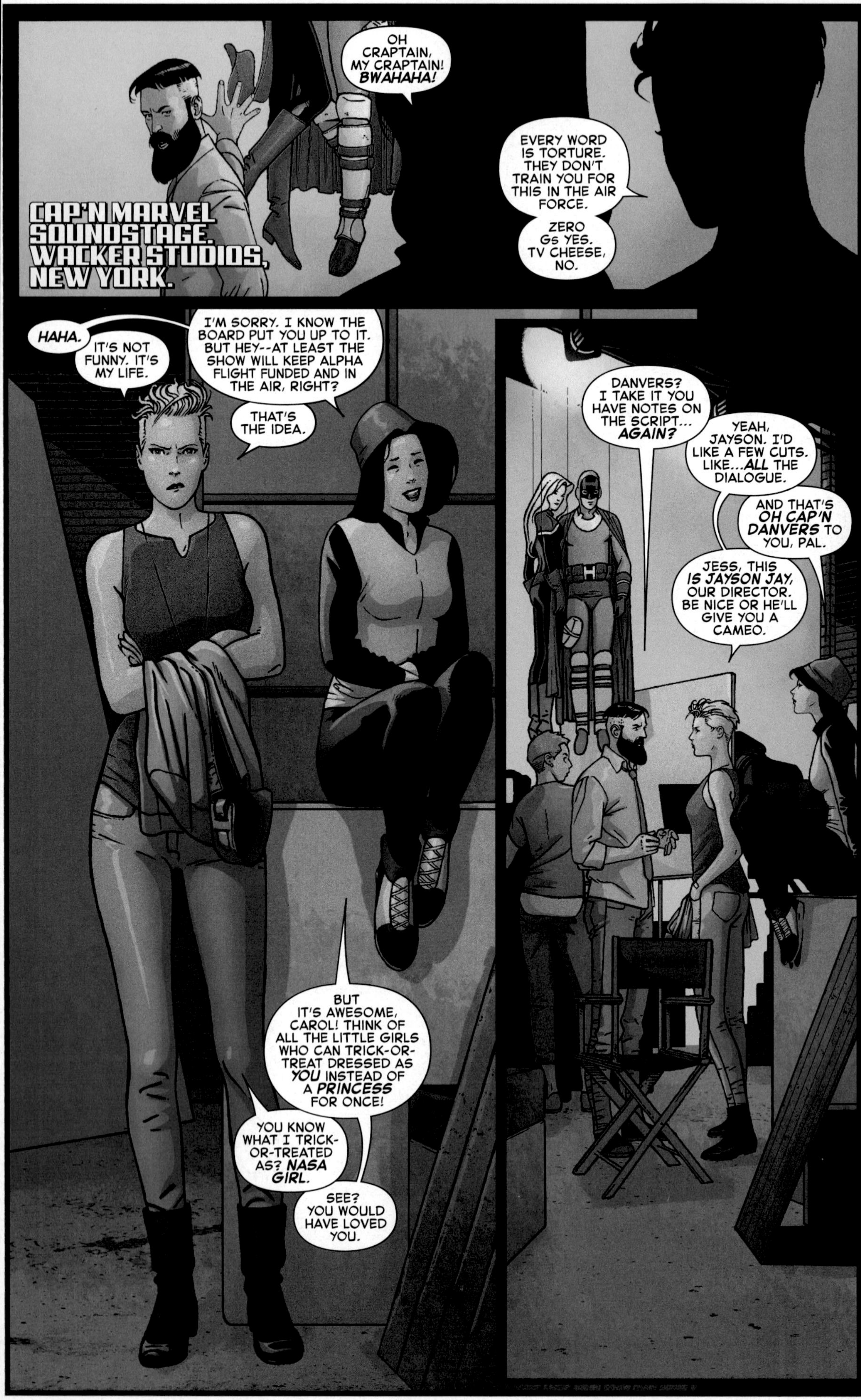
OH CRAPTAIN, MY CRAPTAIN! BWAHAHA!
CAP'N MARVEL SOUNDSTAGE. WACKER STUDIOS, NEW YORK.
EVERY WORD IS TORTURE. THEY DON'T TRAIN YOU FOR THIS IN THE AIR FORCE.
ZERO Gs YES. TV CHEESE, NO.
HAHA.
IT'S NOT FUNNY. IT'S MY LIFE.
I'M SORRY. I KNOW THE BOARD PUT YOU UP TO IT. BUT HEY--AT LEAST THE SHOW WILL KEEP ALPHA FLIGHT FUNDED AND IN THE AIR, RIGHT?
THAT'S THE IDEA.
BUT IT'S AWESOME, CAROL! THINK OF ALL THE LITTLE GIRLS WHO CAN TRICK-OR-TREAT DRESSED AS YOU INSTEAD OF A PRINCESS FOR ONCE!
YOU KNOW WHAT I TRICK-OR-TREATED AS? NASA GIRL.
SEE? YOU WOULD HAVE LOVED YOU.
DANVERS? I TAKE IT YOU HAVE NOTES ON THE SCRIPT... AGAIN?
YEAH, JAYSON. I'D LIKE A FEW CUTS. LIKE...ALL THE DIALOGUE.
AND THAT'S OH CAP'N DANVERS TO YOU, PAL.
JESS, THIS IS JAYSON JAY, OUR DIRECTOR. BE NICE OR HE'LL GIVE YOU A CAMEO.

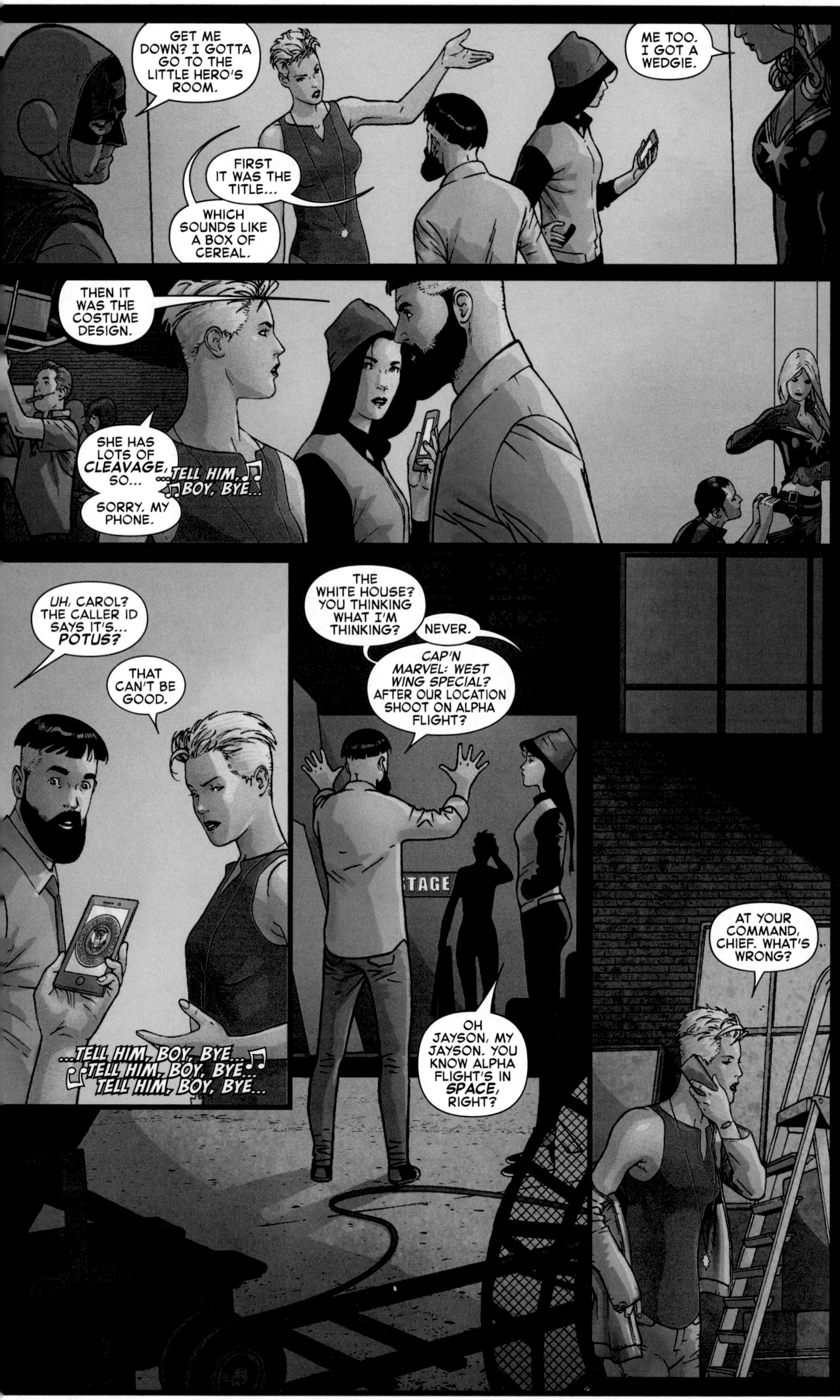
GET ME DOWN? I GOTTA GO TO THE LITTLE HERO'S ROOM.
ME TOO. I GOT A WEDGIE.
FIRST IT WAS THE TITLE...
WHICH SOUNDS LIKE A BOX OF CEREAL.
THEN IT WAS THE COSTUME DESIGN.
SHE HAS LOTS OF CLEAVAGE, SO...
...TELL HIM, BOY, BYE...
SORRY. MY PHONE.
UH, CAROL? THE CALLER ID SAYS IT'S... POTUS?
THAT CAN'T BE GOOD.
...TELL HIM, BOY, BYE...
TELL HIM, BOY, BYE...
TELL HIM, BOY, BYE...
THE WHITE HOUSE? YOU THINKING WHAT I'M THINKING?
NEVER.
CAP'N MARVEL: WEST WING SPECIAL? AFTER OUR LOCATION SHOOT ON ALPHA FLIGHT?
STAGE
OH JAYSON, MY JAYSON. YOU KNOW ALPHA FLIGHT'S IN SPACE, RIGHT?
AT YOUR COMMAND, CHIEF. WHAT'S WRONG?

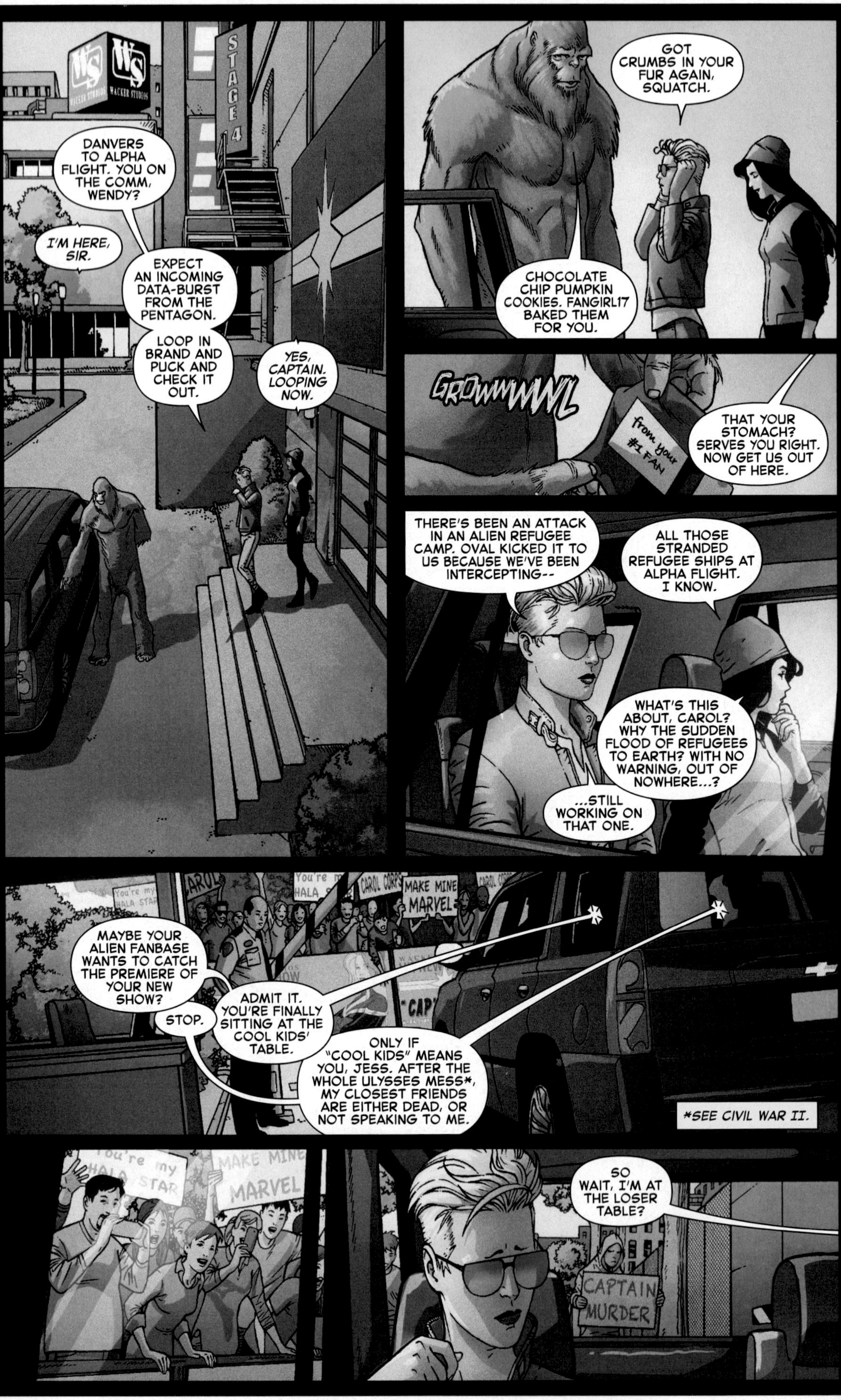

WS
WACKER STUDIOS
STAGE 4
DANVERS TO ALPHA FLIGHT. YOU ON THE COMM, WENDY?
I'M HERE, SIR.
EXPECT AN INCOMING DATA-BURST FROM THE PENTAGON.
LOOP IN BRAND AND PUCK AND CHECK IT OUT.
YES, CAPTAIN. LOOPING NOW.
GOT CRUMBS IN YOUR FUR AGAIN, SQUATCH.
CHOCOLATE CHIP PUMPKIN COOKIES. FANGIRL17 BAKED THEM FOR YOU.
GROWWWWL
from your #1 FAN
THAT YOUR STOMACH? SERVES YOU RIGHT. NOW GET US OUT OF HERE.
THERE'S BEEN AN ATTACK IN AN ALIEN REFUGEE CAMP. OVAL KICKED IT TO US BECAUSE WE'VE BEEN INTERCEPTING--
ALL THOSE STRANDED REFUGEE SHIPS AT ALPHA FLIGHT. I KNOW.
WHAT'S THIS ABOUT, CAROL? WHY THE SUDDEN FLOOD OF REFUGEES TO EARTH? WITH NO WARNING, OUT OF NOWHERE...?
...STILL WORKING ON THAT ONE.
You're my HALA STAR
CAROL CORPS
MAKE MINE MARVEL
MAYBE YOUR ALIEN FANBASE WANTS TO CATCH THE PREMIERE OF YOUR NEW SHOW?
ADMIT IT. YOU'RE FINALLY SITTING AT THE COOL KIDS' TABLE.
STOP.
ONLY IF "COOL KIDS" MEANS YOU, JESS. AFTER THE WHOLE ULYSSES MESS*, MY CLOSEST FRIENDS ARE EITHER DEAD, OR NOT SPEAKING TO ME.
*SEE CIVIL WAR II.
You're my HALA STAR
MAKE MINE MARVEL
SO WAIT, I'M AT THE LOSER TABLE?
CAPTAIN MURDER

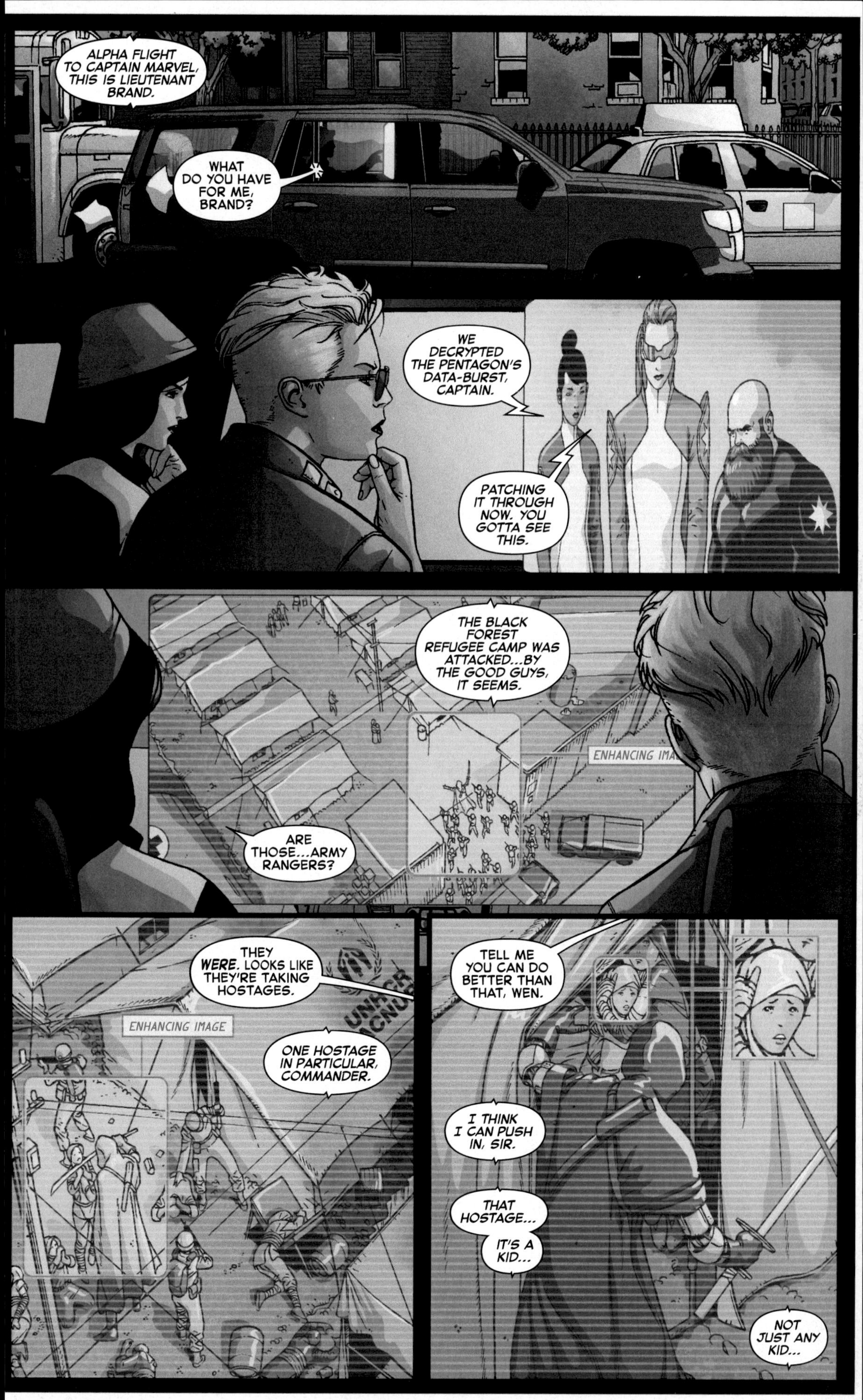
ALPHA FLIGHT TO CAPTAIN MARVEL, THIS IS LIEUTENANT BRAND.
WHAT DO YOU HAVE FOR ME, BRAND?
WE DECRYPTED THE PENTAGON'S DATA-BURST, CAPTAIN.
PATCHING IT THROUGH NOW. YOU GOTTA SEE THIS.
THE BLACK FOREST REFUGEE CAMP WAS ATTACKED...BY THE GOOD GUYS, IT SEEMS.
ENHANCING IMA
ARE THOSE...ARMY RANGERS?
THEY WERE. LOOKS LIKE THEY'RE TAKING HOSTAGES.
ENHANCING IMAGE
UNHCR
ONE HOSTAGE IN PARTICULAR, COMMANDER.
TELL ME YOU CAN DO BETTER THAN THAT, WEN.
I THINK I CAN PUSH IN, SIR.
THAT HOSTAGE...
IT'S A KID...
NOT JUST ANY KID...

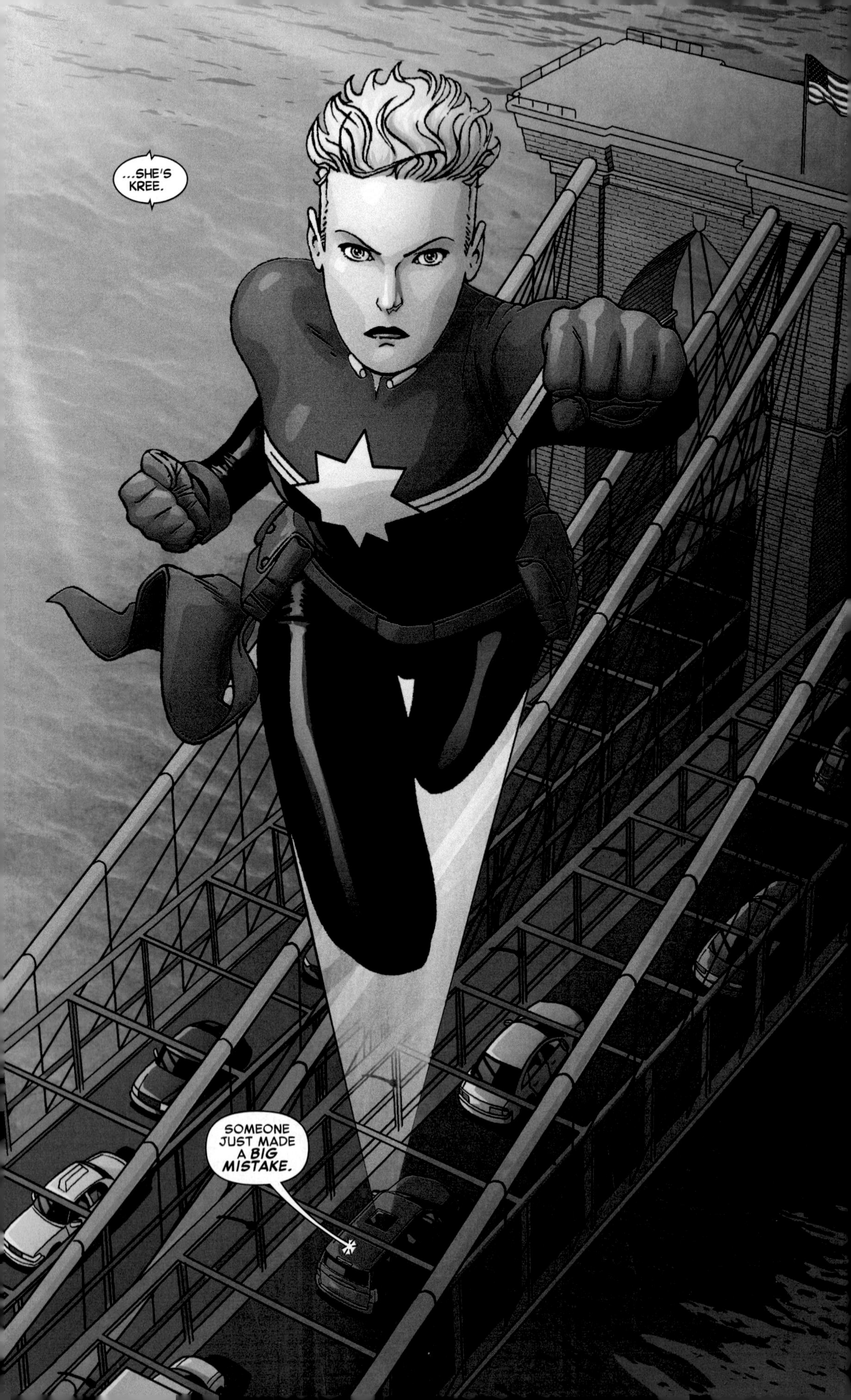
...SHE'S KREE.
SOMEONE JUST MADE A *BIG* MISTAKE.

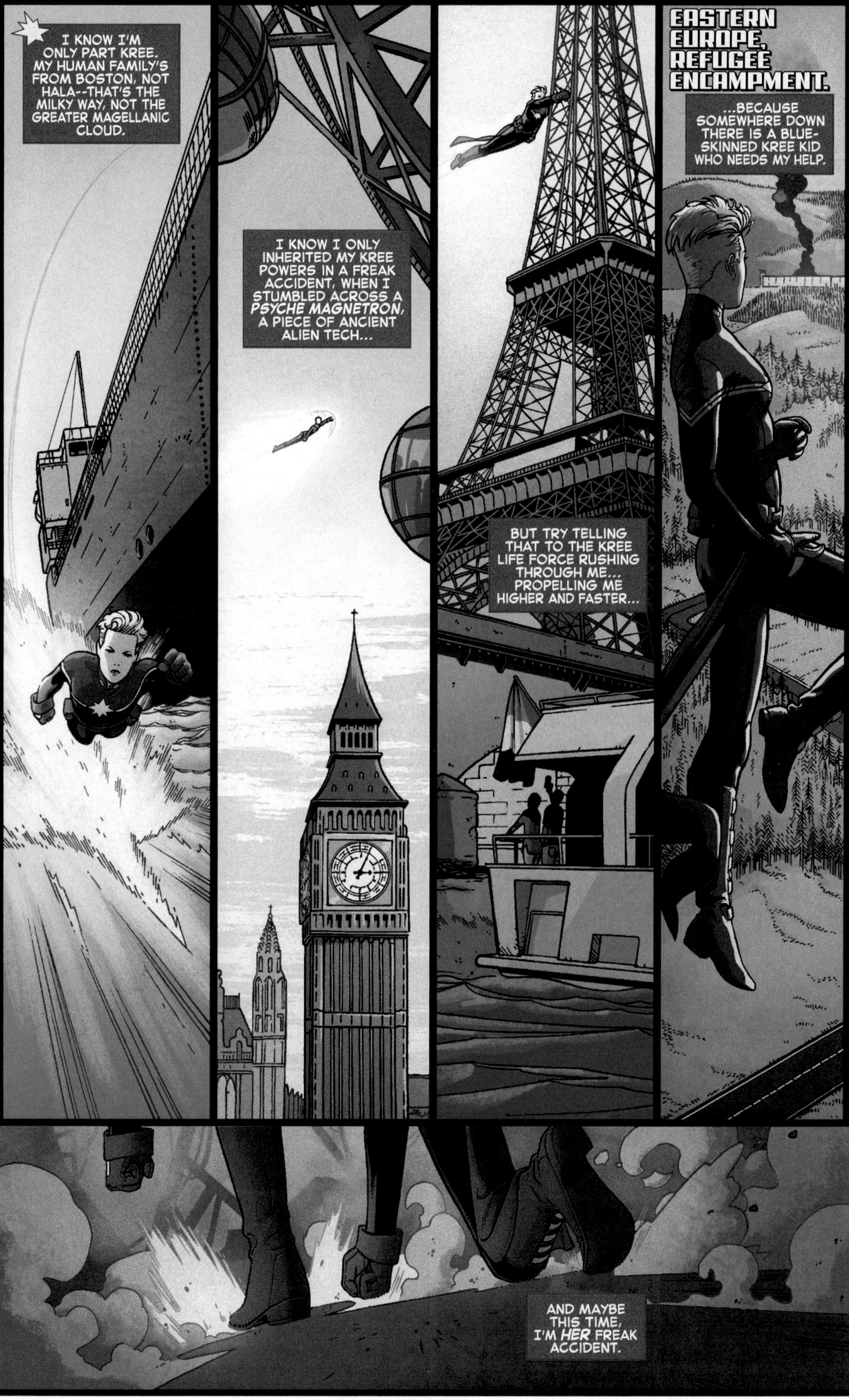
I KNOW I'M ONLY PART KREE. MY HUMAN FAMILY'S FROM BOSTON, NOT HALA--THAT'S THE MILKY WAY, NOT THE GREATER MAGELLANIC CLOUD.
I KNOW I ONLY INHERITED MY KREE POWERS IN A FREAK ACCIDENT, WHEN I STUMBLED ACROSS A *PSYCHE MAGNETRON*, A PIECE OF ANCIENT ALIEN TECH...
BUT TRY TELLING THAT TO THE KREE LIFE FORCE RUSHING THROUGH ME... PROPELLING ME HIGHER AND FASTER...
EASTERN EUROPE, REFUGEE ENCAMPMENT.
...BECAUSE SOMEWHERE DOWN THERE IS A BLUE-SKINNED KREE KID WHO NEEDS MY HELP.
AND MAYBE THIS TIME, I'M *HER* FREAK ACCIDENT.

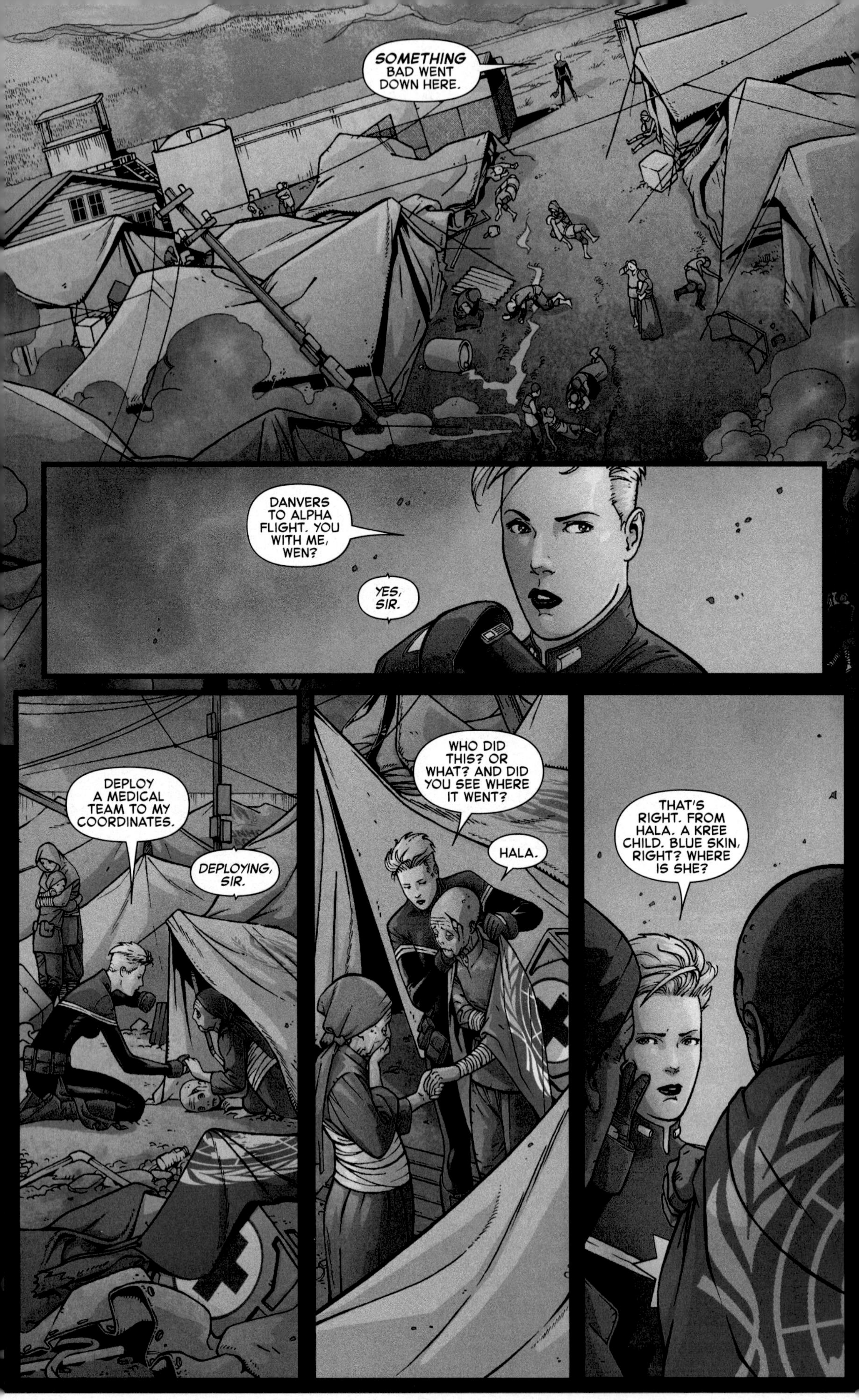
SOMETHING BAD WENT DOWN HERE.
DANVERS TO ALPHA FLIGHT. YOU WITH ME, WEN?
YES, SIR.
DEPLOY A MEDICAL TEAM TO MY COORDINATES.
DEPLOYING, SIR.
WHO DID THIS? OR WHAT? AND DID YOU SEE WHERE IT WENT?
HALA.
THAT'S RIGHT. FROM HALA. A KREE CHILD. BLUE SKIN, RIGHT? WHERE IS SHE?

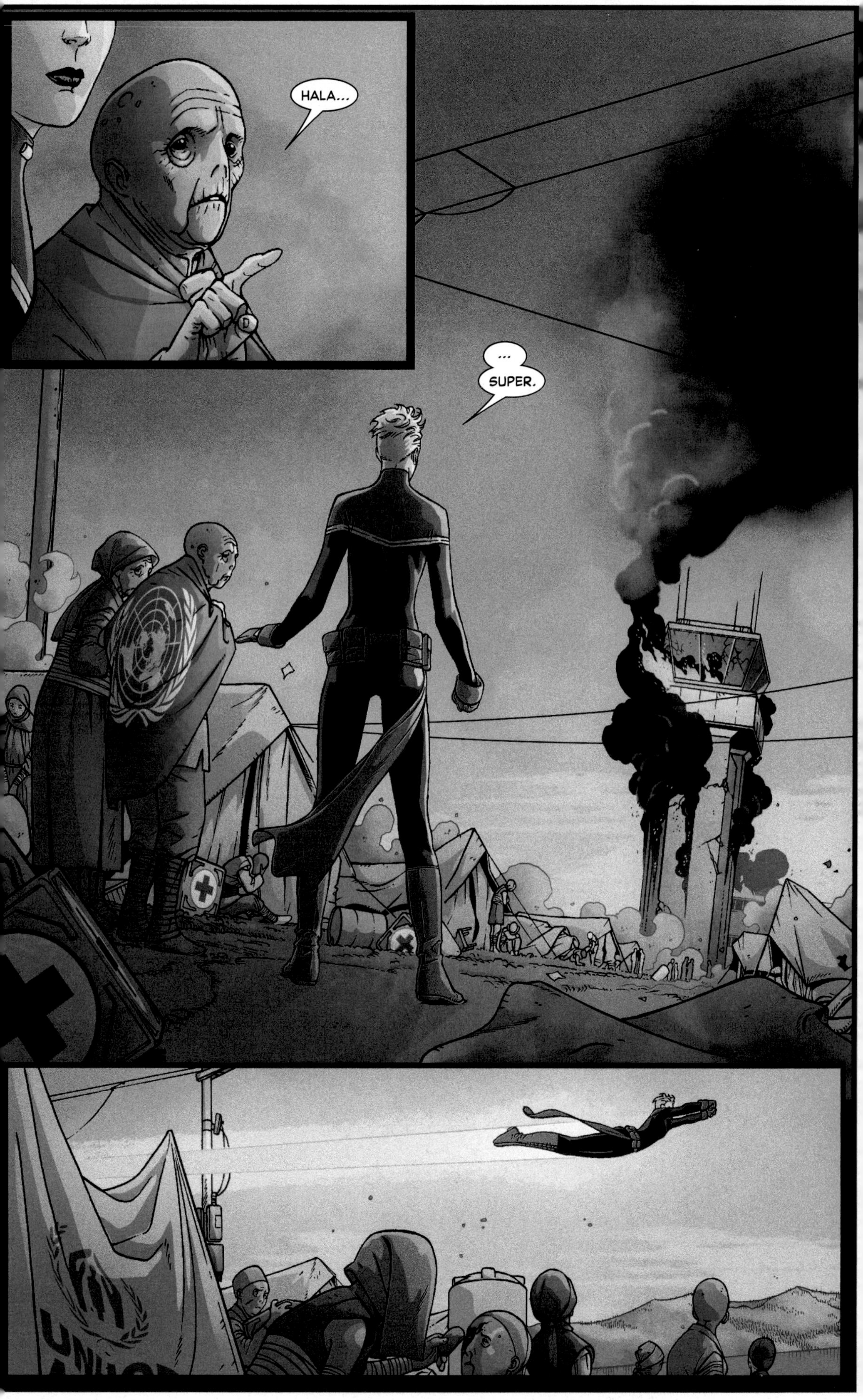
HALA...
...
SUPER.

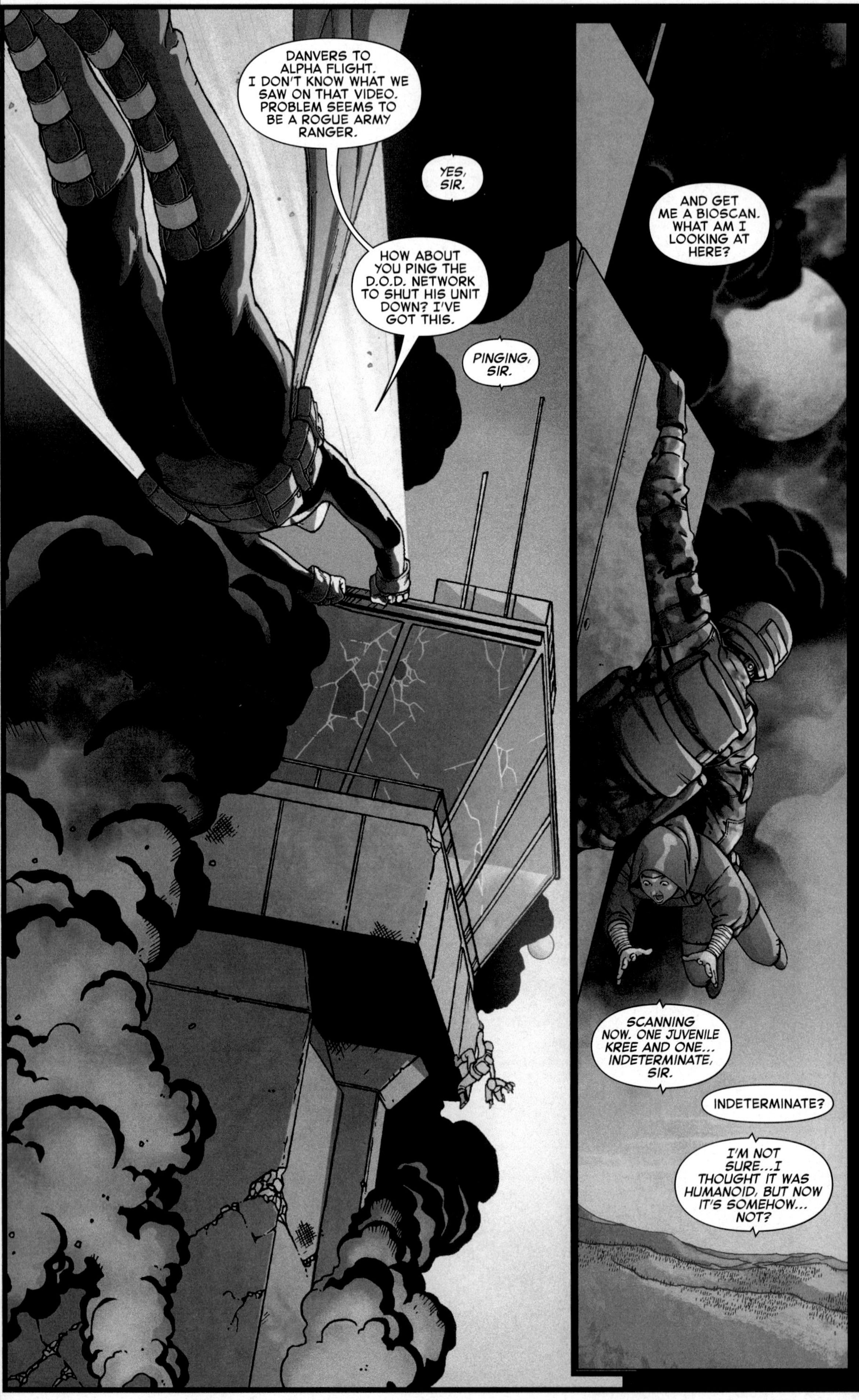
DANVERS TO ALPHA FLIGHT. I DON'T KNOW WHAT WE SAW ON THAT VIDEO. PROBLEM SEEMS TO BE A ROGUE ARMY RANGER.
YES, SIR.
HOW ABOUT YOU PING THE D.O.D. NETWORK TO SHUT HIS UNIT DOWN? I'VE GOT THIS.
PINGING, SIR.
AND GET ME A BIOSCAN. WHAT AM I LOOKING AT HERE?
SCANNING NOW. ONE JUVENILE KREE AND ONE... INDETERMINATE, SIR.
INDETERMINATE?
I'M NOT SURE...I THOUGHT IT WAS HUMANOID, BUT NOW IT'S SOMEHOW... NOT?

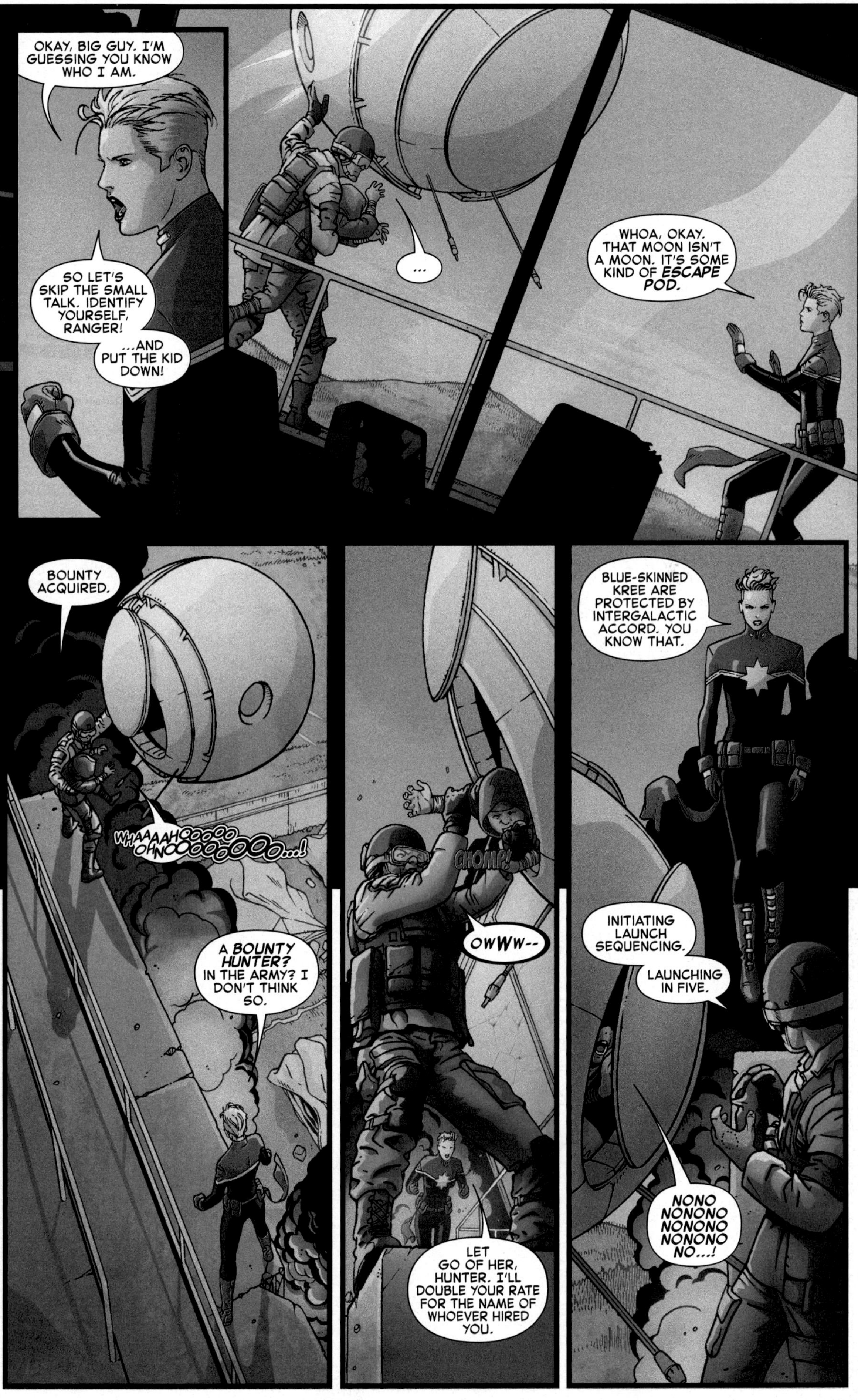
OKAY, BIG GUY. I'M GUESSING YOU KNOW WHO I AM.
SO LET'S SKIP THE SMALL TALK. IDENTIFY YOURSELF, RANGER!
...AND PUT THE KID DOWN!
...
WHOA, OKAY. THAT MOON ISN'T A MOON. IT'S SOME KIND OF ESCAPE POD.
BOUNTY ACQUIRED.
WHAAAAHOOOOO OHNOOOOOOOO...!
A BOUNTY HUNTER? IN THE ARMY? I DON'T THINK SO.
CHOMP!
OWWW--
LET GO OF HER, HUNTER. I'LL DOUBLE YOUR RATE FOR THE NAME OF WHOEVER HIRED YOU.
BLUE-SKINNED KREE ARE PROTECTED BY INTERGALACTIC ACCORD. YOU KNOW THAT.
INITIATING LAUNCH SEQUENCING.
LAUNCHING IN FIVE.
NONO NONONO NONONO NONONO NO...!

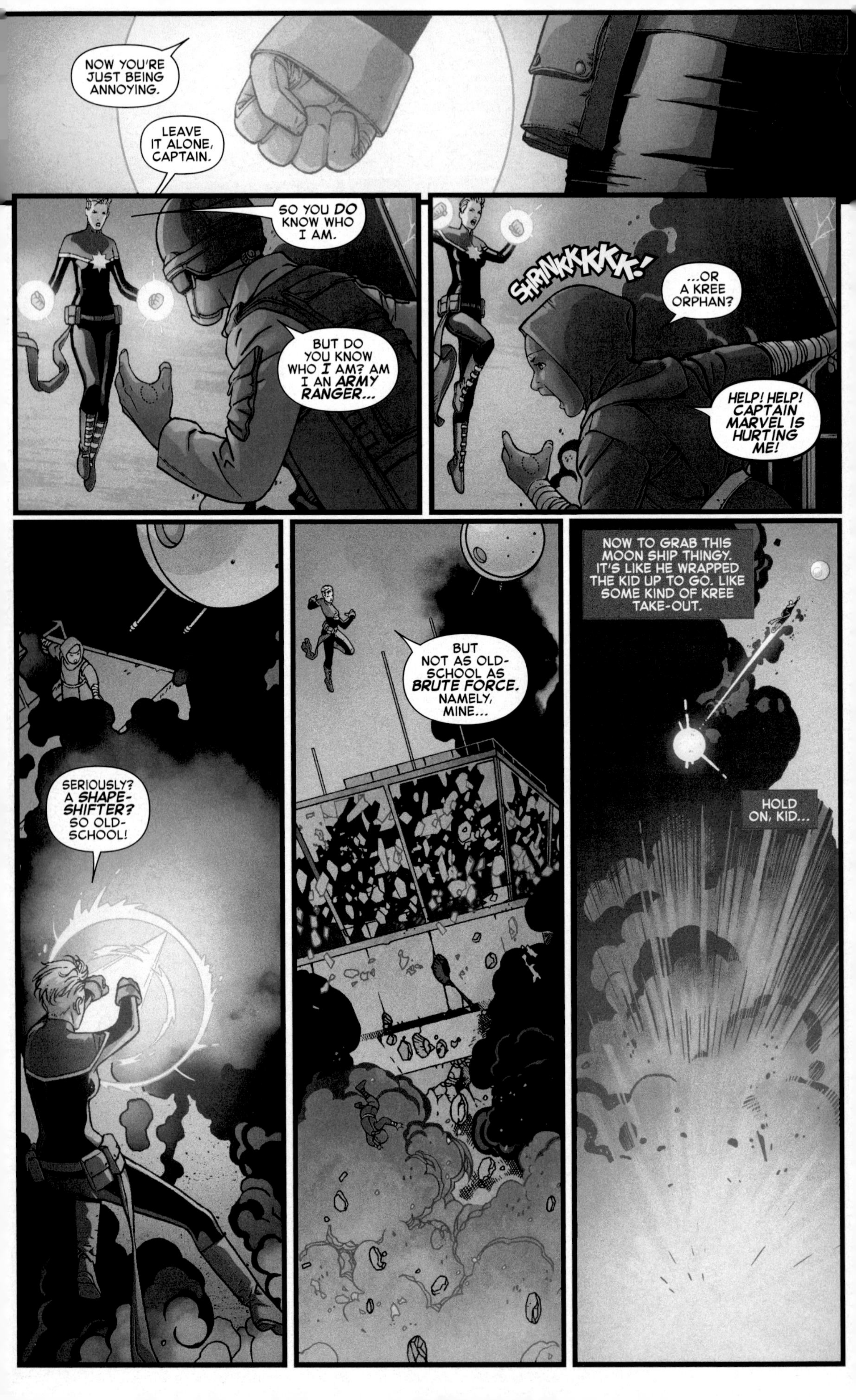
NOW YOU'RE JUST BEING ANNOYING.
LEAVE IT ALONE, CAPTAIN.
SO YOU DO KNOW WHO I AM.
BUT DO YOU KNOW WHO I AM? AM I AN ARMY RANGER...
SHRINKKKKKK!
...OR A KREE ORPHAN?
HELP! HELP! CAPTAIN MARVEL IS HURTING ME!
SERIOUSLY? A SHAPE-SHIFTER? SO OLD-SCHOOL!
BUT NOT AS OLD-SCHOOL AS BRUTE FORCE. NAMELY, MINE...
NOW TO GRAB THIS MOON SHIP THINGY. IT'S LIKE HE WRAPPED THE KID UP TO GO. LIKE SOME KIND OF KREE TAKE-OUT.
HOLD ON, KID...

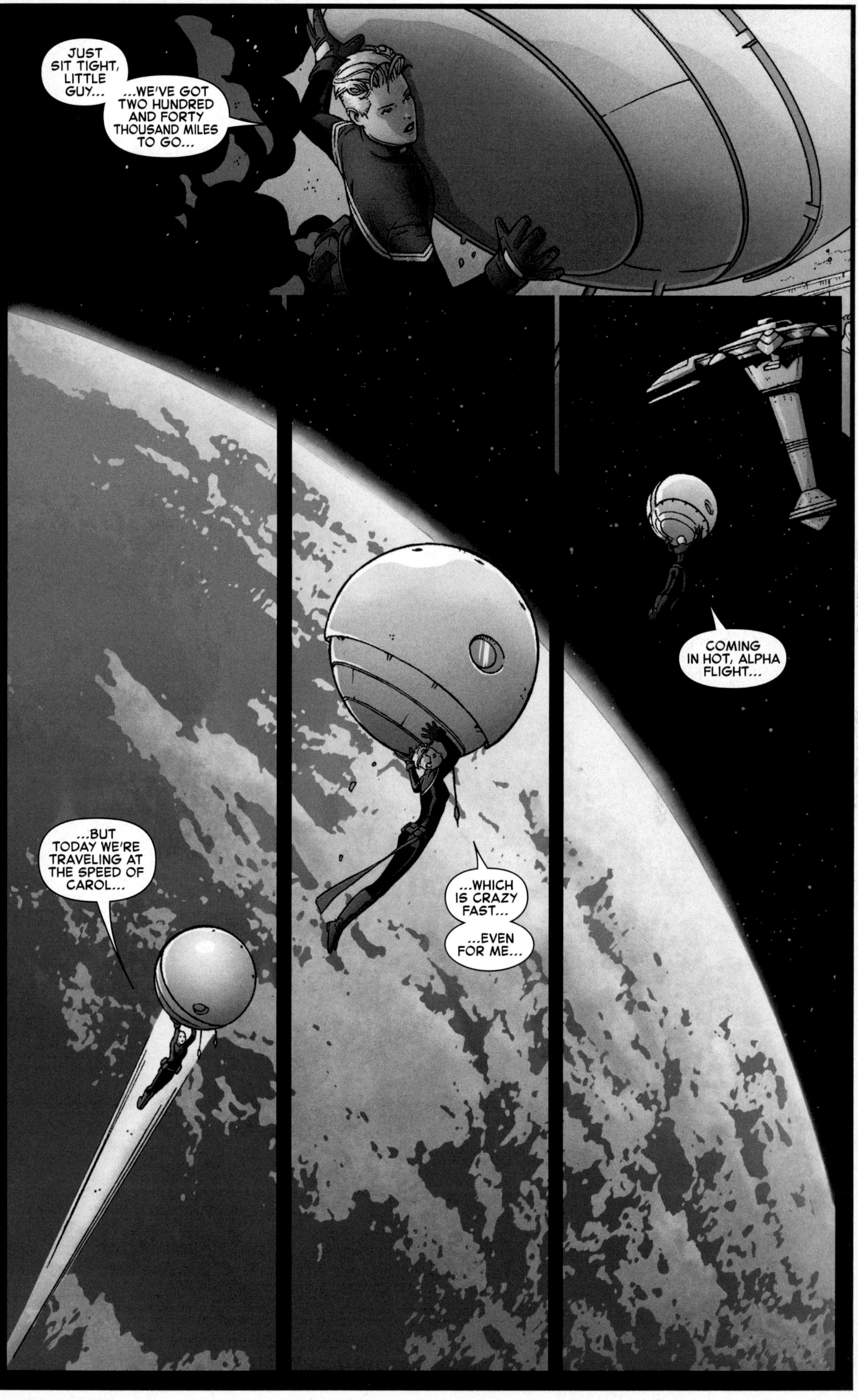
JUST SIT TIGHT, LITTLE GUY...
...WE'VE GOT TWO HUNDRED AND FORTY THOUSAND MILES TO GO...
...BUT TODAY WE'RE TRAVELING AT THE SPEED OF CAROL...
...WHICH IS CRAZY FAST...
...EVEN FOR ME...
COMING IN HOT, ALPHA FLIGHT...

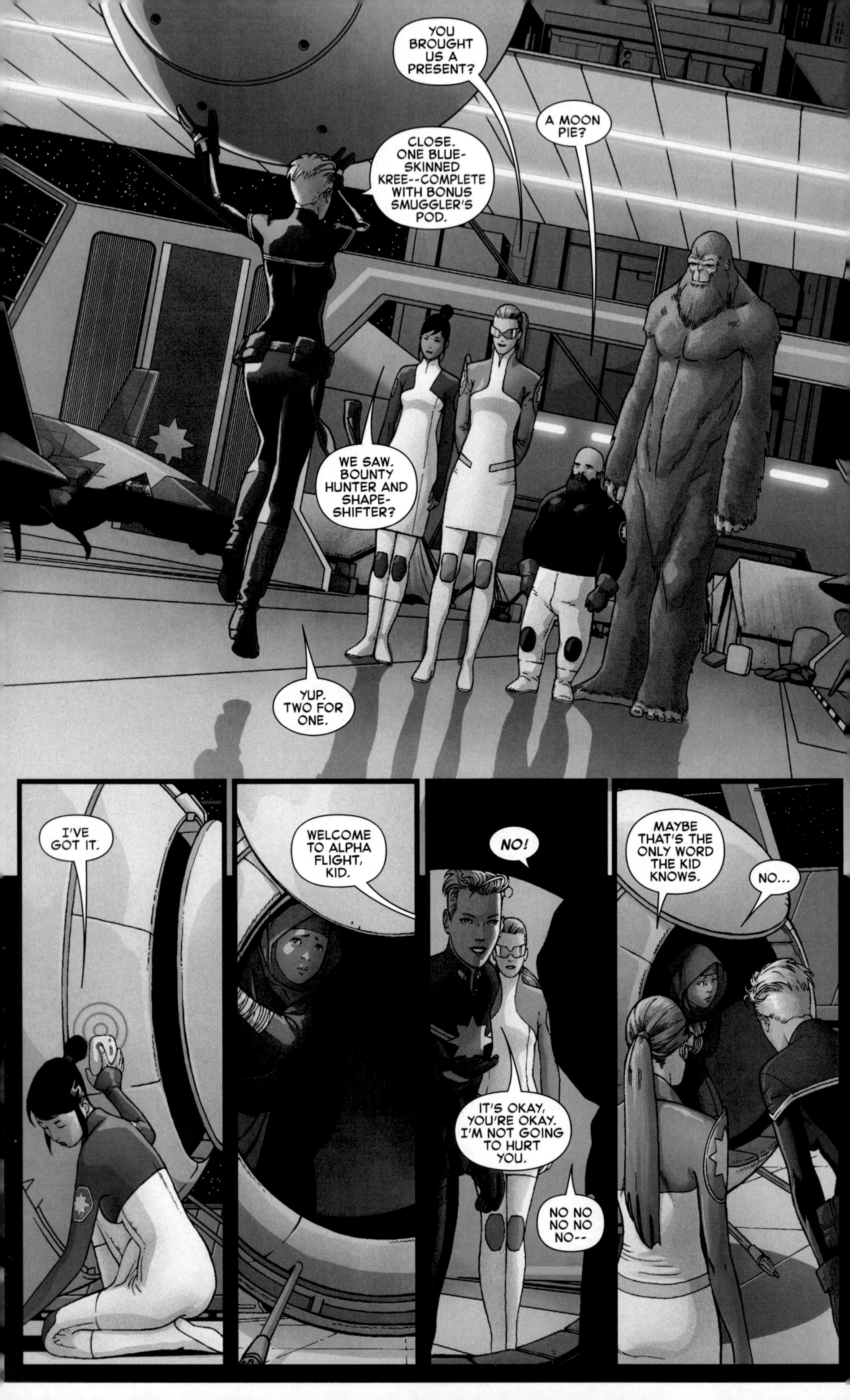
YOU BROUGHT US A PRESENT?
CLOSE. ONE BLUE-SKINNED KREE--COMPLETE WITH BONUS SMUGGLER'S POD.
A MOON PIE?
WE SAW. BOUNTY HUNTER AND SHAPE-SHIFTER?
YUP. TWO FOR ONE.
I'VE GOT IT.
WELCOME TO ALPHA FLIGHT, KID.
NO!
IT'S OKAY, YOU'RE OKAY. I'M NOT GOING TO HURT YOU.
NO NO NO NO NO--
MAYBE THAT'S THE ONLY WORD THE KID KNOWS.
NO...

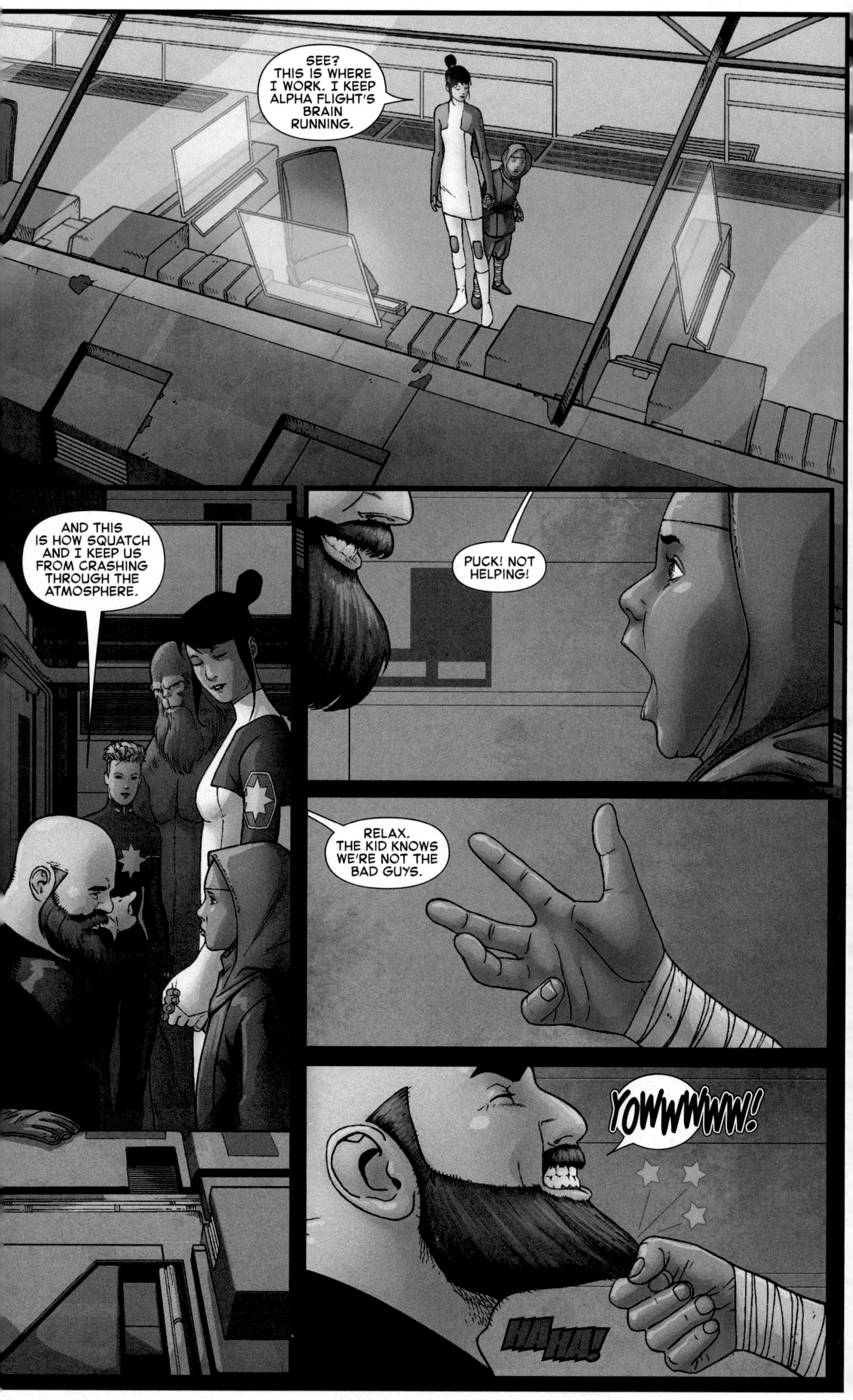
SEE? THIS IS WHERE I WORK. I KEEP ALPHA FLIGHT'S BRAIN RUNNING.
AND THIS IS HOW SQUATCH AND I KEEP US FROM CRASHING THROUGH THE ATMOSPHERE.
PUCK! NOT HELPING!
RELAX. THE KID KNOWS WE'RE NOT THE BAD GUYS.
YOWWWWW!
HAHA!

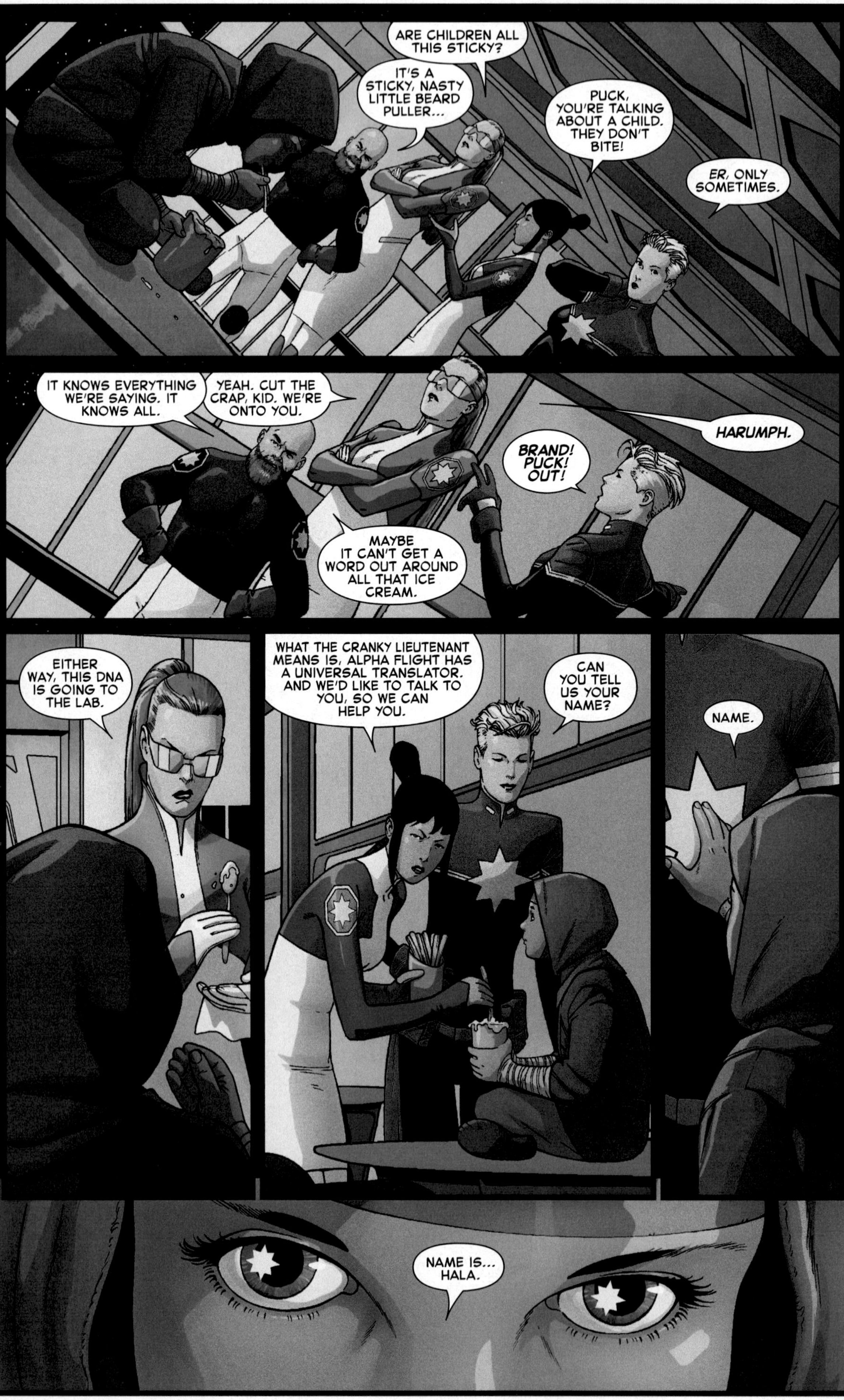
ARE CHILDREN ALL THIS STICKY?
IT'S A STICKY, NASTY LITTLE BEARD PULLER...
PUCK, YOU'RE TALKING ABOUT A CHILD. THEY DON'T BITE!
ER, ONLY SOMETIMES.
IT KNOWS EVERYTHING WE'RE SAYING. IT KNOWS ALL.
YEAH. CUT THE CRAP, KID. WE'RE ONTO YOU.
HARUMPH.
BRAND! PUCK! OUT!
MAYBE IT CAN'T GET A WORD OUT AROUND ALL THAT ICE CREAM.
EITHER WAY, THIS DNA IS GOING TO THE LAB.
WHAT THE CRANKY LIEUTENANT MEANS IS, ALPHA FLIGHT HAS A UNIVERSAL TRANSLATOR. AND WE'D LIKE TO TALK TO YOU, SO WE CAN HELP YOU.
CAN YOU TELL US YOUR NAME?
NAME.
NAME IS... HALA.

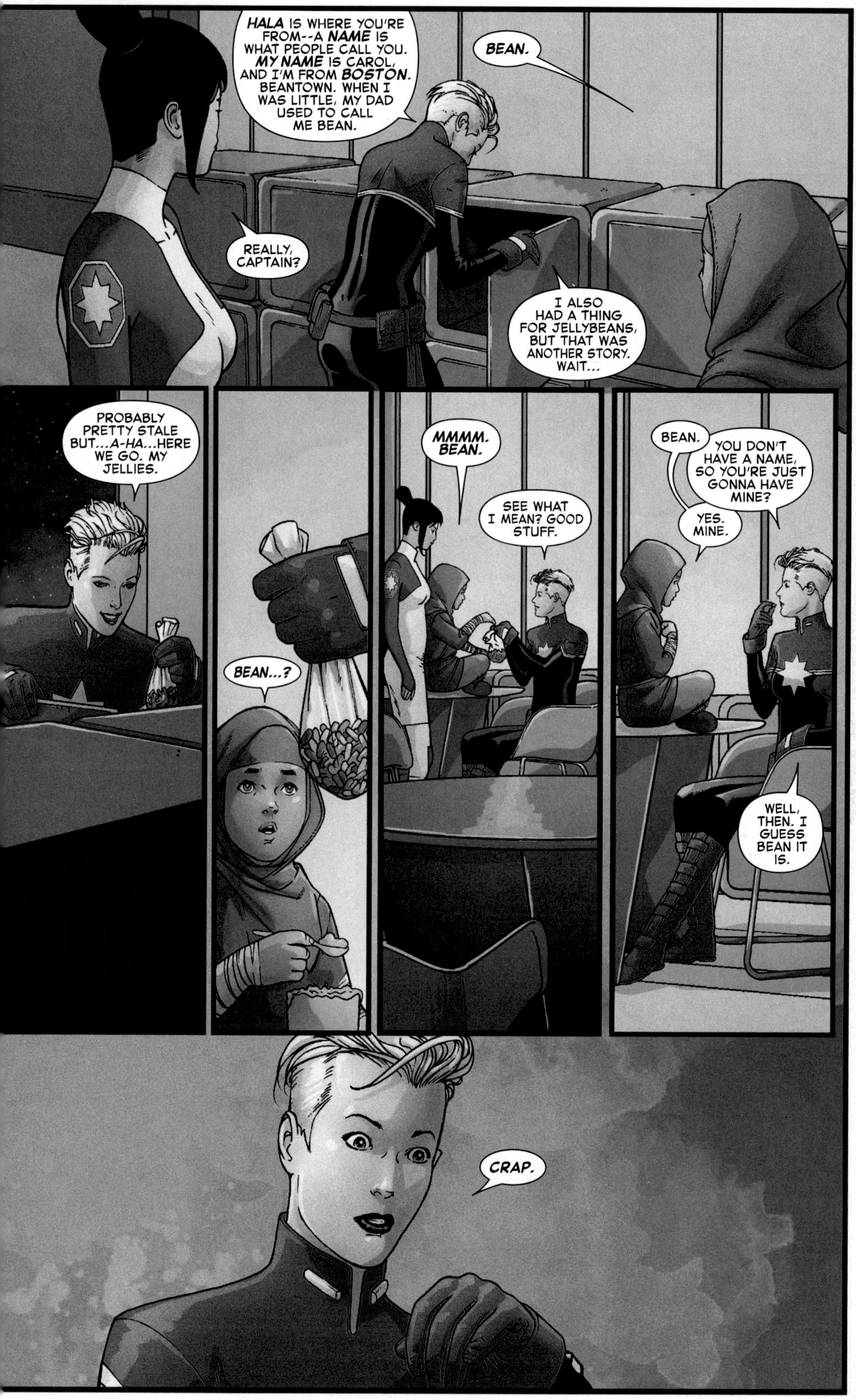
HALA IS WHERE YOU'RE FROM--A NAME IS WHAT PEOPLE CALL YOU. MY NAME IS CAROL, AND I'M FROM BOSTON. BEANTOWN. WHEN I WAS LITTLE, MY DAD USED TO CALL ME BEAN.
BEAN.
REALLY, CAPTAIN?
I ALSO HAD A THING FOR JELLYBEANS, BUT THAT WAS ANOTHER STORY. WAIT...
PROBABLY PRETTY STALE BUT...A-HA...HERE WE GO. MY JELLIES.
BEAN...?
MMMM. BEAN.
SEE WHAT I MEAN? GOOD STUFF.
BEAN.
YOU DON'T HAVE A NAME, SO YOU'RE JUST GONNA HAVE MINE?
YES. MINE.
WELL, THEN. I GUESS BEAN IT IS.
CRAP.

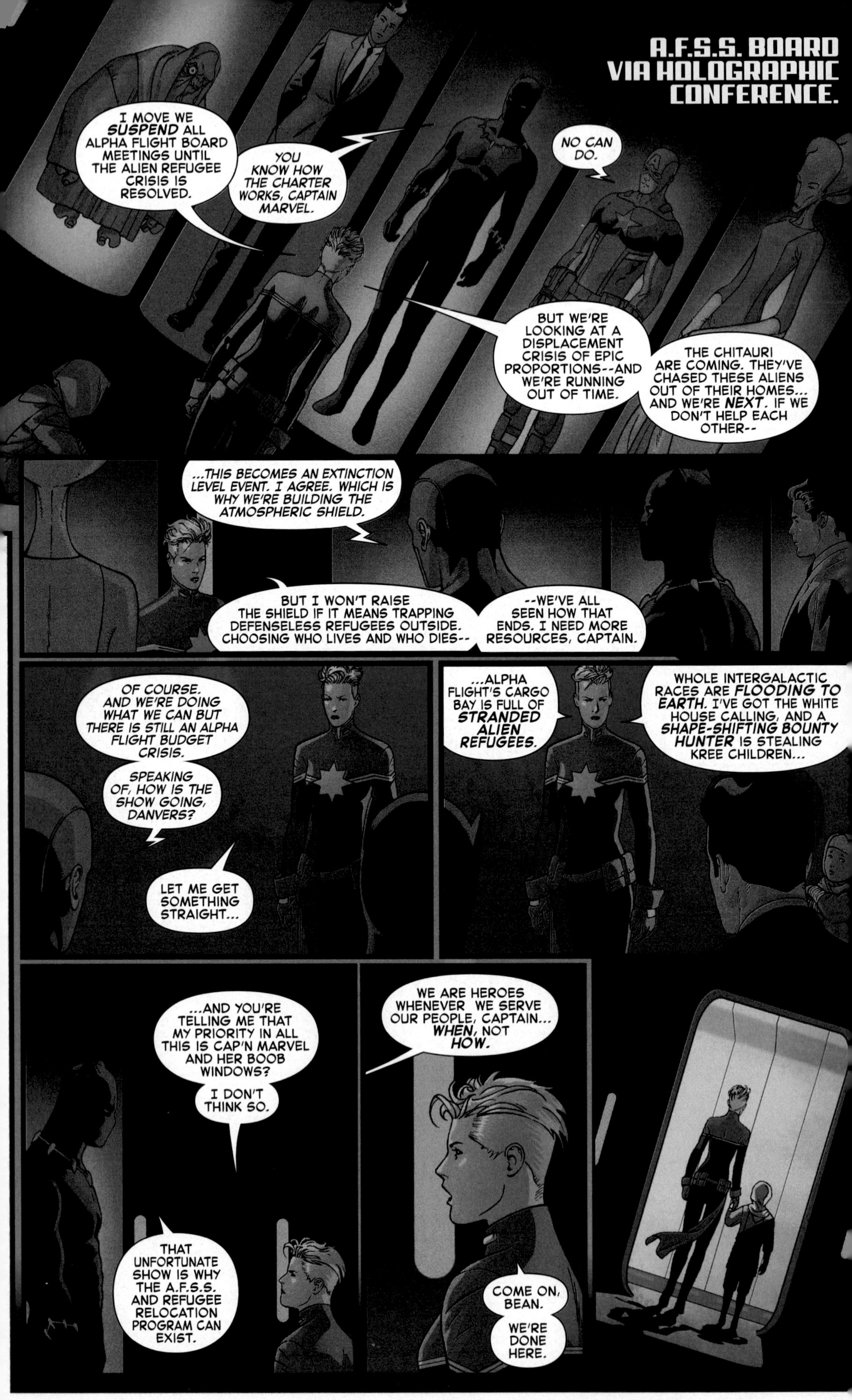
A.F.S.S. BOARD VIA HOLOGRAPHIC CONFERENCE.
I MOVE WE SUSPEND ALL ALPHA FLIGHT BOARD MEETINGS UNTIL THE ALIEN REFUGEE CRISIS IS RESOLVED.
YOU KNOW HOW THE CHARTER WORKS, CAPTAIN MARVEL.
NO CAN DO.
BUT WE'RE LOOKING AT A DISPLACEMENT CRISIS OF EPIC PROPORTIONS--AND WE'RE RUNNING OUT OF TIME.
THE CHITAURI ARE COMING. THEY'VE CHASED THESE ALIENS OUT OF THEIR HOMES... AND WE'RE NEXT. IF WE DON'T HELP EACH OTHER--
...THIS BECOMES AN EXTINCTION LEVEL EVENT. I AGREE. WHICH IS WHY WE'RE BUILDING THE ATMOSPHERIC SHIELD.
BUT I WON'T RAISE THE SHIELD IF IT MEANS TRAPPING DEFENSELESS REFUGEES OUTSIDE. CHOOSING WHO LIVES AND WHO DIES--
--WE'VE ALL SEEN HOW THAT ENDS. I NEED MORE RESOURCES, CAPTAIN.
OF COURSE. AND WE'RE DOING WHAT WE CAN BUT THERE IS STILL AN ALPHA FLIGHT BUDGET CRISIS.
SPEAKING OF, HOW IS THE SHOW GOING, DANVERS?
LET ME GET SOMETHING STRAIGHT...
...ALPHA FLIGHT'S CARGO BAY IS FULL OF STRANDED ALIEN REFUGEES.
WHOLE INTERGALACTIC RACES ARE FLOODING TO EARTH. I'VE GOT THE WHITE HOUSE CALLING, AND A SHAPE-SHIFTING BOUNTY HUNTER IS STEALING KREE CHILDREN...
...AND YOU'RE TELLING ME THAT MY PRIORITY IN ALL THIS IS CAP'N MARVEL AND HER BOOB WINDOWS?
I DON'T THINK SO.
THAT UNFORTUNATE SHOW IS WHY THE A.F.S.S. AND REFUGEE RELOCATION PROGRAM CAN EXIST.
WE ARE HEROES WHENEVER WE SERVE OUR PEOPLE, CAPTAIN... WHEN, NOT HOW.
COME ON, BEAN.
WE'RE DONE HERE.

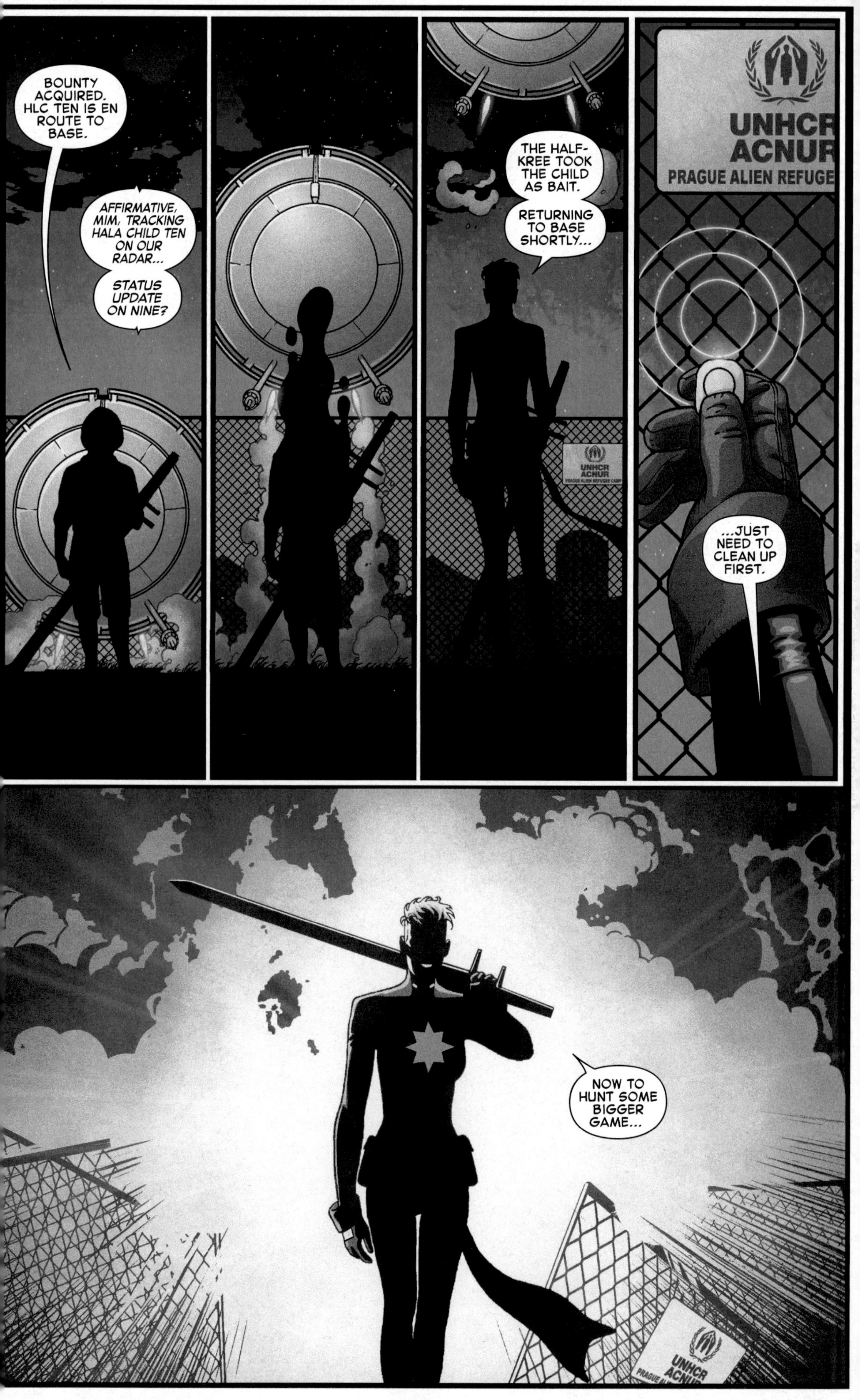
BOUNTY ACQUIRED. HLC TEN IS EN ROUTE TO BASE.
AFFIRMATIVE, MIM, TRACKING HALA CHILD TEN ON OUR RADAR...
STATUS UPDATE ON NINE?
THE HALF-KREE TOOK THE CHILD AS BAIT.
RETURNING TO BASE SHORTLY...
UNHCR
ACNUR
PRAGUE ALIEN REFUGE
...JUST NEED TO CLEAN UP FIRST.
NOW TO HUNT SOME BIGGER GAME...

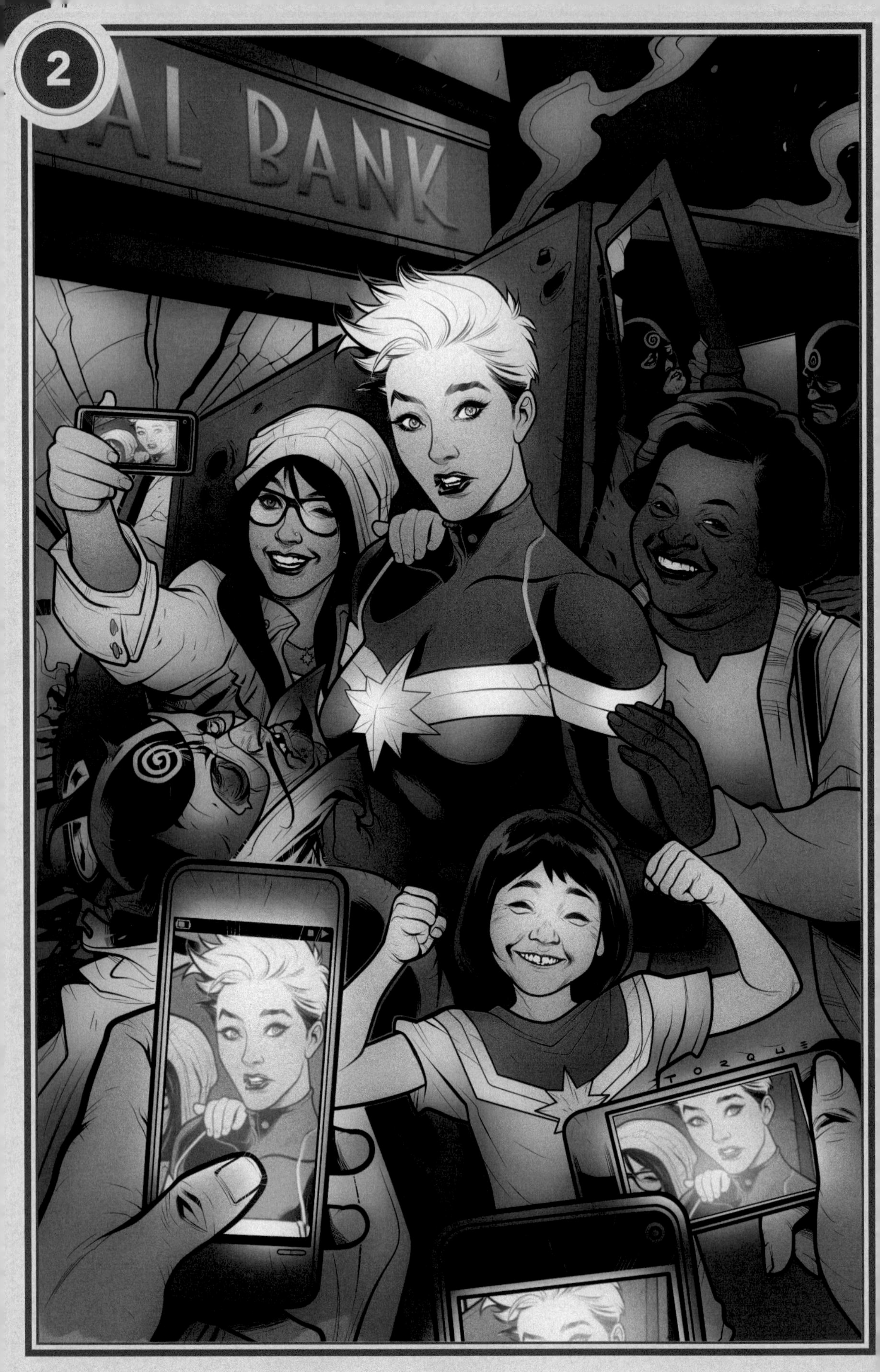
2
AL BANK
TORQUE

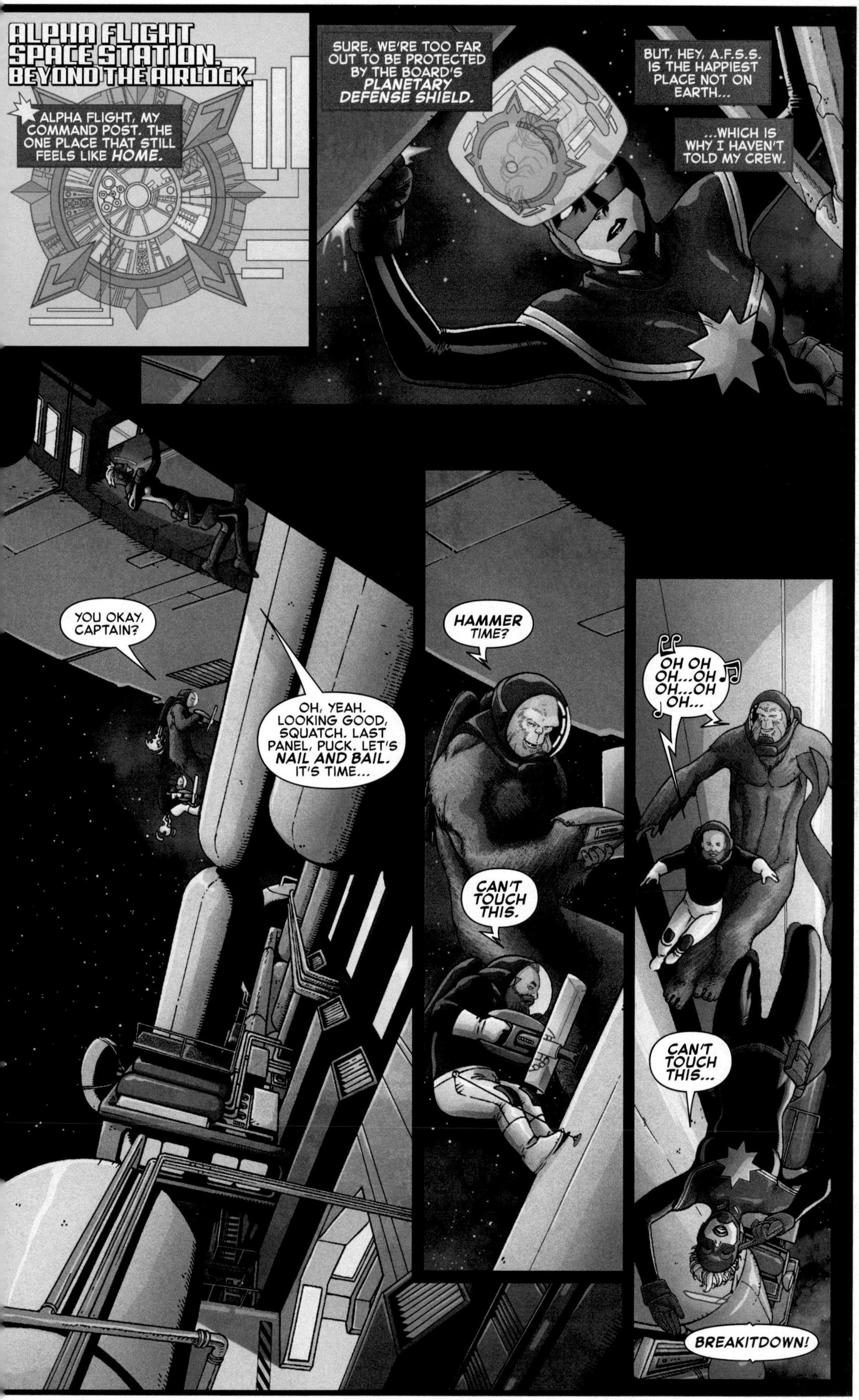
ALPHA FLIGHT SPACE STATION. BEYOND THE AIRLOCK.
ALPHA FLIGHT, MY COMMAND POST. THE ONE PLACE THAT STILL FEELS LIKE HOME.
SURE, WE'RE TOO FAR OUT TO BE PROTECTED BY THE BOARD'S PLANETARY DEFENSE SHIELD.
BUT, HEY, A.F.S.S. IS THE HAPPIEST PLACE NOT ON EARTH...
...WHICH IS WHY I HAVEN'T TOLD MY CREW.
YOU OKAY, CAPTAIN?
OH, YEAH. LOOKING GOOD, SQUATCH. LAST PANEL, PUCK. LET'S NAIL AND BAIL. IT'S TIME...
HAMMER TIME?
CAN'T TOUCH THIS.
OH OH OH...OH OH...OH OH...
CAN'T TOUCH THIS...
BREAKITDOWN!

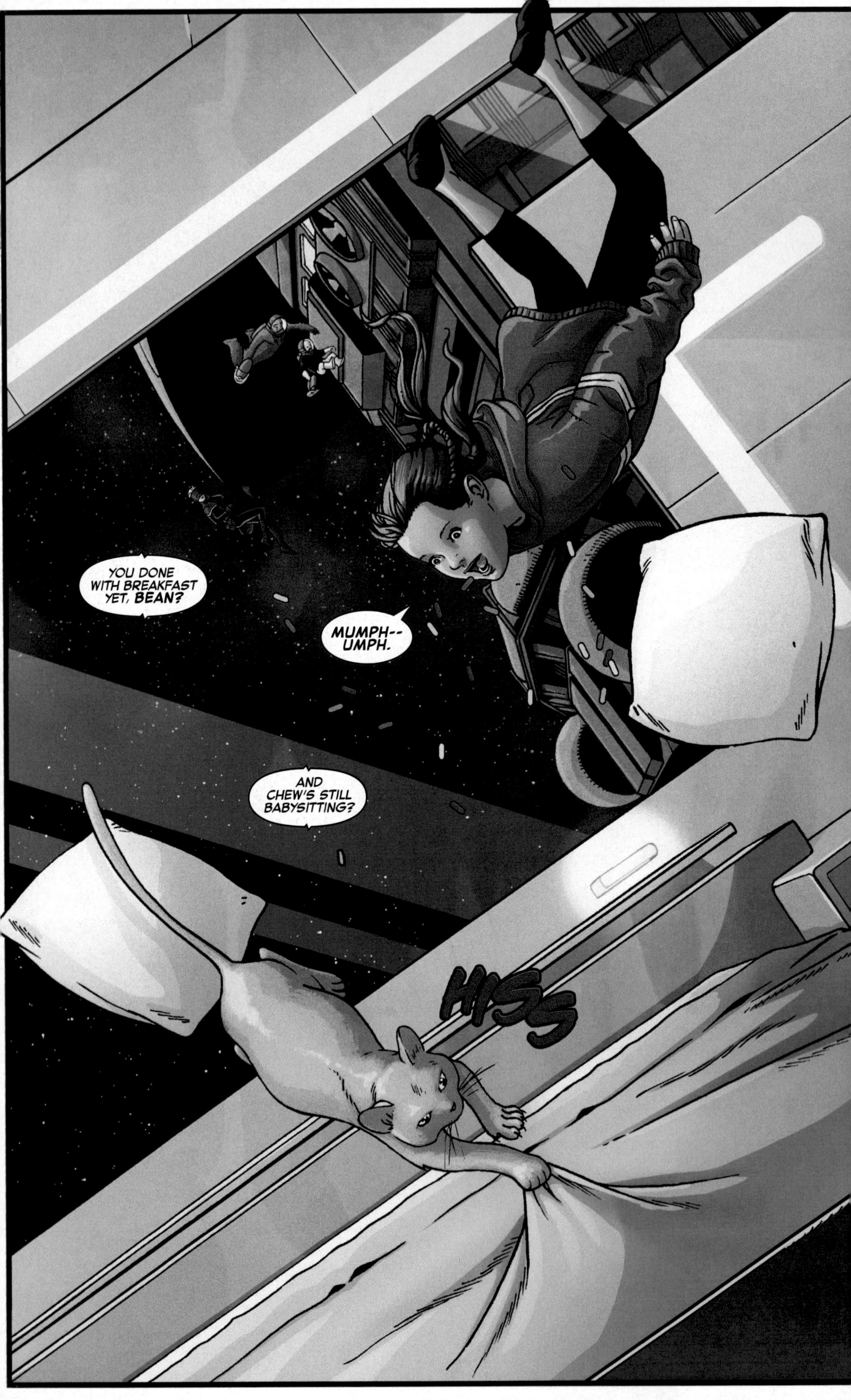
YOU DONE WITH BREAKFAST YET, BEAN?
MUMPH--UMPH.
AND CHEW'S STILL BABYSITTING?
HISS

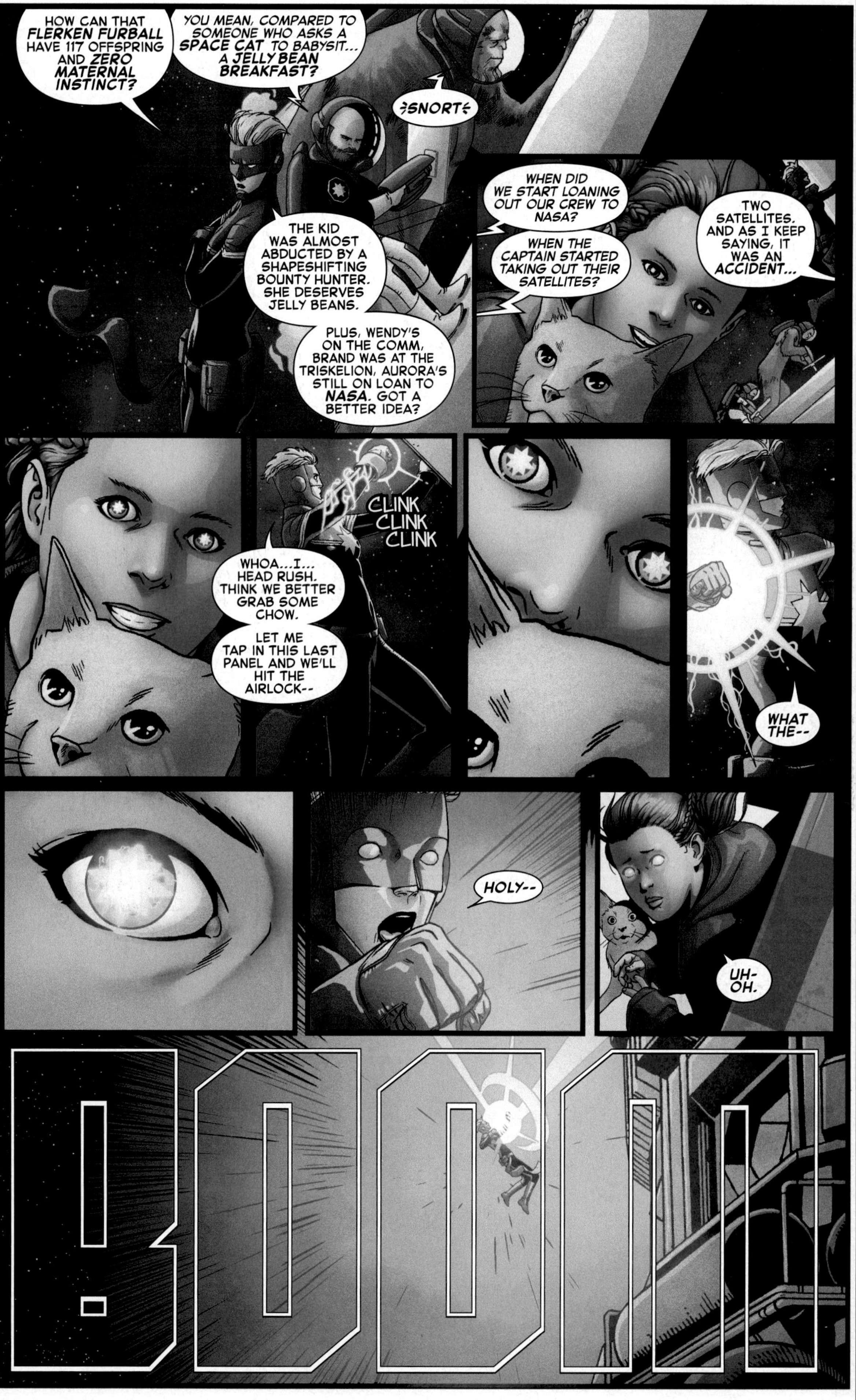
HOW CAN THAT FLERKEN FURBALL HAVE 117 OFFSPRING AND ZERO MATERNAL INSTINCT?
YOU MEAN, COMPARED TO SOMEONE WHO ASKS A SPACE CAT TO BABYSIT... A JELLY BEAN BREAKFAST?
SNORT
THE KID WAS ALMOST ABDUCTED BY A SHAPESHIFTING BOUNTY HUNTER. SHE DESERVES JELLY BEANS.
PLUS, WENDY'S ON THE COMM, BRAND WAS AT THE TRISKELION, AURORA'S STILL ON LOAN TO NASA. GOT A BETTER IDEA?
WHEN DID WE START LOANING OUT OUR CREW TO NASA?
WHEN THE CAPTAIN STARTED TAKING OUT THEIR SATELLITES?
TWO SATELLITES. AND AS I KEEP SAYING, IT WAS AN ACCIDENT...
CLINK CLINK CLINK
WHOA...I... HEAD RUSH. THINK WE BETTER GRAB SOME CHOW.
LET ME TAP IN THIS LAST PANEL AND WE'LL HIT THE AIRLOCK--
WHAT THE--
HOLY--
UH-OH.
BOOM!

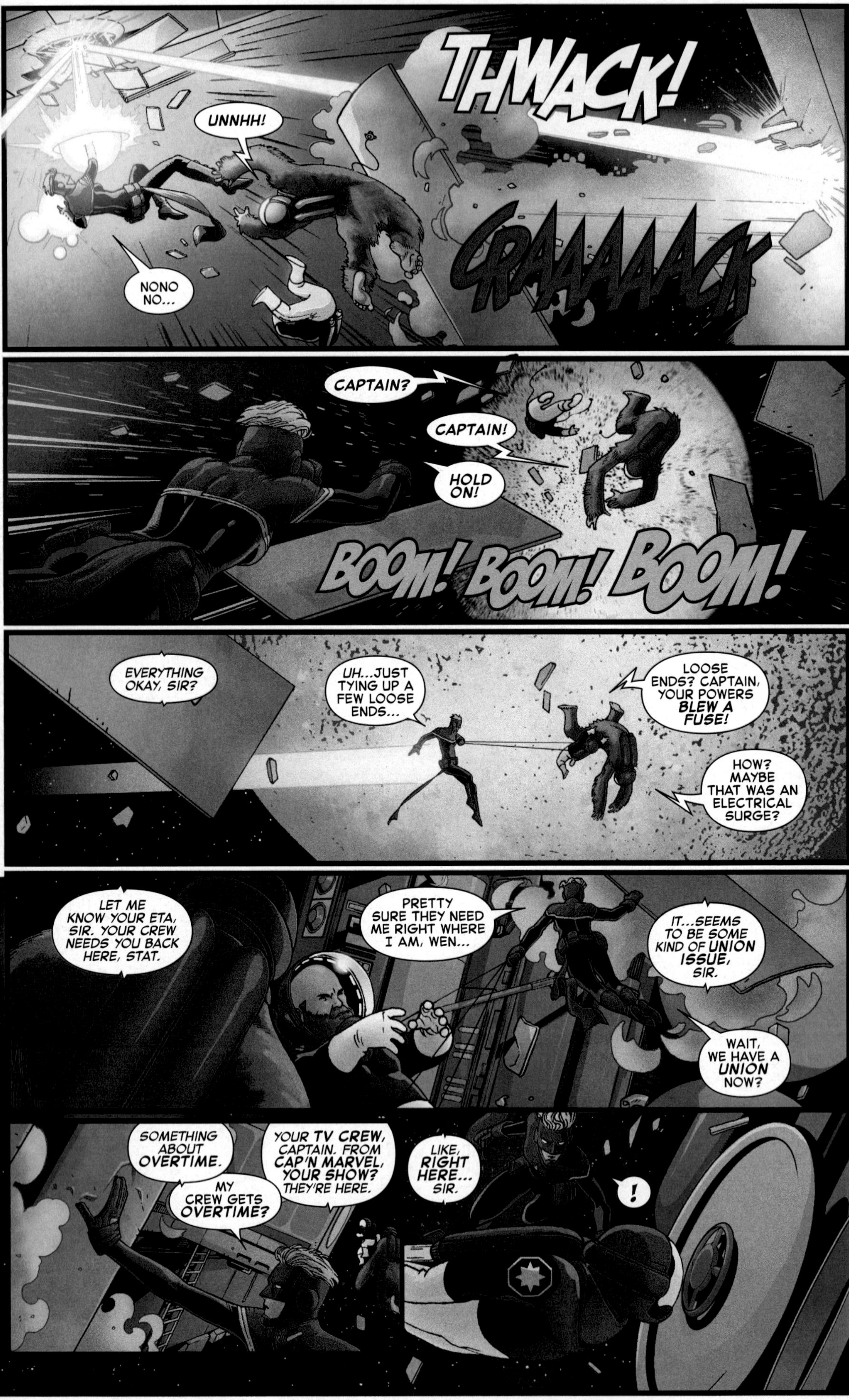
THWACK!
UNNHH!
NONO NO...
CRAAAAACK
CAPTAIN?
CAPTAIN!
HOLD ON!
BOOM! BOOM! BOOM!
EVERYTHING OKAY, SIR?
UH...JUST TYING UP A FEW LOOSE ENDS...
LOOSE ENDS? CAPTAIN, YOUR POWERS BLEW A FUSE!
HOW? MAYBE THAT WAS AN ELECTRICAL SURGE?
LET ME KNOW YOUR ETA, SIR. YOUR CREW NEEDS YOU BACK HERE, STAT.
PRETTY SURE THEY NEED ME RIGHT WHERE I AM, WEN...
IT...SEEMS TO BE SOME KIND OF UNION ISSUE, SIR.
WAIT, WE HAVE A UNION NOW?
SOMETHING ABOUT OVERTIME.
MY CREW GETS OVERTIME?
YOUR TV CREW, CAPTAIN. FROM CAP'N MARVEL, YOUR SHOW? THEY'RE HERE.
LIKE, RIGHT HERE... SIR.
!

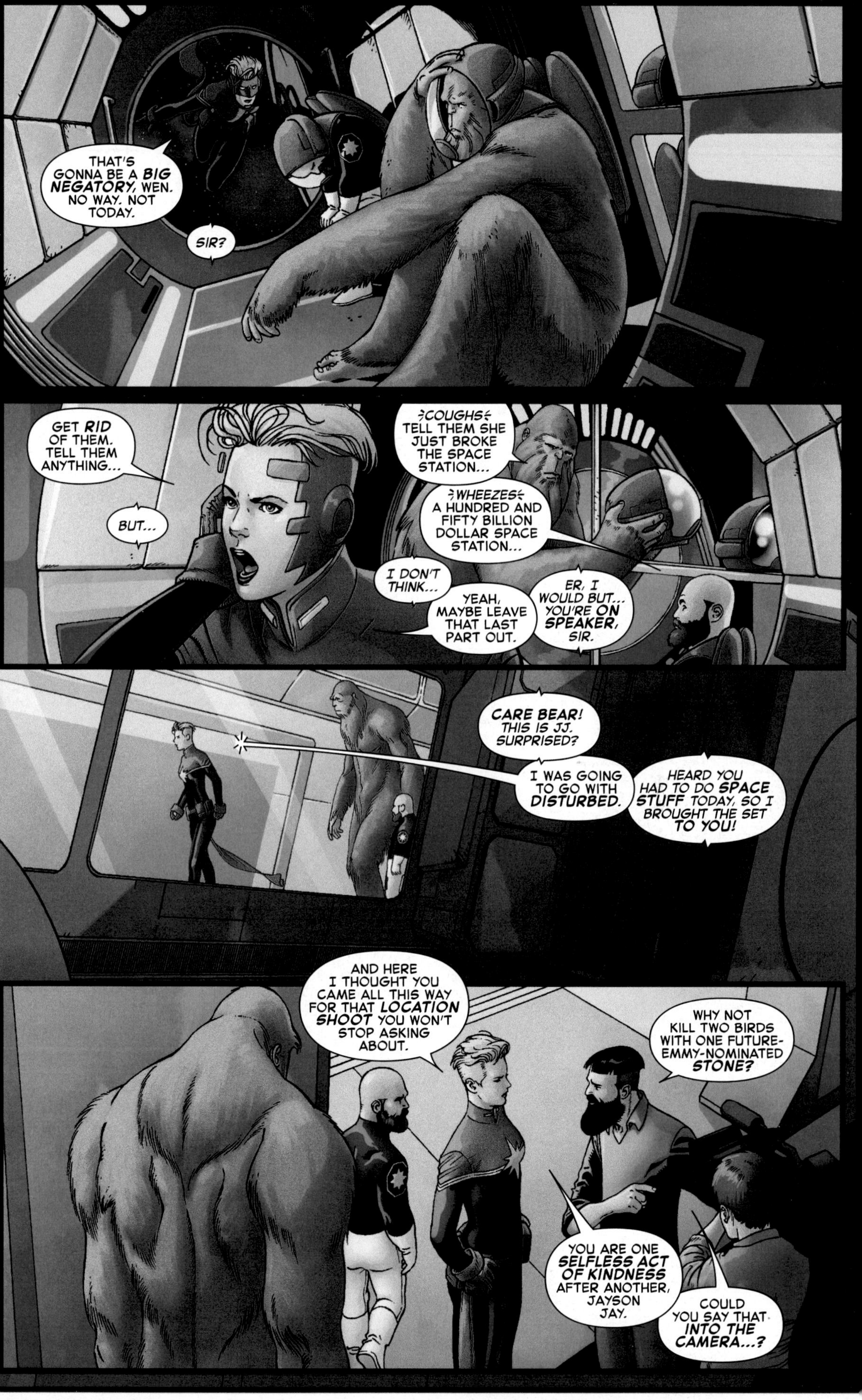

THAT'S GONNA BE A BIG NEGATORY, WEN. NO WAY. NOT TODAY.
SIR?
GET RID OF THEM. TELL THEM ANYTHING...
BUT...
COUGHS TELL THEM SHE JUST BROKE THE SPACE STATION...
WHEEZES A HUNDRED AND FIFTY BILLION DOLLAR SPACE STATION...
I DON'T THINK...
YEAH, MAYBE LEAVE THAT LAST PART OUT.
ER, I WOULD BUT... YOU'RE ON SPEAKER, SIR.
CARE BEAR! THIS IS JJ. SURPRISED?
I WAS GOING TO GO WITH DISTURBED.
HEARD YOU HAD TO DO SPACE STUFF TODAY, SO I BROUGHT THE SET TO YOU!
AND HERE I THOUGHT YOU CAME ALL THIS WAY FOR THAT LOCATION SHOOT YOU WON'T STOP ASKING ABOUT.
WHY NOT KILL TWO BIRDS WITH ONE FUTURE-EMMY-NOMINATED STONE?
YOU ARE ONE SELFLESS ACT OF KINDNESS AFTER ANOTHER, JAYSON JAY.
COULD YOU SAY THAT INTO THE CAMERA...?

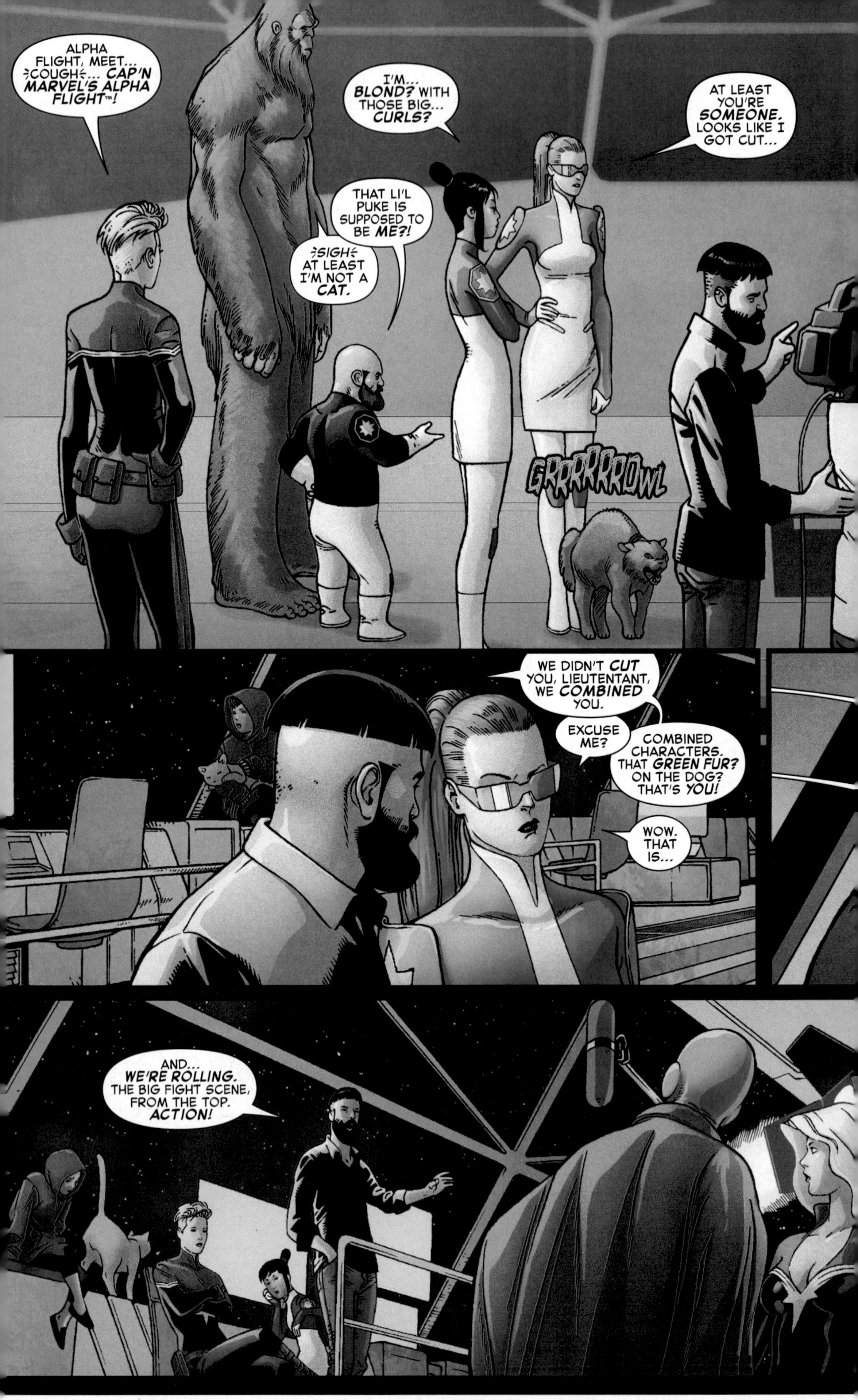
ALPHA FLIGHT, MEET... ⁓COUGH⁓... CAP'N MARVEL'S ALPHA FLIGHT™!
I'M... BLOND? WITH THOSE BIG... CURLS?
AT LEAST YOU'RE SOMEONE. LOOKS LIKE I GOT CUT...
THAT LI'L PUKE IS SUPPOSED TO BE ME?!
⁓SIGH⁓ AT LEAST I'M NOT A CAT.
GRRRRRROWL
WE DIDN'T CUT YOU, LIEUTENTANT, WE COMBINED YOU.
EXCUSE ME?
COMBINED CHARACTERS. THAT GREEN FUR? ON THE DOG? THAT'S YOU!
WOW. THAT IS...
AND... WE'RE ROLLING. THE BIG FIGHT SCENE, FROM THE TOP. ACTION!

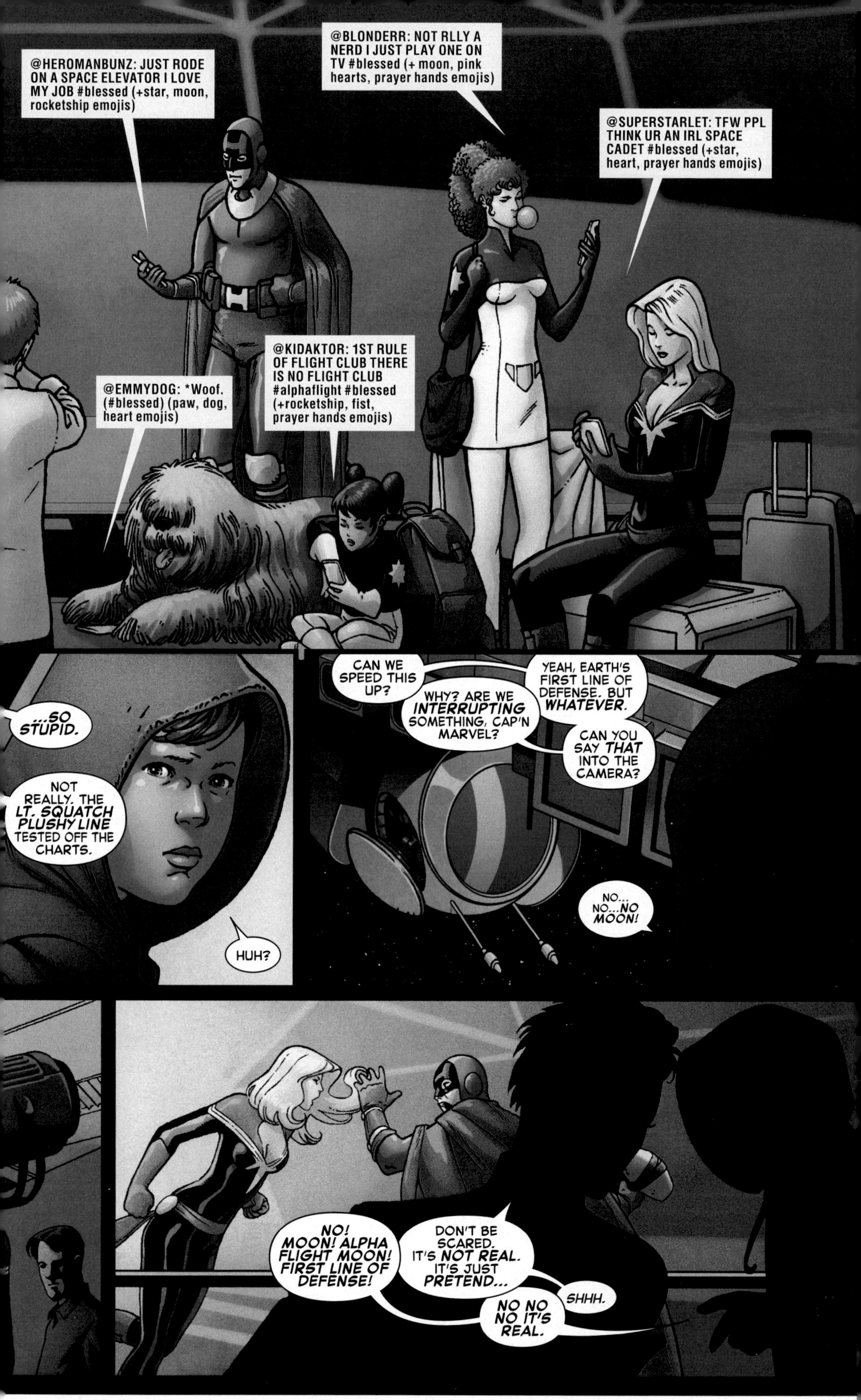
@HEROMANBUNZ: JUST RODE ON A SPACE ELEVATOR I LOVE MY JOB #blessed (+star, moon, rocketship emojis)
@BLONDERR: NOT RLLY A NERD I JUST PLAY ONE ON TV #blessed (+ moon, pink hearts, prayer hands emojis)
@SUPERSTARLET: TFW PPL THINK UR AN IRL SPACE CADET #blessed (+star, heart, prayer hands emojis)
@EMMYDOG: *Woof. (#blessed) (paw, dog, heart emojis)
@KIDAKTOR: 1ST RULE OF FLIGHT CLUB THERE IS NO FLIGHT CLUB #alphaflight #blessed (+rocketship, fist, prayer hands emojis)
...SO STUPID.
NOT REALLY. THE LT. SQUATCH PLUSHY LINE TESTED OFF THE CHARTS.
HUH?
CAN WE SPEED THIS UP?
WHY? ARE WE INTERRUPTING SOMETHING, CAP'N MARVEL?
YEAH, EARTH'S FIRST LINE OF DEFENSE. BUT WHATEVER.
CAN YOU SAY THAT INTO THE CAMERA?
NO... NO...NO MOON!
NO! MOON! ALPHA FLIGHT MOON! FIRST LINE OF DEFENSE!
DON'T BE SCARED. IT'S NOT REAL. IT'S JUST PRETEND...
SHHH.
NO NO NO IT'S REAL.

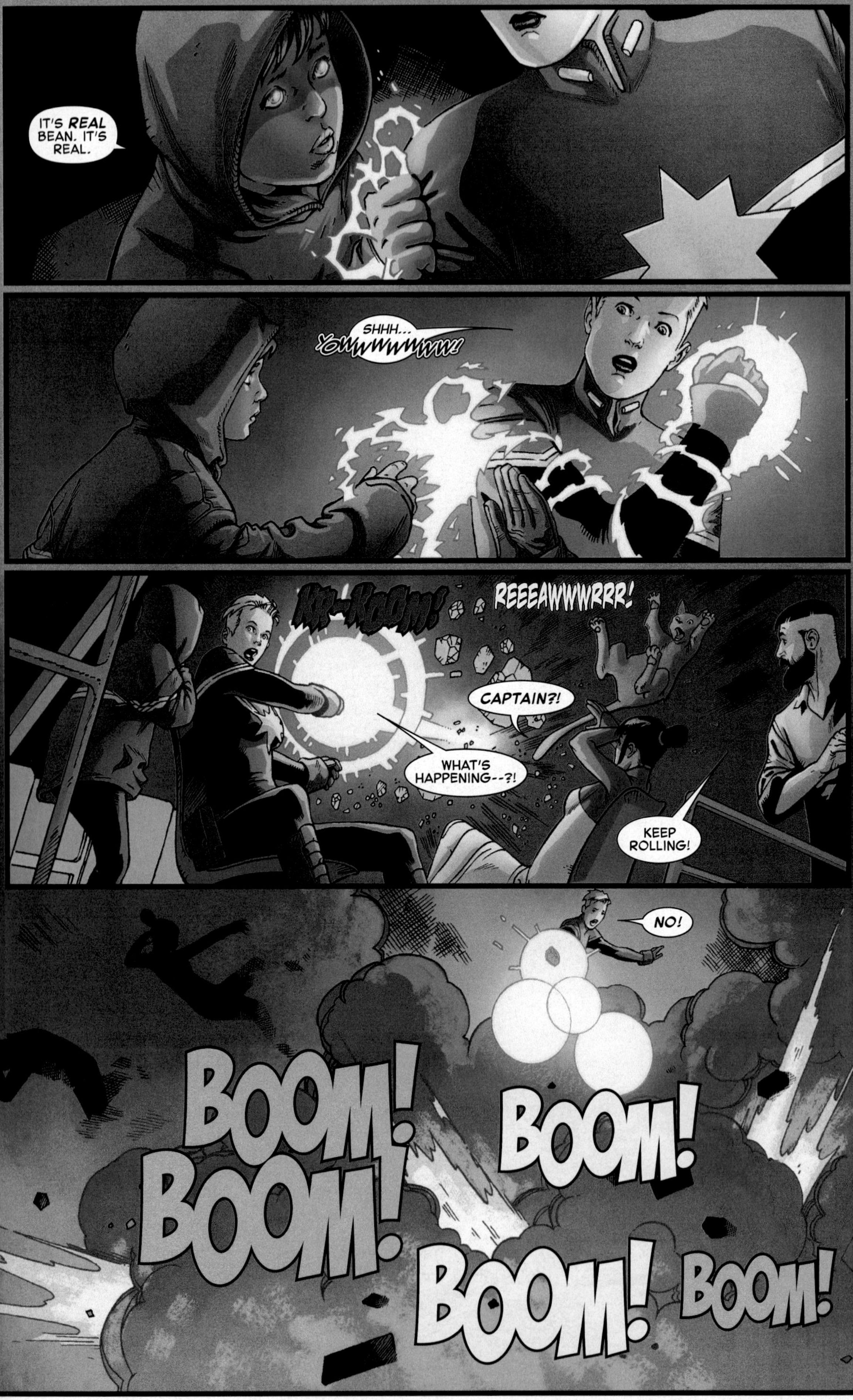
IT'S *REAL* BEAN. IT'S REAL.
SHHH...
YOWWWWWW!
KR-KOOM!
REEEAWWWRRR!
CAPTAIN?!
WHAT'S HAPPENING--?!
KEEP ROLLING!
NO!
BOOM! BOOM!
BOOM!
BOOM! BOOM!

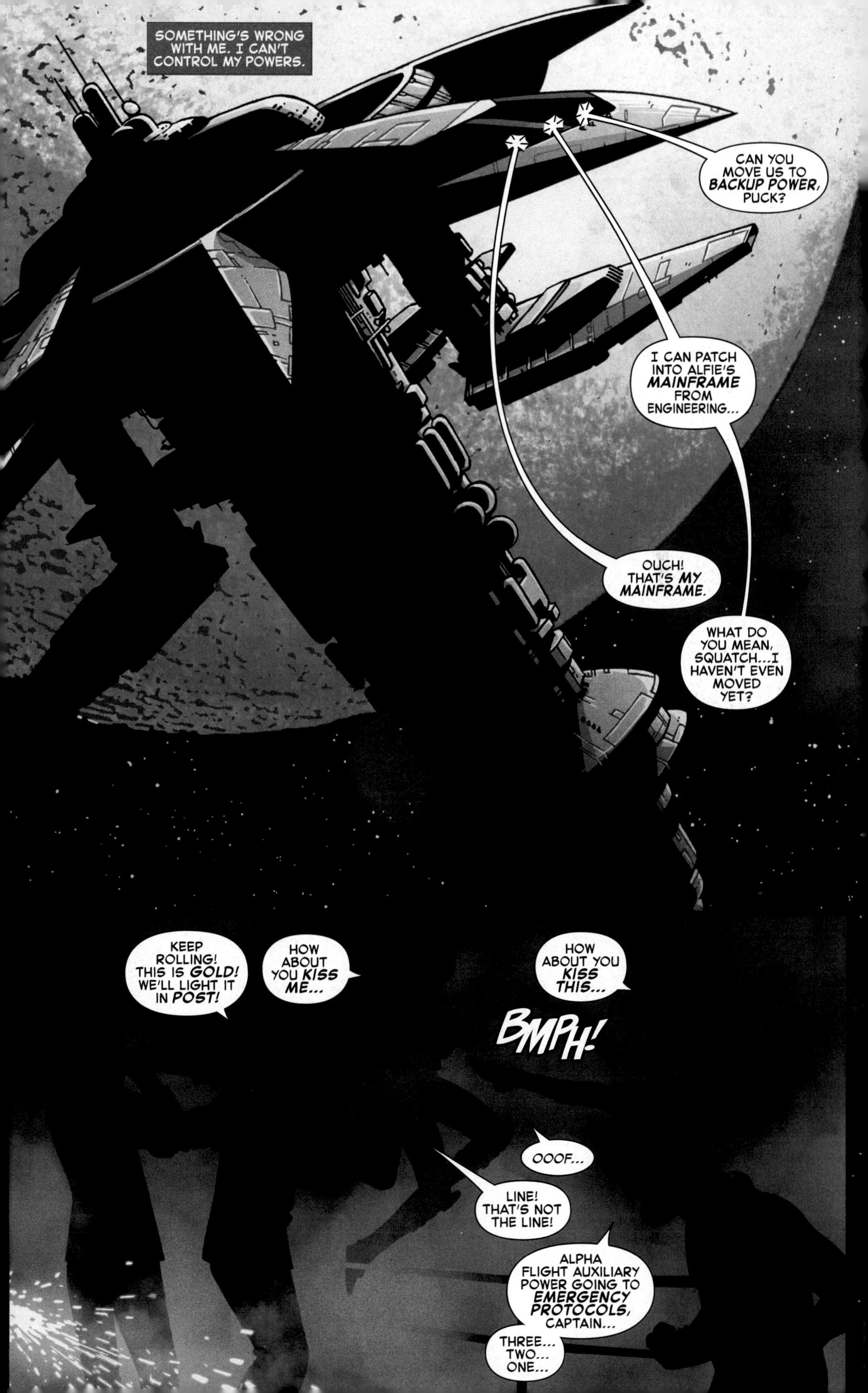
SOMETHING'S WRONG WITH ME. I CAN'T CONTROL MY POWERS.
CAN YOU MOVE US TO BACKUP POWER, PUCK?
I CAN PATCH INTO ALFIE'S MAINFRAME FROM ENGINEERING...
OUCH! THAT'S MY MAINFRAME.
WHAT DO YOU MEAN, SQUATCH...I HAVEN'T EVEN MOVED YET?
KEEP ROLLING! THIS IS GOLD! WE'LL LIGHT IT IN POST!
HOW ABOUT YOU KISS ME...
HOW ABOUT YOU KISS THIS...
BMPH!
OOOF...
LINE! THAT'S NOT THE LINE!
ALPHA FLIGHT AUXILIARY POWER GOING TO EMERGENCY PROTOCOLS, CAPTAIN...
THREE... TWO... ONE...

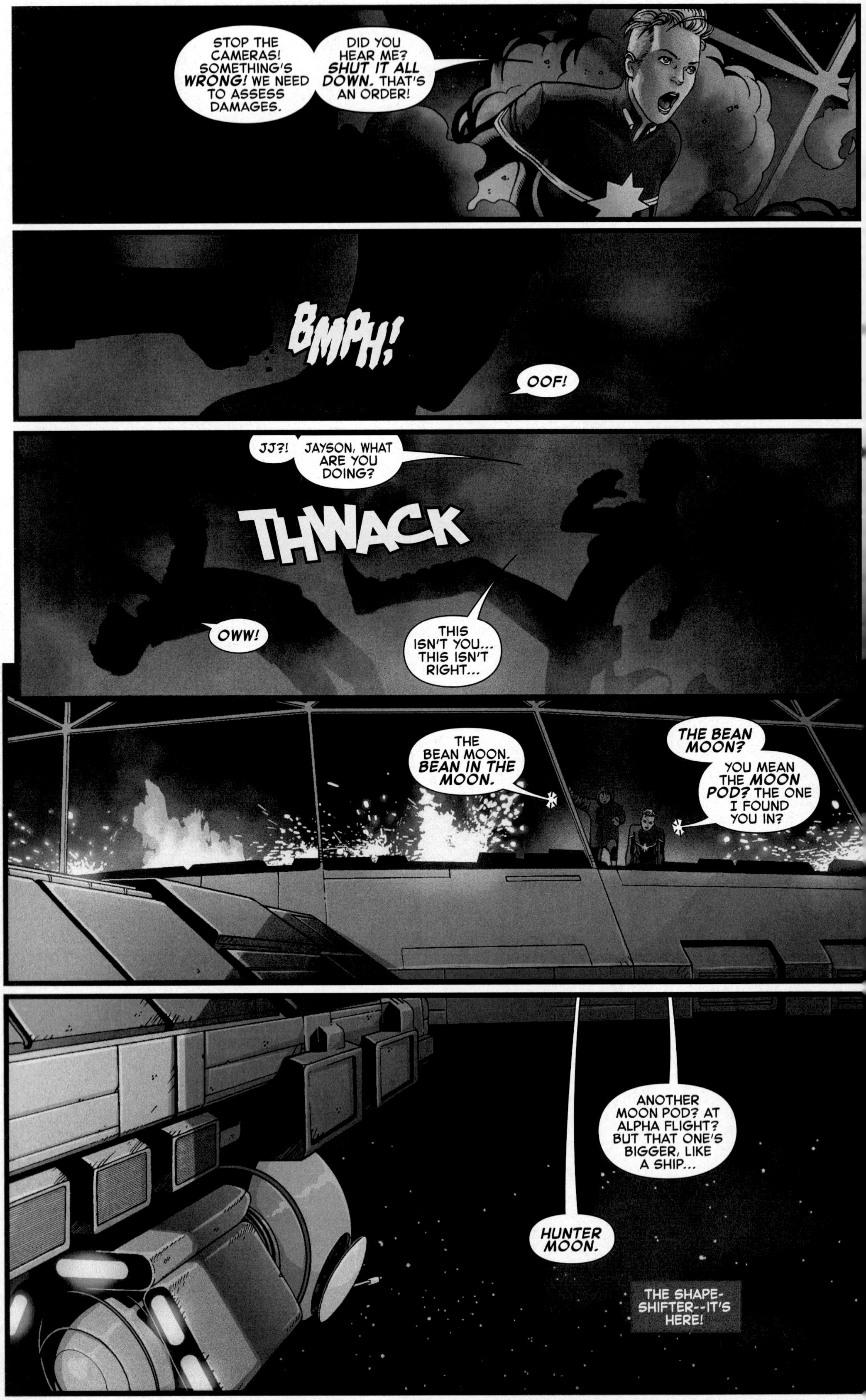
STOP THE CAMERAS! SOMETHING'S WRONG! WE NEED TO ASSESS DAMAGES.
DID YOU HEAR ME? SHUT IT ALL DOWN. THAT'S AN ORDER!
BMPH!
OOF!
JJ?!
JAYSON, WHAT ARE YOU DOING?
THWACK
OWW!
THIS ISN'T YOU... THIS ISN'T RIGHT...
THE BEAN MOON. BEAN IN THE MOON.
THE BEAN MOON?
YOU MEAN THE MOON POD? THE ONE I FOUND YOU IN?
ANOTHER MOON POD? AT ALPHA FLIGHT? BUT THAT ONE'S BIGGER, LIKE A SHIP...
HUNTER MOON.
THE SHAPE-SHIFTER--IT'S HERE!

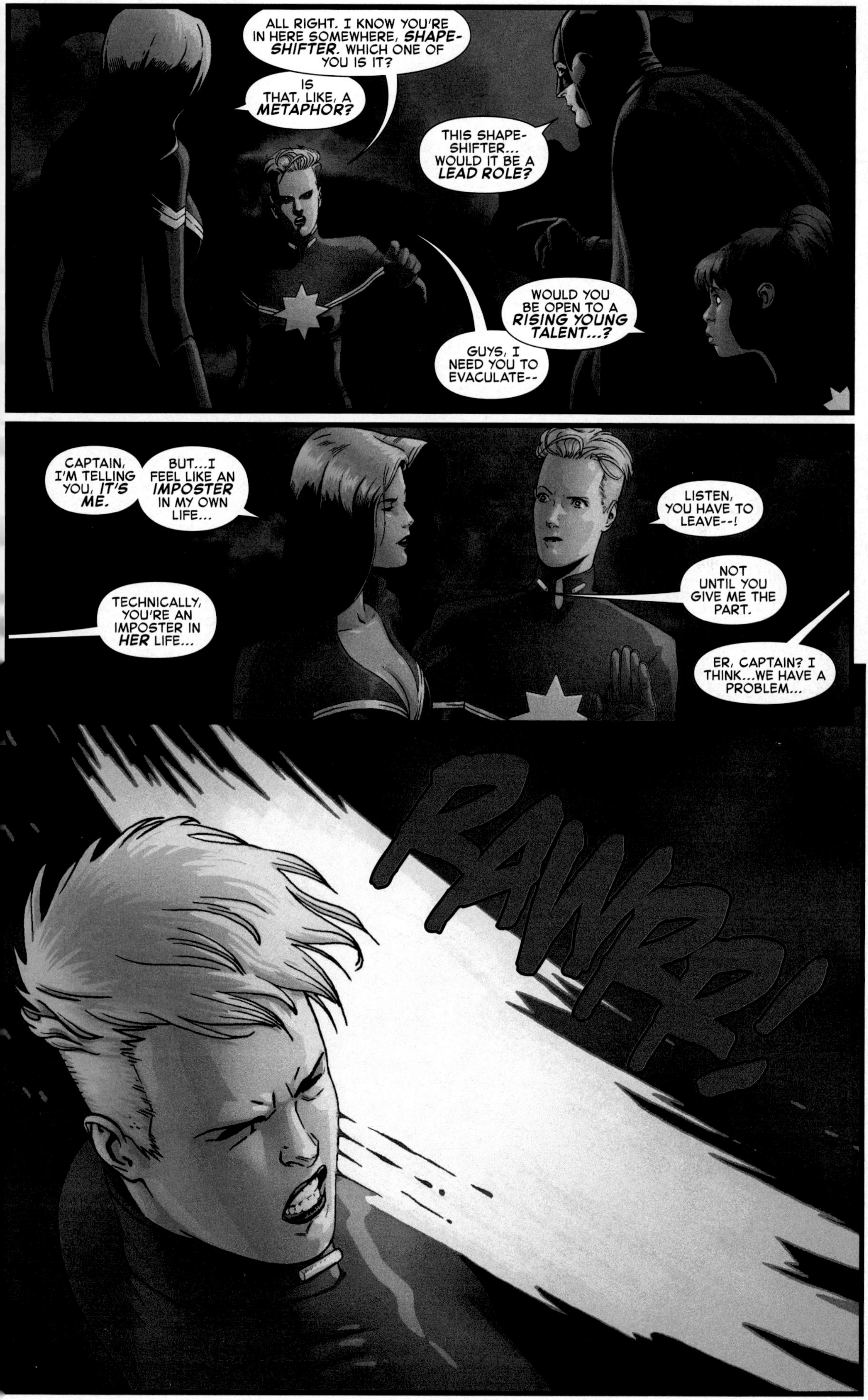
ALL RIGHT. I KNOW YOU'RE IN HERE SOMEWHERE, SHAPE-SHIFTER. WHICH ONE OF YOU IS IT?
IS THAT, LIKE, A METAPHOR?
THIS SHAPE-SHIFTER... WOULD IT BE A LEAD ROLE?
WOULD YOU BE OPEN TO A RISING YOUNG TALENT...?
GUYS, I NEED YOU TO EVACUATE--
CAPTAIN, I'M TELLING YOU, IT'S ME.
BUT...I FEEL LIKE AN IMPOSTER IN MY OWN LIFE...
LISTEN, YOU HAVE TO LEAVE--!
TECHNICALLY, YOU'RE AN IMPOSTER IN HER LIFE...
NOT UNTIL YOU GIVE ME THE PART.
ER, CAPTAIN? I THINK...WE HAVE A PROBLEM...
RAWRR!

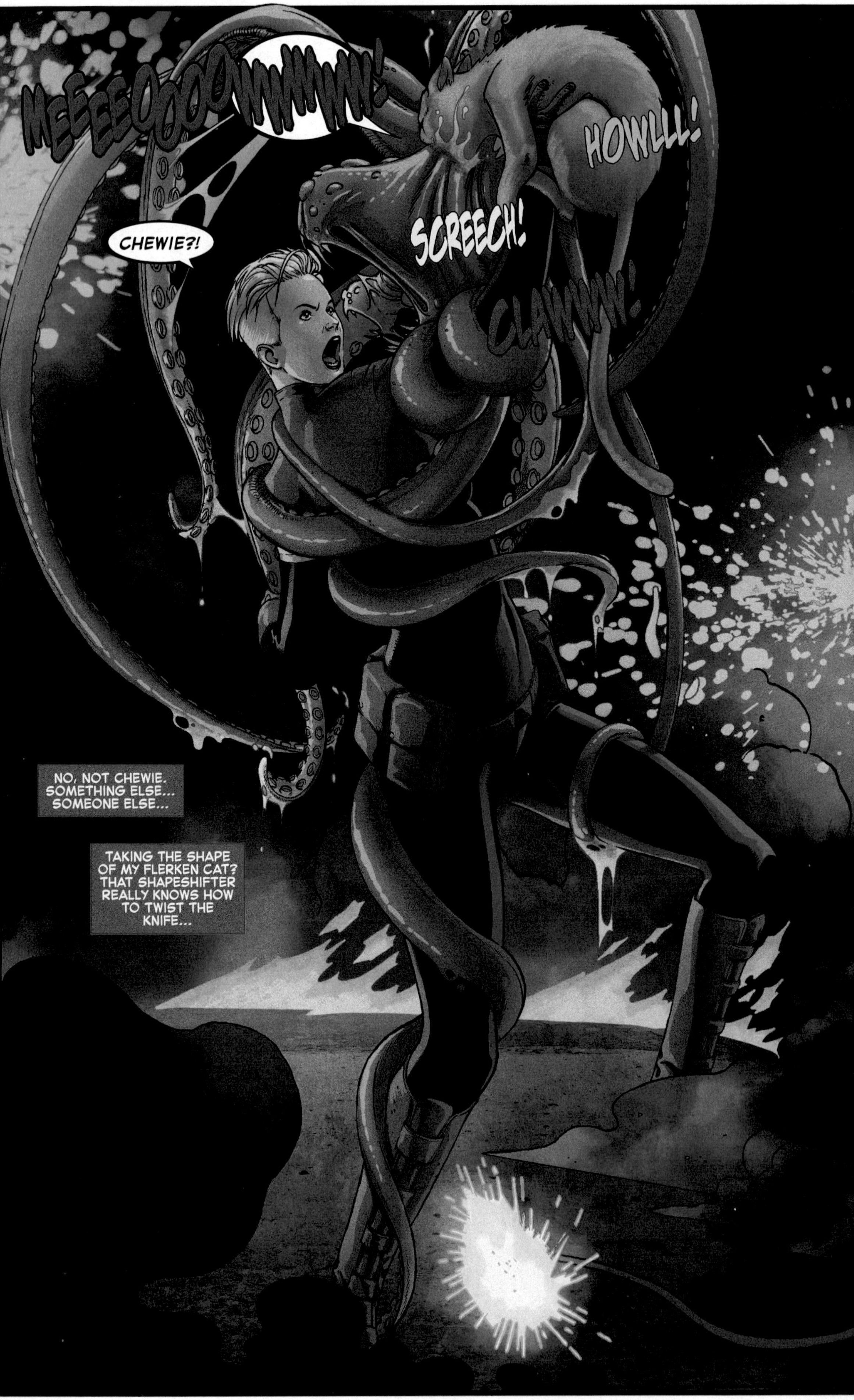
MEEEEEOOOOWWWWW!
CHEWIE?!
HOWLLL!
SCREECH!
CLAWWW!
NO, NOT CHEWIE. SOMETHING ELSE... SOMEONE ELSE...
TAKING THE SHAPE OF MY FLERKEN CAT? THAT SHAPESHIFTER REALLY KNOWS HOW TO TWIST THE KNIFE...

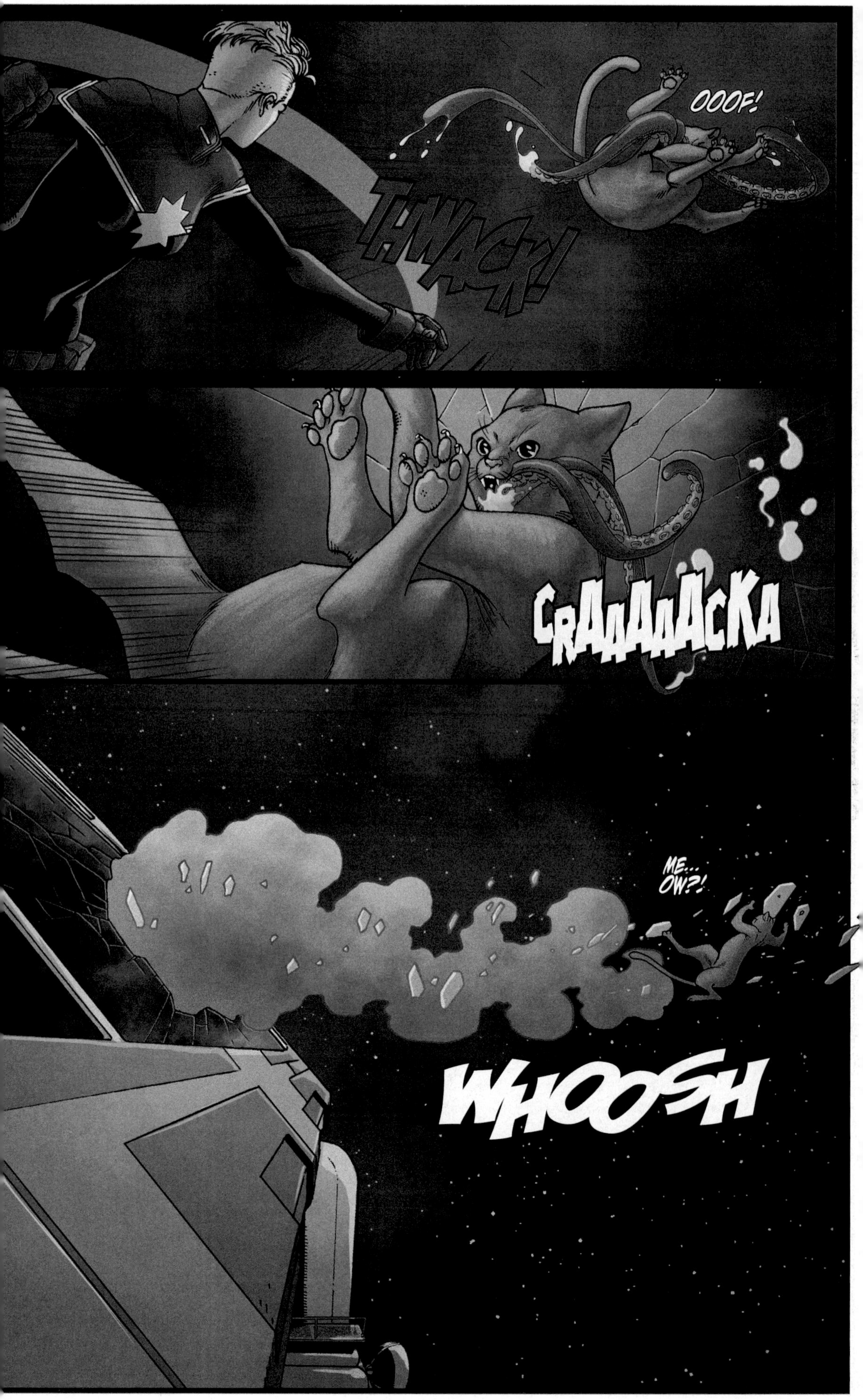
OOOF!
THWACK!
CRAAAAACKA
ME... OW?!
WHOOSH

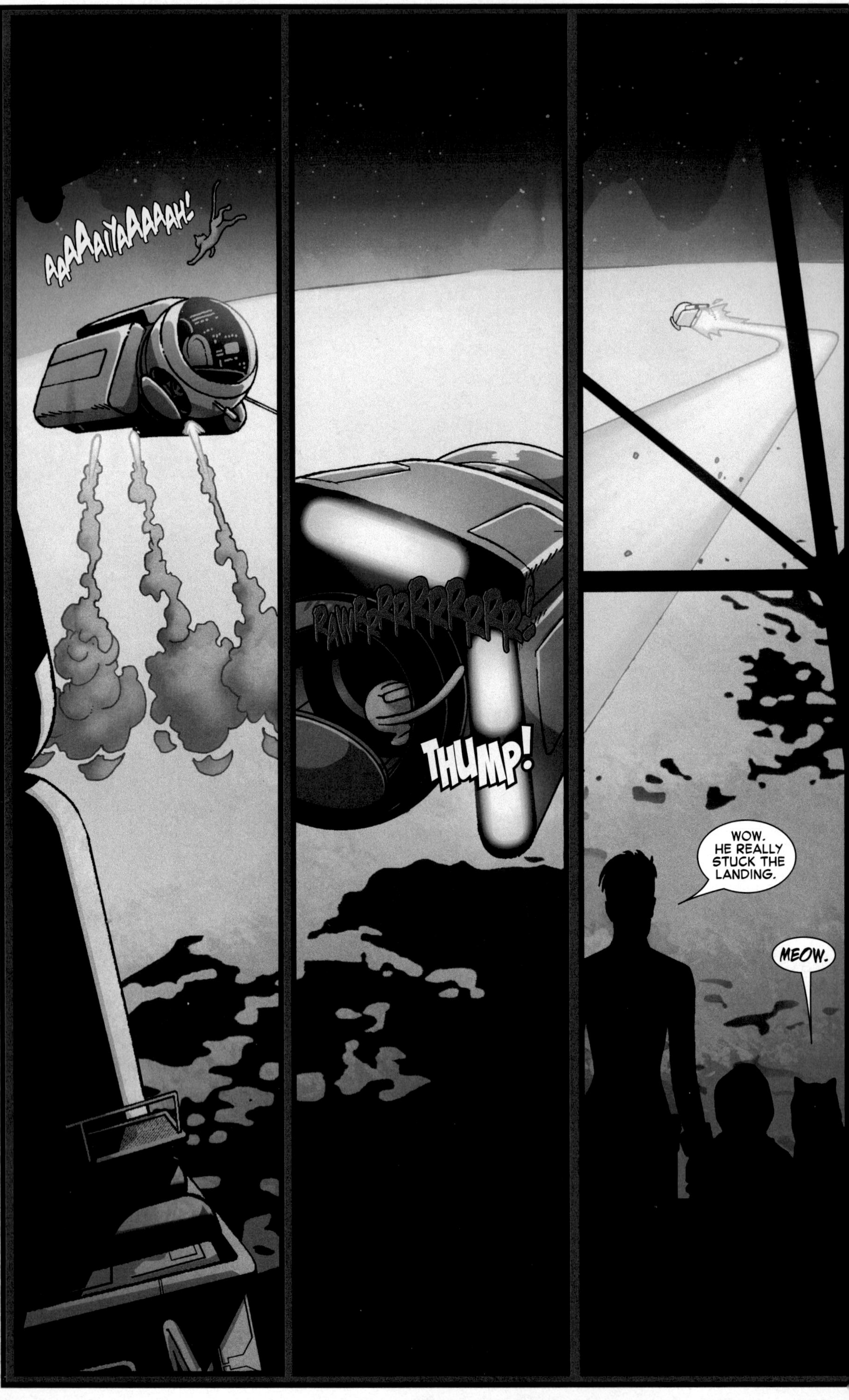
AaAAaiYaAAAAH!
RAWRRRRRRRRR!
THUMP!
WOW. HE REALLY STUCK THE LANDING.
MEOW.

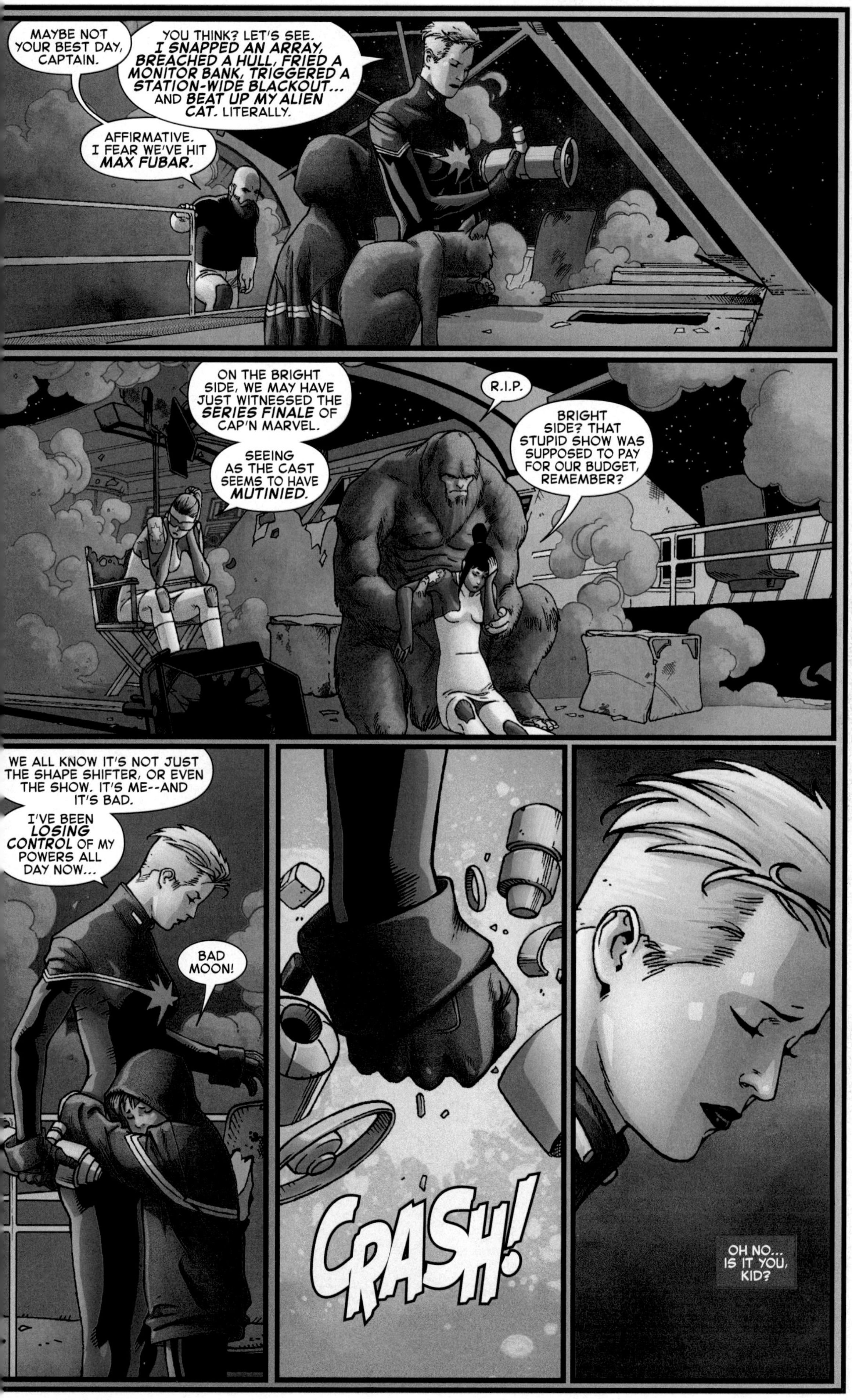
MAYBE NOT YOUR BEST DAY, CAPTAIN.
YOU THINK? LET'S SEE. I SNAPPED AN ARRAY, BREACHED A HULL, FRIED A MONITOR BANK, TRIGGERED A STATION-WIDE BLACKOUT... AND BEAT UP MY ALIEN CAT. LITERALLY.
AFFIRMATIVE. I FEAR WE'VE HIT MAX FUBAR.
ON THE BRIGHT SIDE, WE MAY HAVE JUST WITNESSED THE SERIES FINALE OF CAP'N MARVEL.
SEEING AS THE CAST SEEMS TO HAVE MUTINIED.
R.I.P.
BRIGHT SIDE? THAT STUPID SHOW WAS SUPPOSED TO PAY FOR OUR BUDGET, REMEMBER?
WE ALL KNOW IT'S NOT JUST THE SHAPE SHIFTER, OR EVEN THE SHOW. IT'S ME--AND IT'S BAD.
I'VE BEEN LOSING CONTROL OF MY POWERS ALL DAY NOW...
BAD MOON!
CRASH!
OH NO... IS IT YOU, KID?

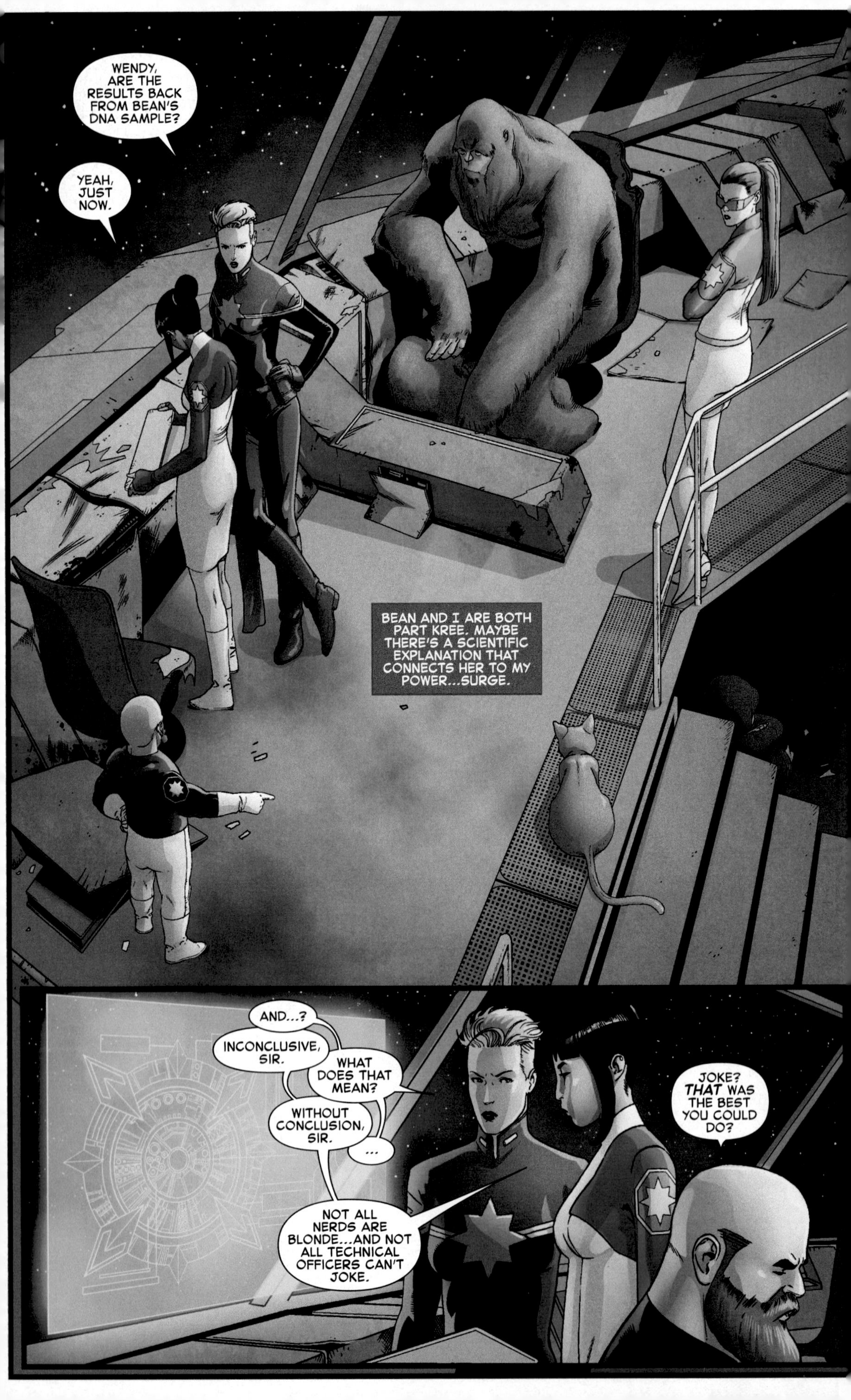
WENDY, ARE THE RESULTS BACK FROM BEAN'S DNA SAMPLE?
YEAH, JUST NOW.
BEAN AND I ARE BOTH PART KREE. MAYBE THERE'S A SCIENTIFIC EXPLANATION THAT CONNECTS HER TO MY POWER...SURGE.
AND...?
INCONCLUSIVE, SIR.
WHAT DOES THAT MEAN?
WITHOUT CONCLUSION, SIR.
...
NOT ALL NERDS ARE BLONDE...AND NOT ALL TECHNICAL OFFICERS CAN'T JOKE.
JOKE? THAT WAS THE BEST YOU COULD DO?

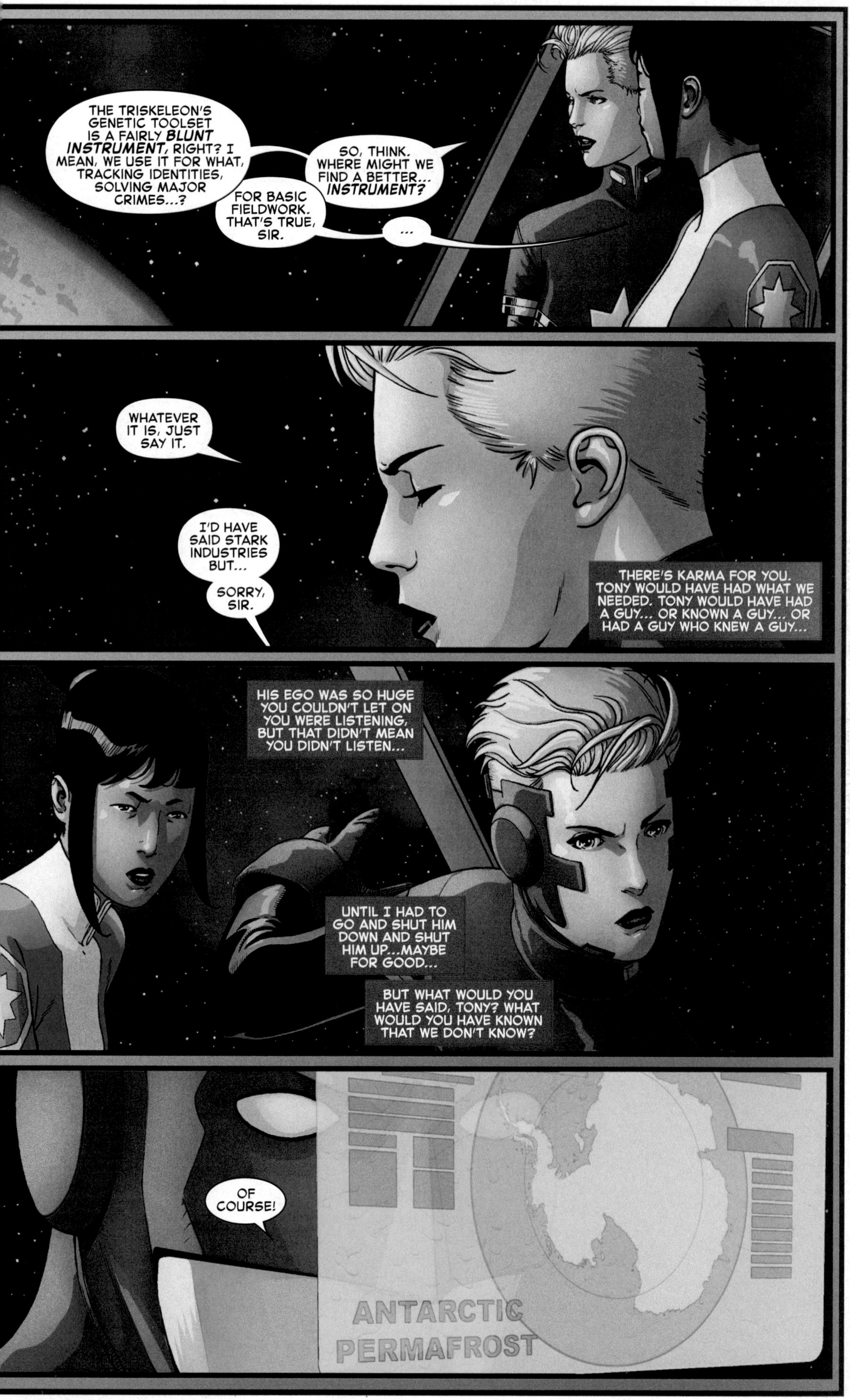
THE TRISKELEON'S GENETIC TOOLSET IS A FAIRLY BLUNT INSTRUMENT, RIGHT? I MEAN, WE USE IT FOR WHAT, TRACKING IDENTITIES, SOLVING MAJOR CRIMES...?
FOR BASIC FIELDWORK. THAT'S TRUE, SIR.
SO, THINK. WHERE MIGHT WE FIND A BETTER... INSTRUMENT?
...
WHATEVER IT IS, JUST SAY IT.
I'D HAVE SAID STARK INDUSTRIES BUT...
SORRY, SIR.
THERE'S KARMA FOR YOU. TONY WOULD HAVE HAD WHAT WE NEEDED. TONY WOULD HAVE HAD A GUY... OR KNOWN A GUY... OR HAD A GUY WHO KNEW A GUY...
HIS EGO WAS SO HUGE YOU COULDN'T LET ON YOU WERE LISTENING, BUT THAT DIDN'T MEAN YOU DIDN'T LISTEN...
UNTIL I HAD TO GO AND SHUT HIM DOWN AND SHUT HIM UP...MAYBE FOR GOOD...
BUT WHAT WOULD YOU HAVE SAID, TONY? WHAT WOULD YOU HAVE KNOWN THAT WE DON'T KNOW?
OF COURSE!
ANTARCTIC PERMAFROST

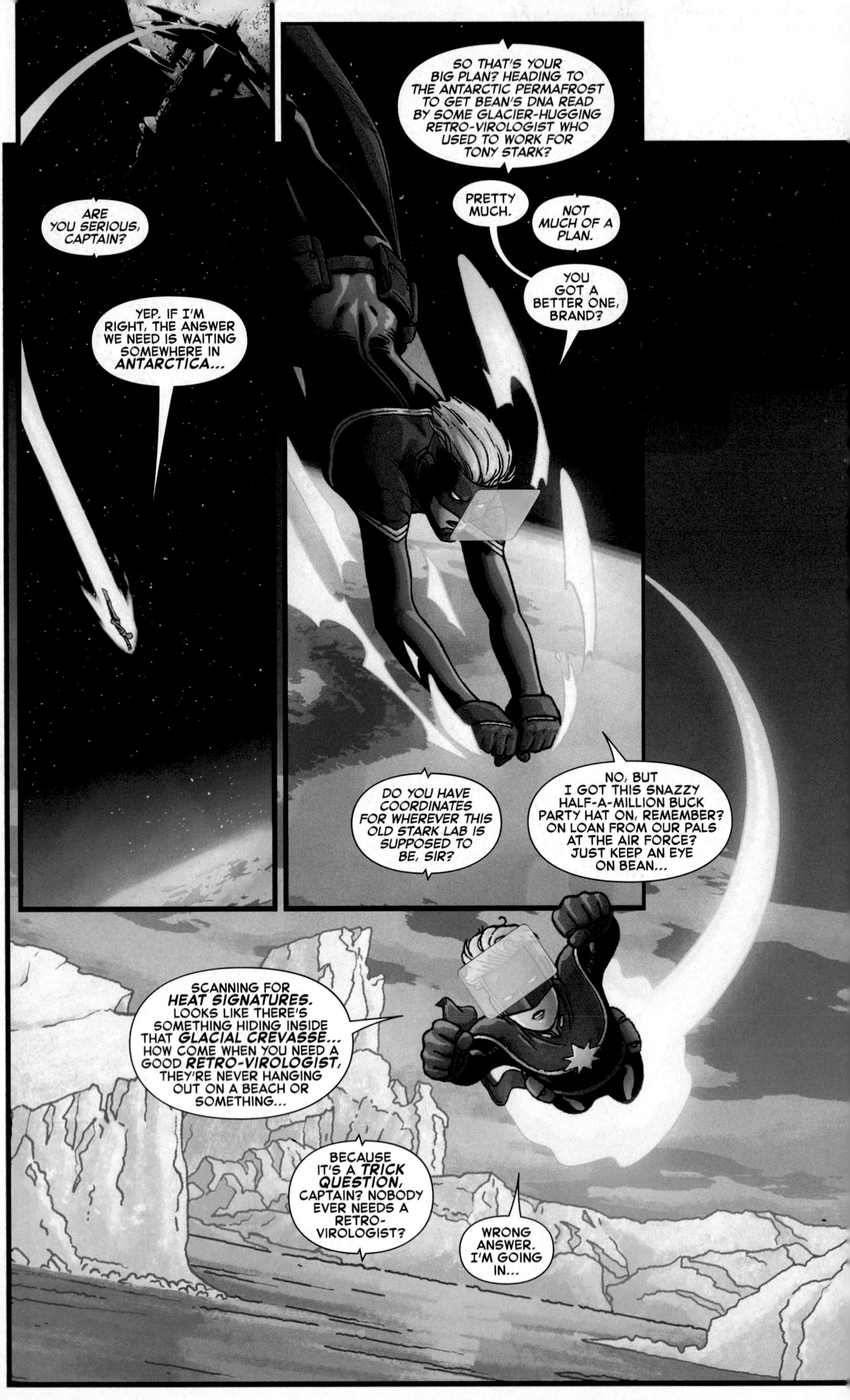
ARE YOU SERIOUS, CAPTAIN?
YEP. IF I'M RIGHT, THE ANSWER WE NEED IS WAITING SOMEWHERE IN ANTARCTICA...
SO THAT'S YOUR BIG PLAN? HEADING TO THE ANTARCTIC PERMAFROST TO GET BEAN'S DNA READ BY SOME GLACIER-HUGGING RETRO-VIROLOGIST WHO USED TO WORK FOR TONY STARK?
PRETTY MUCH.
NOT MUCH OF A PLAN.
YOU GOT A BETTER ONE, BRAND?
DO YOU HAVE COORDINATES FOR WHEREVER THIS OLD STARK LAB IS SUPPOSED TO BE, SIR?
NO, BUT I GOT THIS SNAZZY HALF-A-MILLION BUCK PARTY HAT ON, REMEMBER? ON LOAN FROM OUR PALS AT THE AIR FORCE? JUST KEEP AN EYE ON BEAN...
SCANNING FOR HEAT SIGNATURES. LOOKS LIKE THERE'S SOMETHING HIDING INSIDE THAT GLACIAL CREVASSE... HOW COME WHEN YOU NEED A GOOD RETRO-VIROLOGIST, THEY'RE NEVER HANGING OUT ON A BEACH OR SOMETHING...
BECAUSE IT'S A TRICK QUESTION, CAPTAIN? NOBODY EVER NEEDS A RETRO-VIROLOGIST?
WRONG ANSWER. I'M GOING IN...

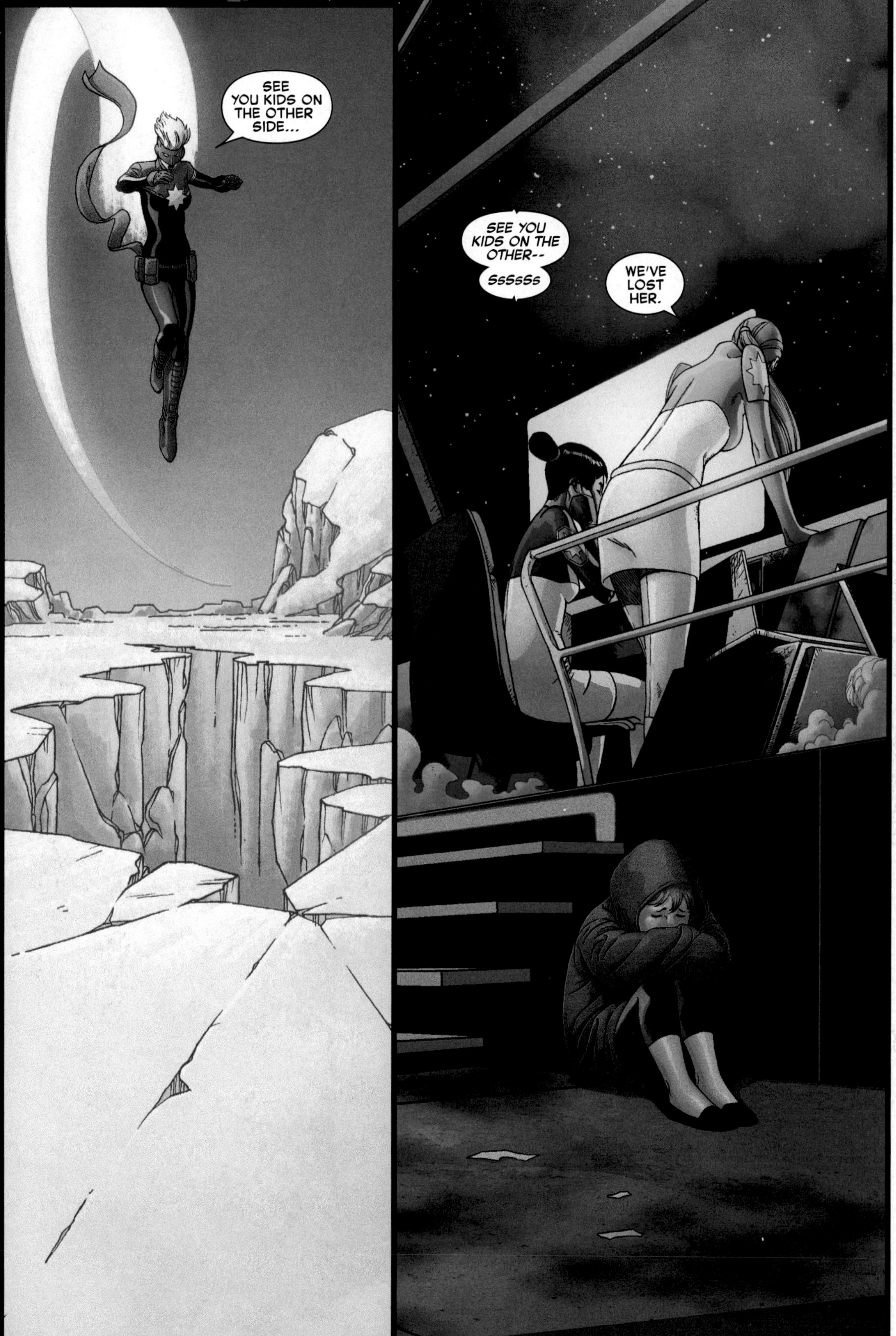
SEE YOU KIDS ON THE OTHER SIDE...
SEE YOU KIDS ON THE OTHER--
SSSSSS
WE'VE LOST HER.

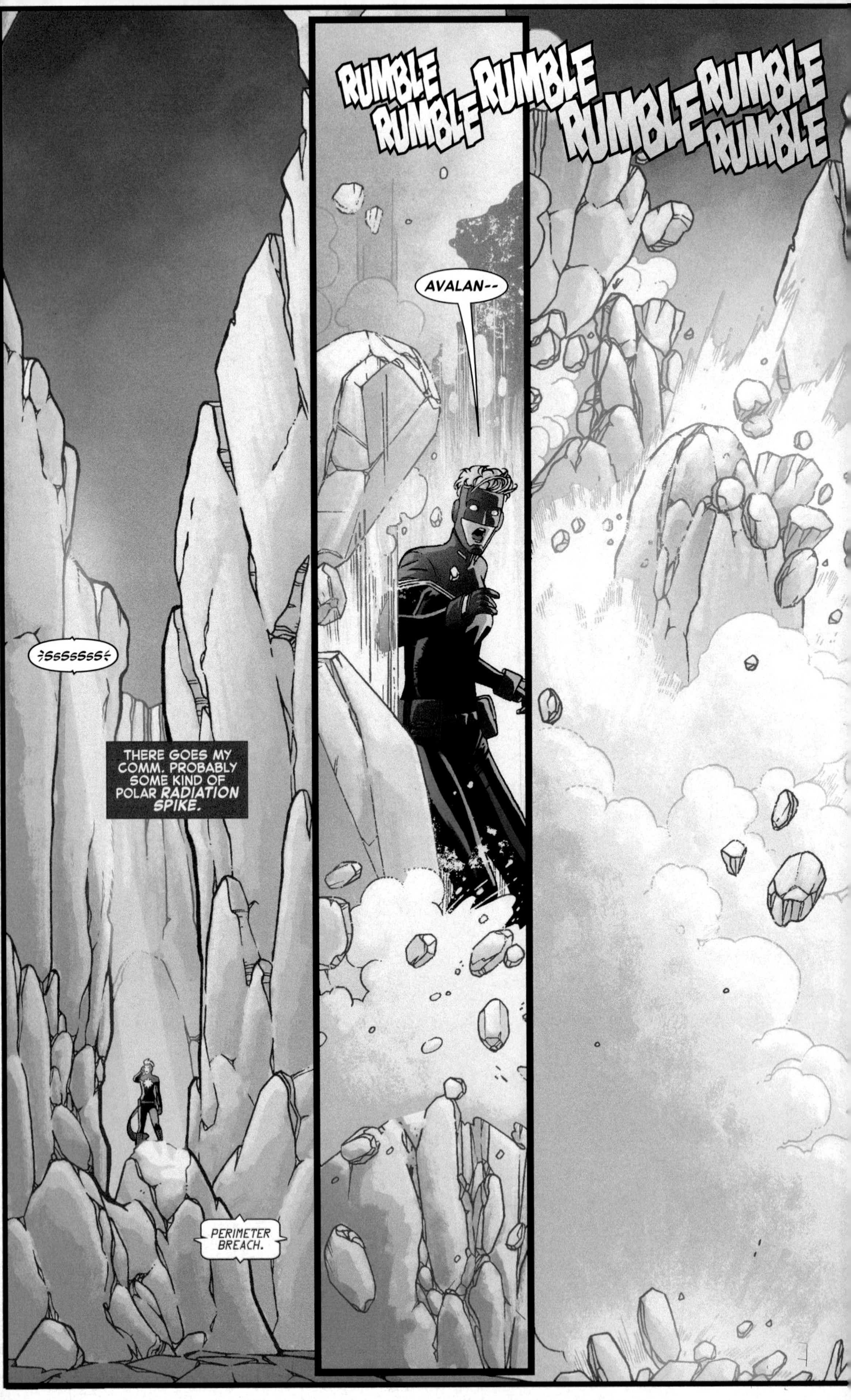
SSSSSSS
THERE GOES MY COMM. PROBABLY SOME KIND OF POLAR *RADIATION SPIKE.*
PERIMETER BREACH.
RUMBLE RUMBLE RUMBLE RUMBLE RUMBLE RUMBLE
AVALAN--

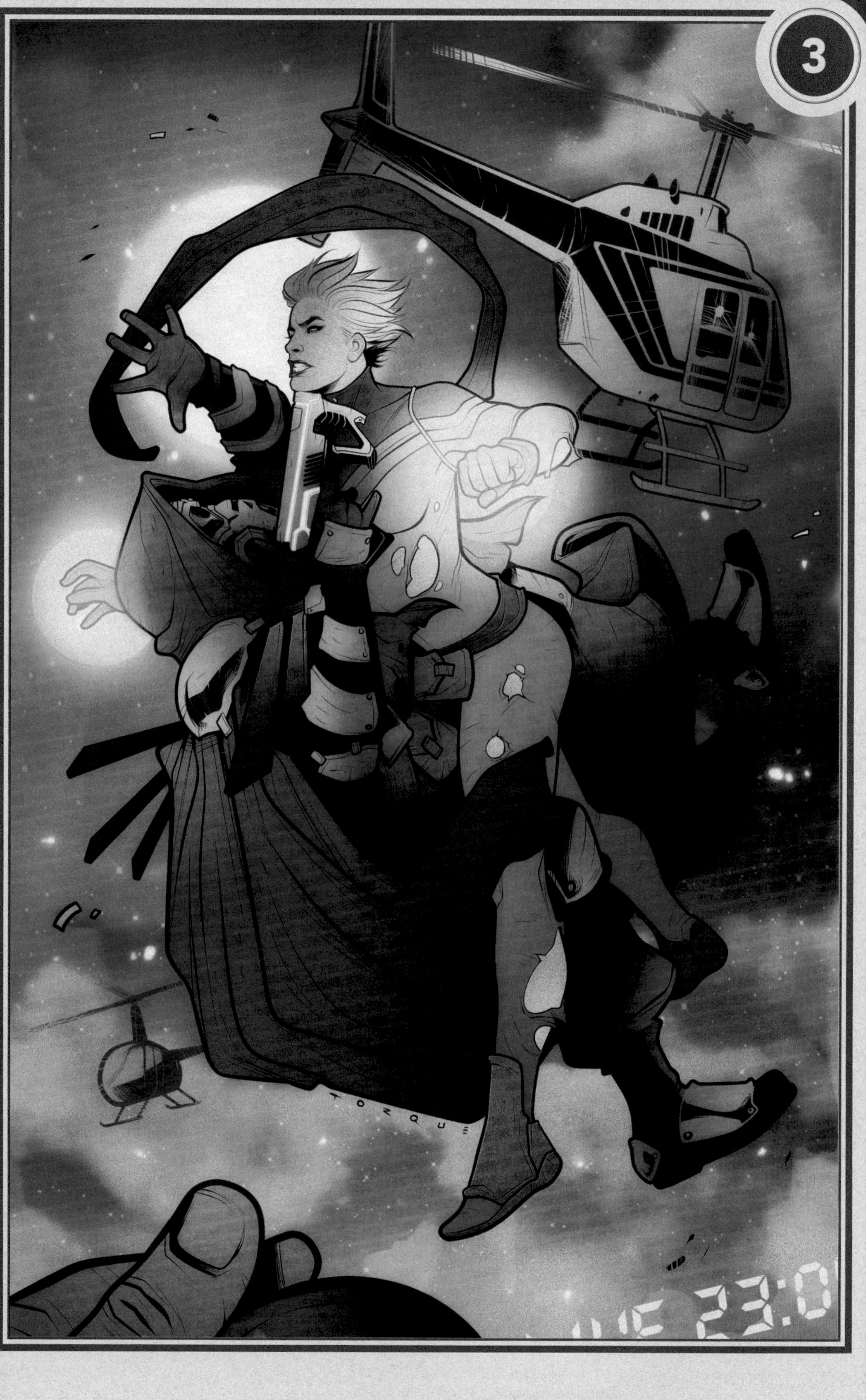
3
TORQUE

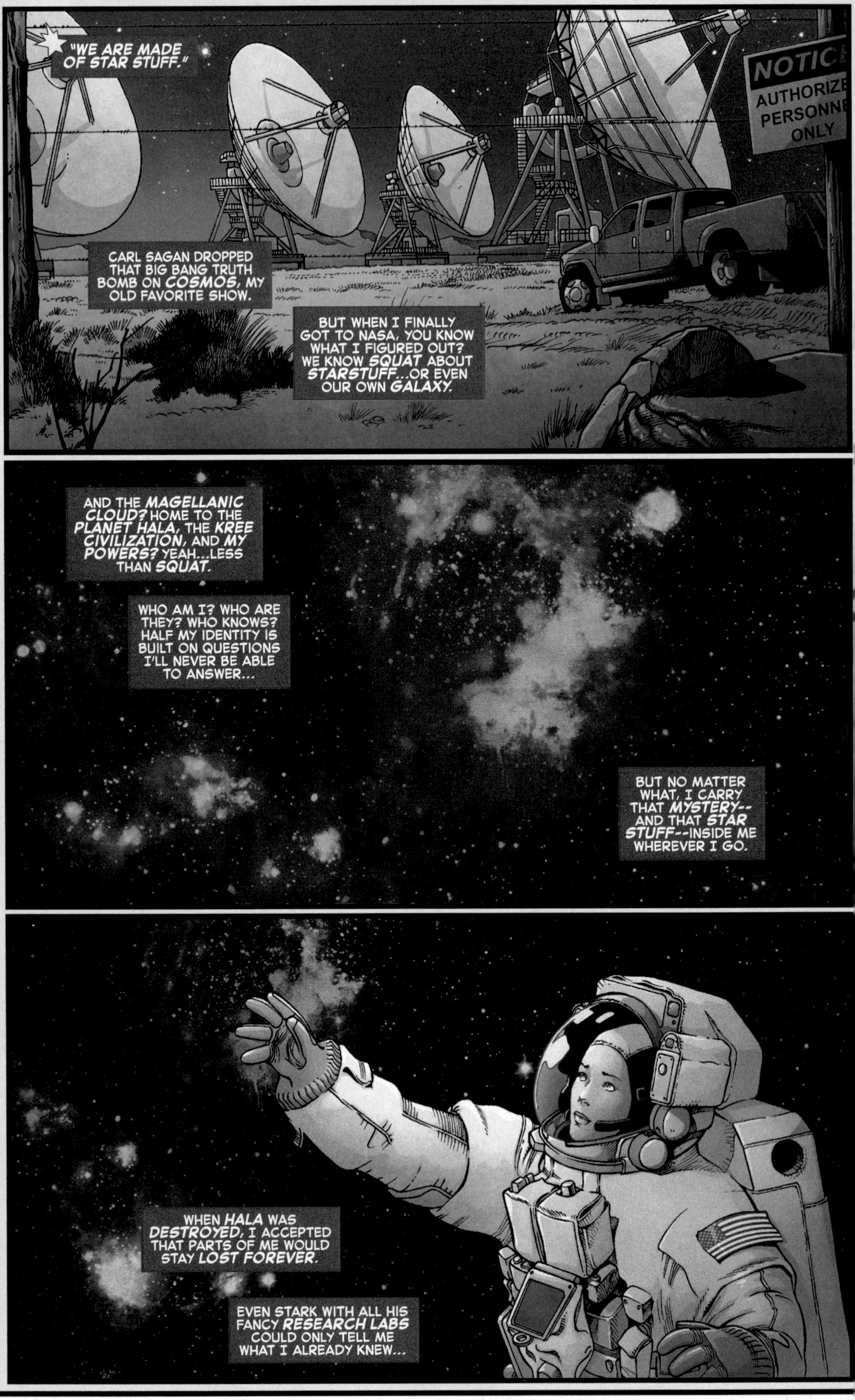
"WE ARE MADE OF STAR STUFF."
NOTICE AUTHORIZE PERSONNE ONLY
CARL SAGAN DROPPED THAT BIG BANG TRUTH BOMB ON COSMOS, MY OLD FAVORITE SHOW.
BUT WHEN I FINALLY GOT TO NASA, YOU KNOW WHAT I FIGURED OUT? WE KNOW SQUAT ABOUT STARSTUFF...OR EVEN OUR OWN GALAXY.
AND THE MAGELLANIC CLOUD? HOME TO THE PLANET HALA, THE KREE CIVILIZATION, AND MY POWERS? YEAH...LESS THAN SQUAT.
WHO AM I? WHO ARE THEY? WHO KNOWS? HALF MY IDENTITY IS BUILT ON QUESTIONS I'LL NEVER BE ABLE TO ANSWER...
BUT NO MATTER WHAT, I CARRY THAT MYSTERY--AND THAT STAR STUFF--INSIDE ME WHEREVER I GO.
WHEN HALA WAS DESTROYED, I ACCEPTED THAT PARTS OF ME WOULD STAY LOST FOREVER.
EVEN STARK WITH ALL HIS FANCY RESEARCH LABS COULD ONLY TELL ME WHAT I ALREADY KNEW...

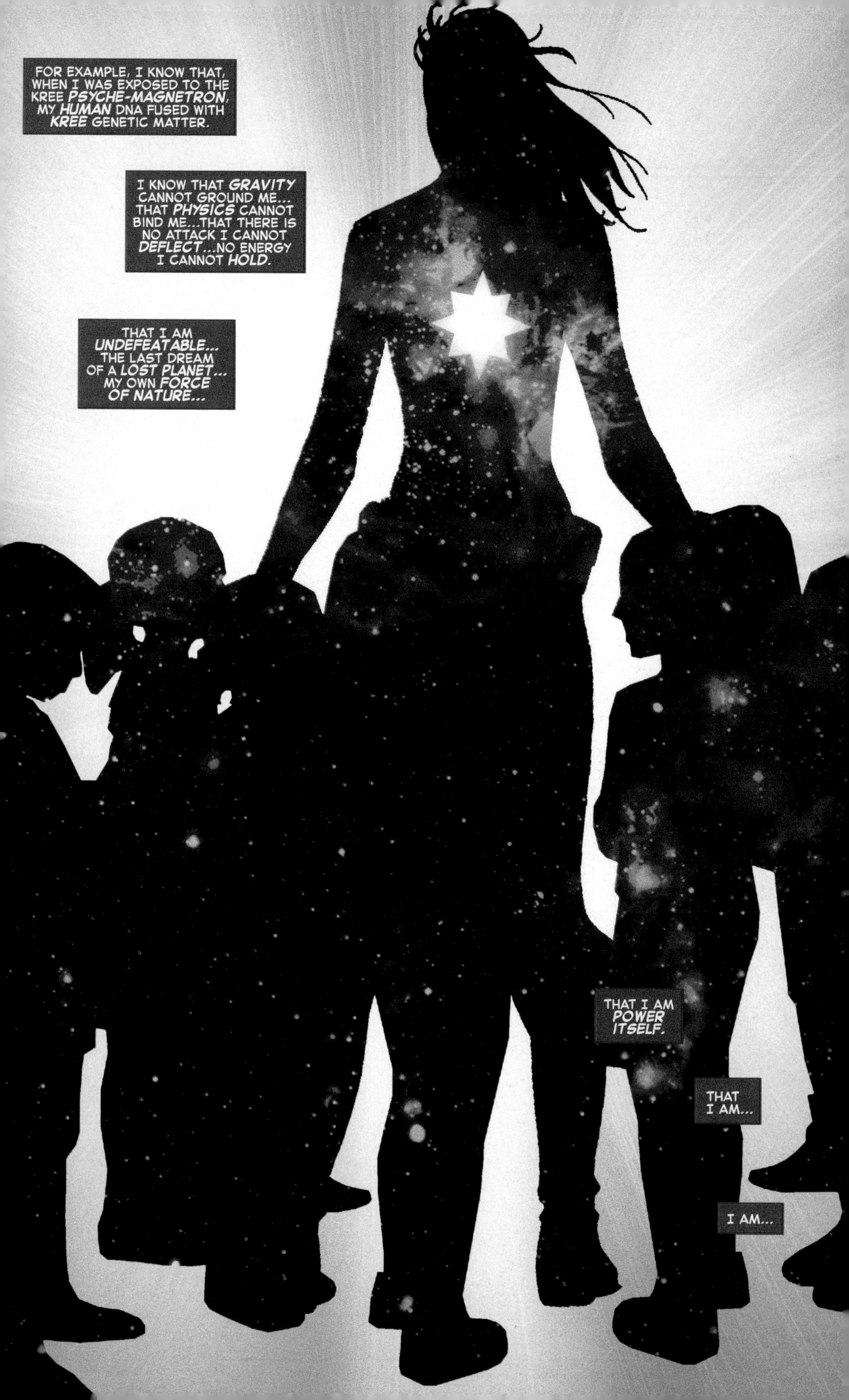
FOR EXAMPLE, I KNOW THAT, WHEN I WAS EXPOSED TO THE KREE PSYCHE-MAGNETRON, MY HUMAN DNA FUSED WITH KREE GENETIC MATTER.
I KNOW THAT GRAVITY CANNOT GROUND ME... THAT PHYSICS CANNOT BIND ME...THAT THERE IS NO ATTACK I CANNOT DEFLECT...NO ENERGY I CANNOT HOLD.
THAT I AM UNDEFEATABLE... THE LAST DREAM OF A LOST PLANET... MY OWN FORCE OF NATURE...
THAT I AM POWER ITSELF.
THAT I AM...
I AM...

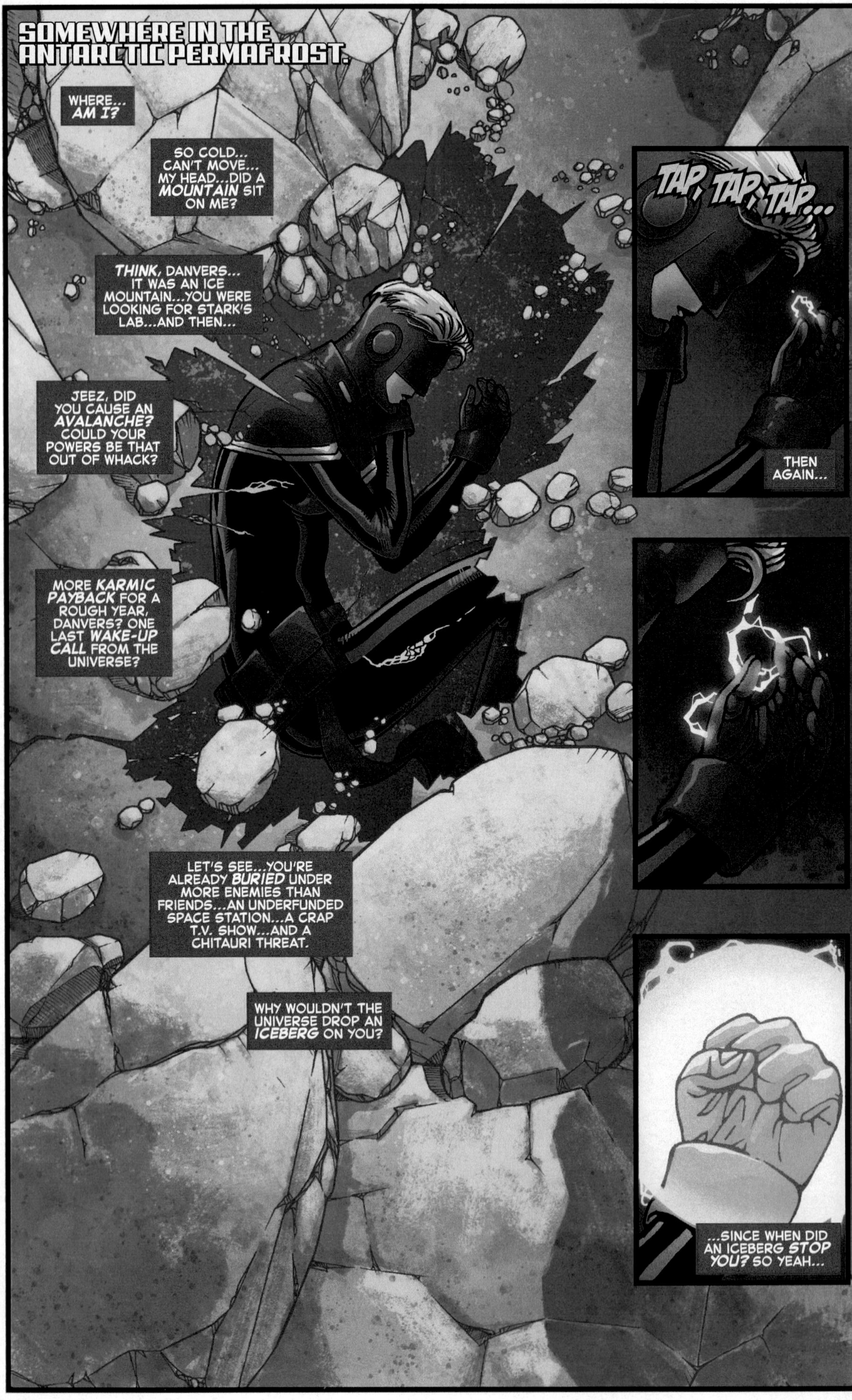
SOMEWHERE IN THE ANTARCTIC PERMAFROST.
WHERE... AM I?
SO COLD... CAN'T MOVE... MY HEAD...DID A MOUNTAIN SIT ON ME?
THINK, DANVERS... IT WAS AN ICE MOUNTAIN...YOU WERE LOOKING FOR STARK'S LAB...AND THEN...
JEEZ, DID YOU CAUSE AN AVALANCHE? COULD YOUR POWERS BE THAT OUT OF WHACK?
MORE KARMIC PAYBACK FOR A ROUGH YEAR, DANVERS? ONE LAST WAKE-UP CALL FROM THE UNIVERSE?
LET'S SEE...YOU'RE ALREADY BURIED UNDER MORE ENEMIES THAN FRIENDS...AN UNDERFUNDED SPACE STATION...A CRAP T.V. SHOW...AND A CHITAURI THREAT.
WHY WOULDN'T THE UNIVERSE DROP AN ICEBERG ON YOU?
TAP, TAP, TAP...
THEN AGAIN...
...SINCE WHEN DID AN ICEBERG STOP YOU? SO YEAH...

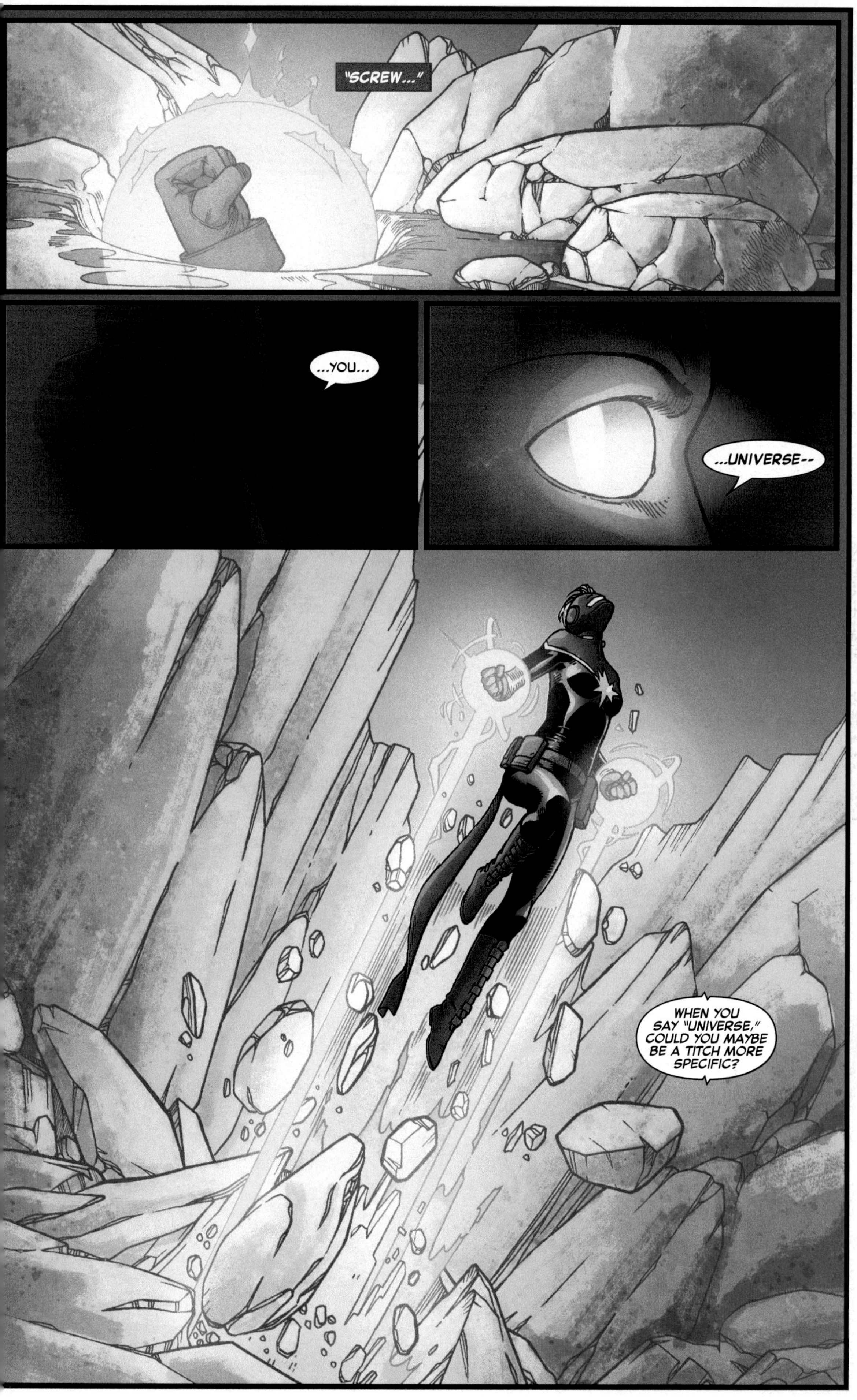
"SCREW..."
...YOU...
...UNIVERSE--
WHEN YOU SAY "UNIVERSE," COULD YOU MAYBE BE A TITCH MORE SPECIFIC?

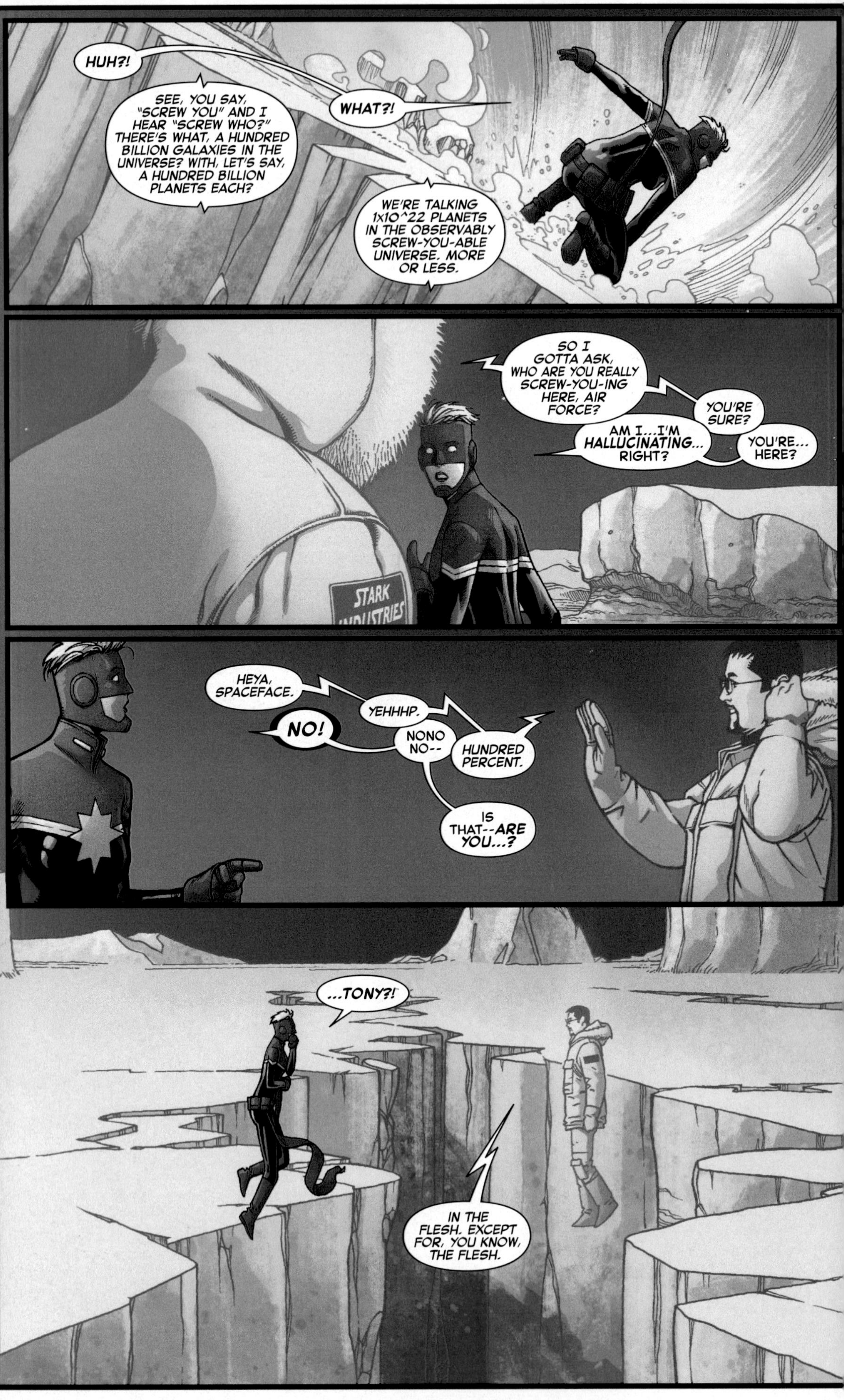
HUH?!
SEE, YOU SAY, "SCREW YOU" AND I HEAR "SCREW WHO?" THERE'S WHAT, A HUNDRED BILLION GALAXIES IN THE UNIVERSE? WITH, LET'S SAY, A HUNDRED BILLION PLANETS EACH?
WHAT?!
WE'RE TALKING 1x10^22 PLANETS IN THE OBSERVABLY SCREW-YOU-ABLE UNIVERSE. MORE OR LESS.
SO I GOTTA ASK, WHO ARE YOU REALLY SCREW-YOU-ING HERE, AIR FORCE?
AM I...I'M HALLUCINATING... RIGHT?
YOU'RE SURE?
YOU'RE... HERE?
STARK INDUSTRIES
HEYA, SPACEFACE.
YEHHHP.
NO!
NONO NO--
HUNDRED PERCENT.
IS THAT--ARE YOU...?
...TONY?!
IN THE FLESH. EXCEPT FOR, YOU KNOW, THE FLESH.

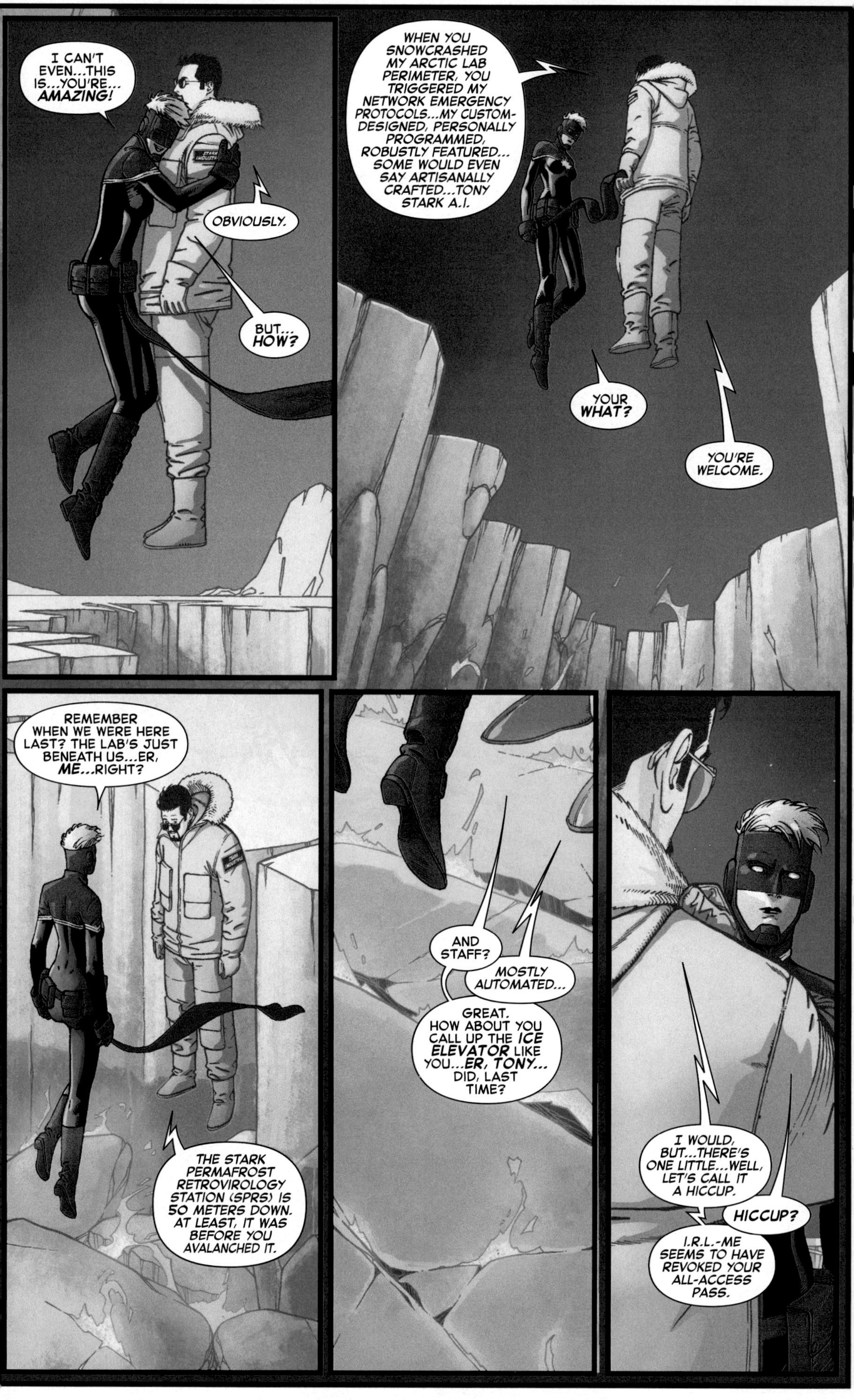
I CAN'T EVEN...THIS IS...YOU'RE... AMAZING!
OBVIOUSLY.
BUT... HOW?
WHEN YOU SNOWCRASHED MY ARCTIC LAB PERIMETER, YOU TRIGGERED MY NETWORK EMERGENCY PROTOCOLS...MY CUSTOM-DESIGNED, PERSONALLY PROGRAMMED, ROBUSTLY FEATURED... SOME WOULD EVEN SAY ARTISANALLY CRAFTED...TONY STARK A.I.
YOUR WHAT?
YOU'RE WELCOME.
REMEMBER WHEN WE WERE HERE LAST? THE LAB'S JUST BENEATH US...ER, ME...RIGHT?
THE STARK PERMAFROST RETROVIROLOGY STATION (SPRS) IS 50 METERS DOWN. AT LEAST, IT WAS BEFORE YOU AVALANCHED IT.
AND STAFF?
MOSTLY AUTOMATED...
GREAT. HOW ABOUT YOU CALL UP THE ICE ELEVATOR LIKE YOU...ER, TONY... DID, LAST TIME?
I WOULD, BUT...THERE'S ONE LITTLE...WELL, LET'S CALL IT A HICCUP.
HICCUP?
I.R.L.-ME SEEMS TO HAVE REVOKED YOUR ALL-ACCESS PASS.

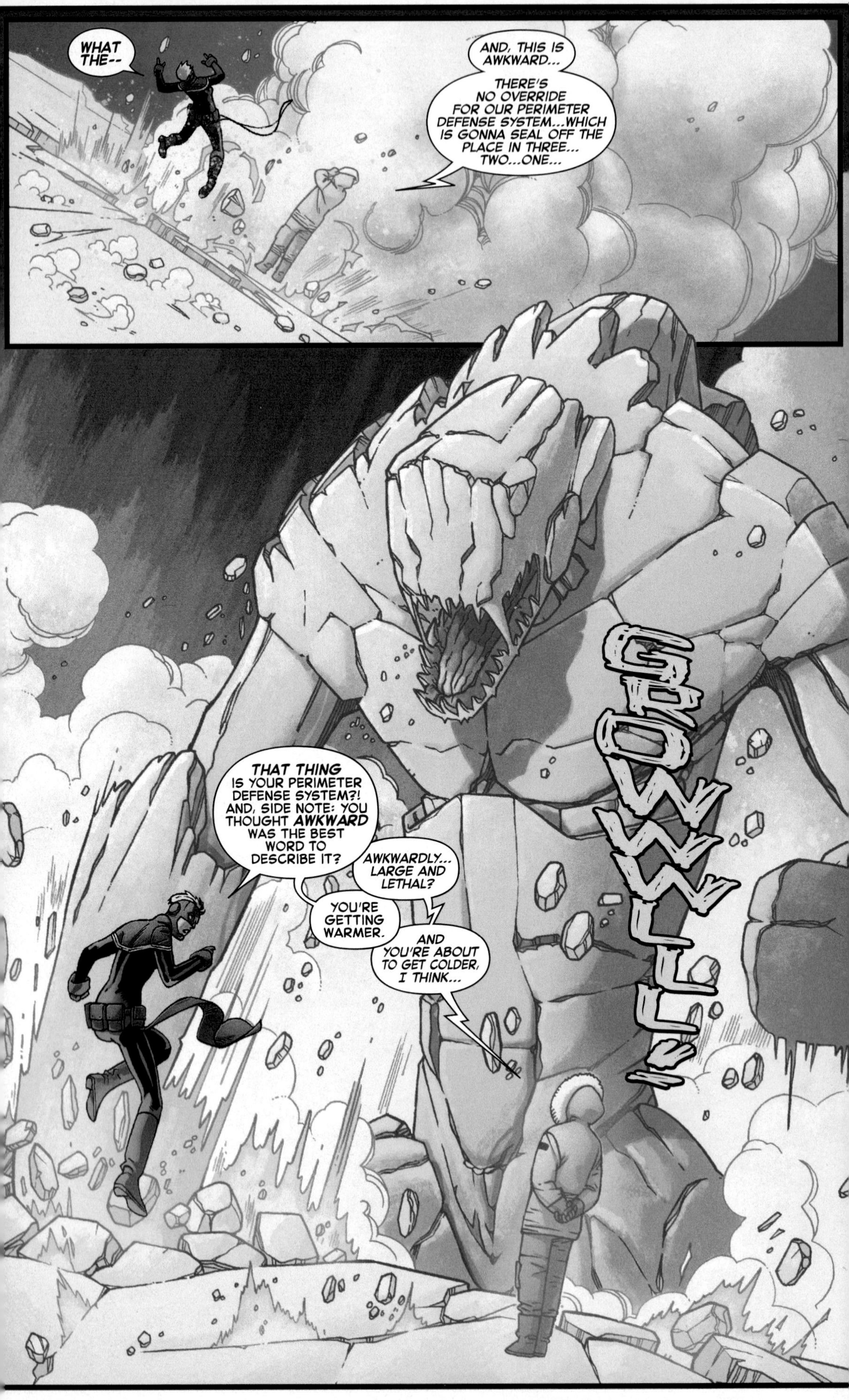
WHAT THE--
AND, THIS IS AWKWARD...
THERE'S NO OVERRIDE FOR OUR PERIMETER DEFENSE SYSTEM...WHICH IS GONNA SEAL OFF THE PLACE IN THREE... TWO...ONE...
THAT THING IS YOUR PERIMETER DEFENSE SYSTEM?! AND, SIDE NOTE: YOU THOUGHT AWKWARD WAS THE BEST WORD TO DESCRIBE IT?
AWKWARDLY... LARGE AND LETHAL?
YOU'RE GETTING WARMER.
AND YOU'RE ABOUT TO GET COLDER, I THINK...
GROWWLLL!!

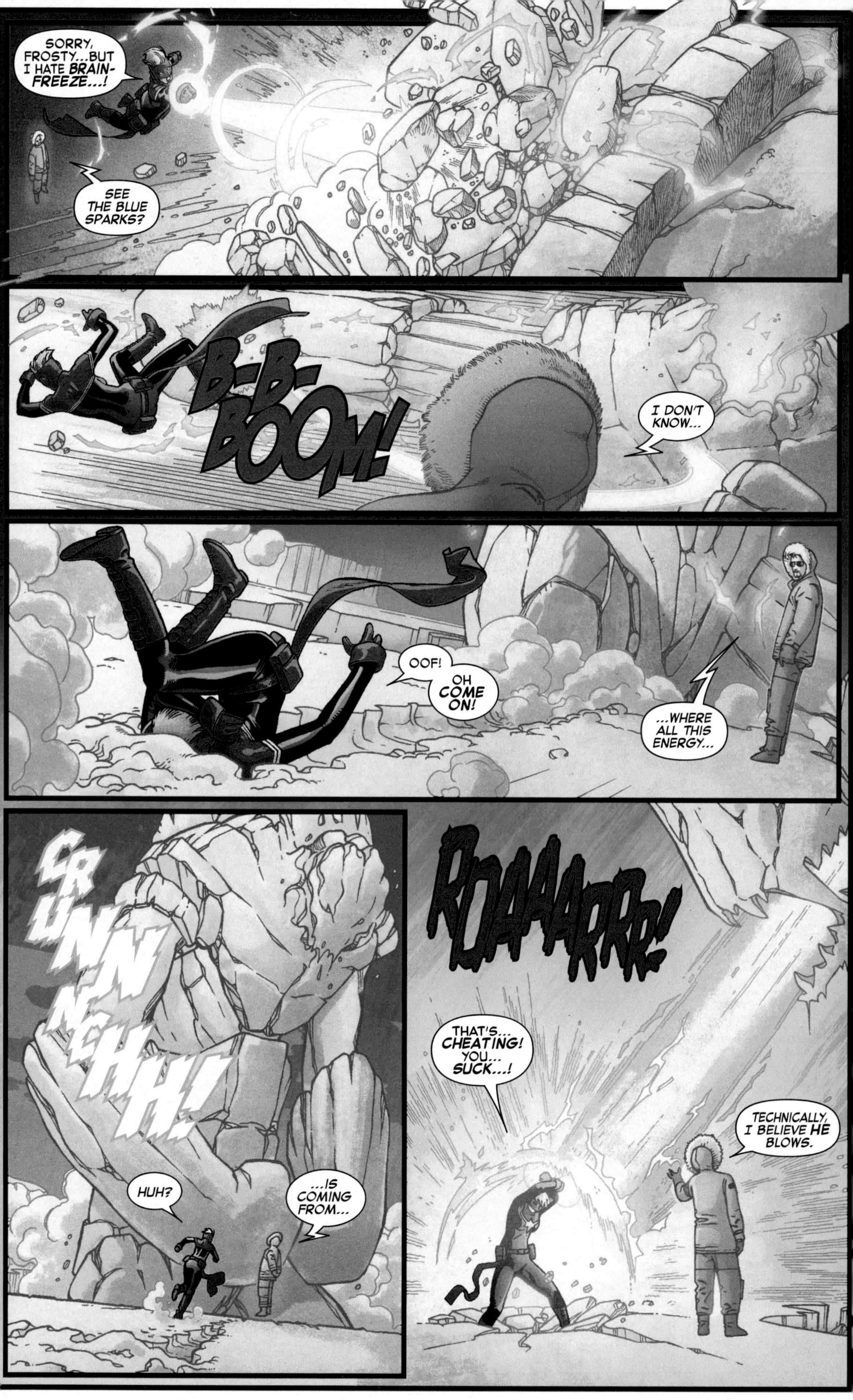
SORRY, FROSTY...BUT I HATE BRAIN-FREEZE...!
SEE THE BLUE SPARKS?
B-B-BOOM!
I DON'T KNOW...
OOF!
OH COME ON!
...WHERE ALL THIS ENERGY...
CRUNNNCHH!
HUH?
...IS COMING FROM...
ROAAARRR!
THAT'S... CHEATING! YOU... SUCK...!
TECHNICALLY, I BELIEVE HE BLOWS.

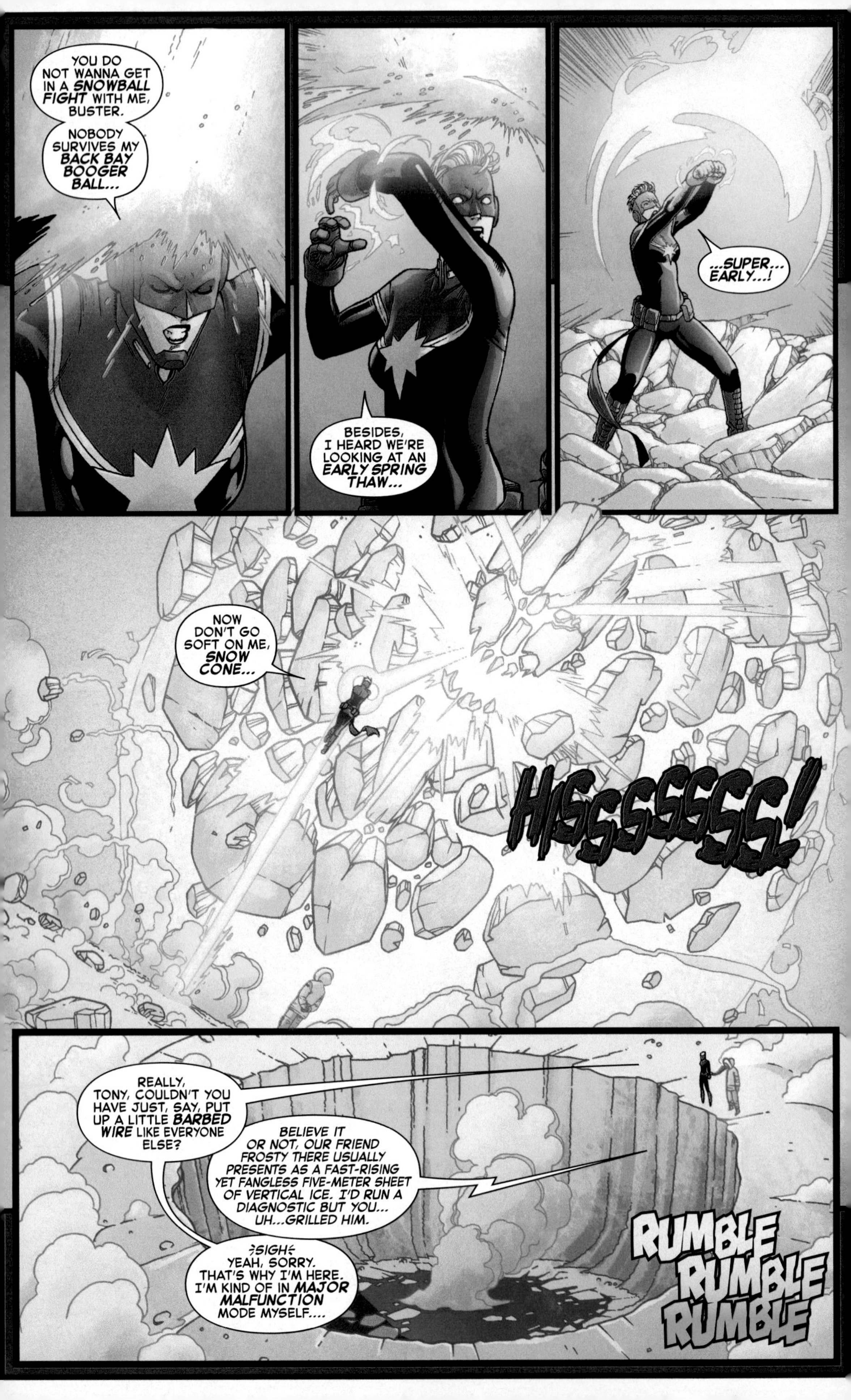
YOU DO NOT WANNA GET IN A SNOWBALL FIGHT WITH ME, BUSTER.
NOBODY SURVIVES MY BACK BAY BOOGER BALL...
BESIDES, I HEARD WE'RE LOOKING AT AN EARLY SPRING THAW...
...SUPER... EARLY...!
NOW DON'T GO SOFT ON ME, SNOW CONE...
HISSSSSSS!
REALLY, TONY, COULDN'T YOU HAVE JUST, SAY, PUT UP A LITTLE BARBED WIRE LIKE EVERYONE ELSE?
BELIEVE IT OR NOT, OUR FRIEND FROSTY THERE USUALLY PRESENTS AS A FAST-RISING YET FANGLESS FIVE-METER SHEET OF VERTICAL ICE. I'D RUN A DIAGNOSTIC BUT YOU... UH...GRILLED HIM.
SIGH YEAH, SORRY. THAT'S WHY I'M HERE. I'M KIND OF IN MAJOR MALFUNCTION MODE MYSELF....
RUMBLE RUMBLE RUMBLE

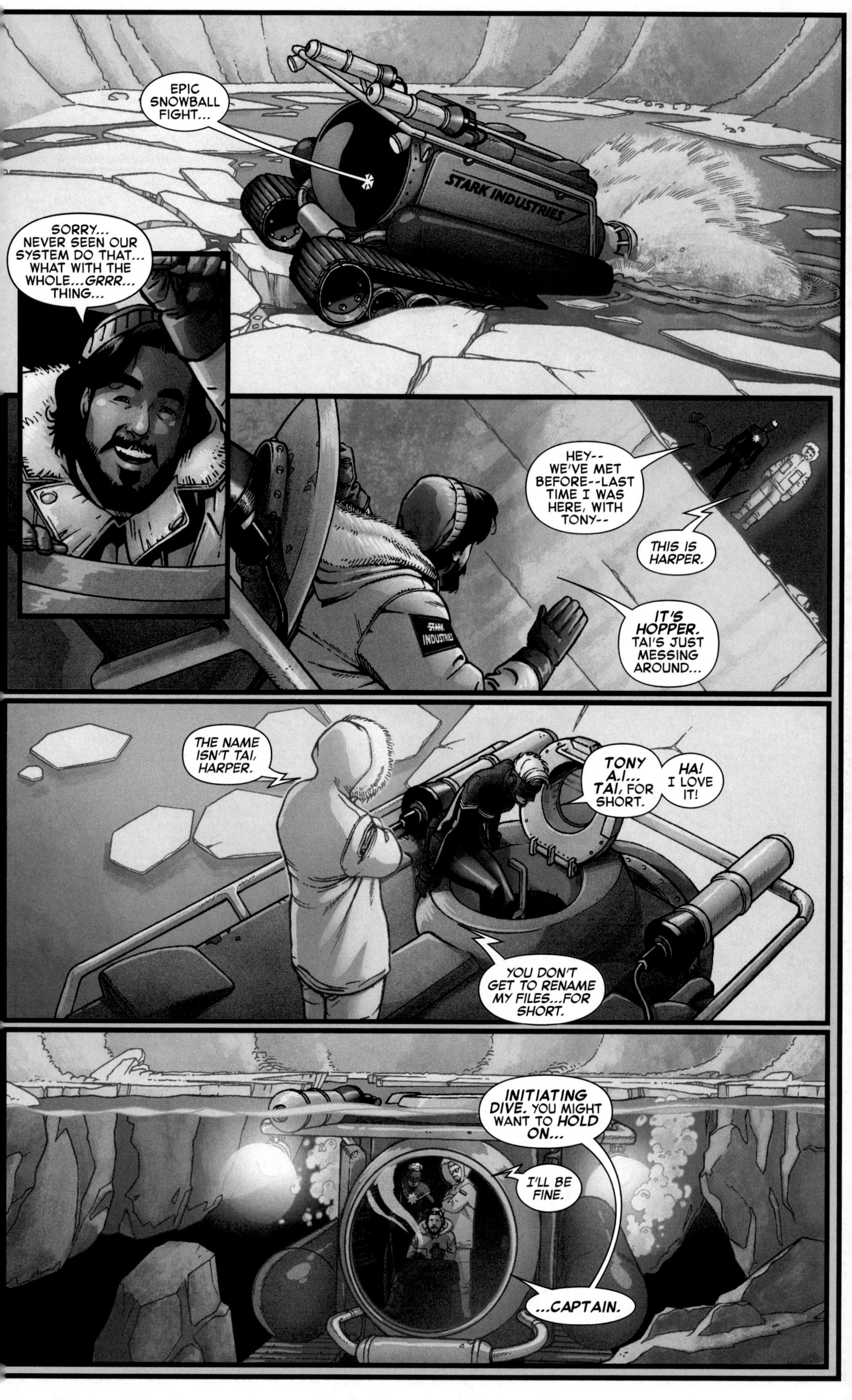
EPIC SNOWBALL FIGHT...
STARK INDUSTRIES
SORRY... NEVER SEEN OUR SYSTEM DO THAT... WHAT WITH THE WHOLE...GRRR... THING...
HEY-- WE'VE MET BEFORE--LAST TIME I WAS HERE, WITH TONY--
THIS IS HARPER.
IT'S HOPPER. TAI'S JUST MESSING AROUND...
STARK INDUSTRIES
THE NAME ISN'T TAI, HARPER.
TONY A.I... TAI, FOR SHORT.
HA! I LOVE IT!
YOU DON'T GET TO RENAME MY FILES...FOR SHORT.
INITIATING DIVE. YOU MIGHT WANT TO HOLD ON...
I'LL BE FINE.
...CAPTAIN.

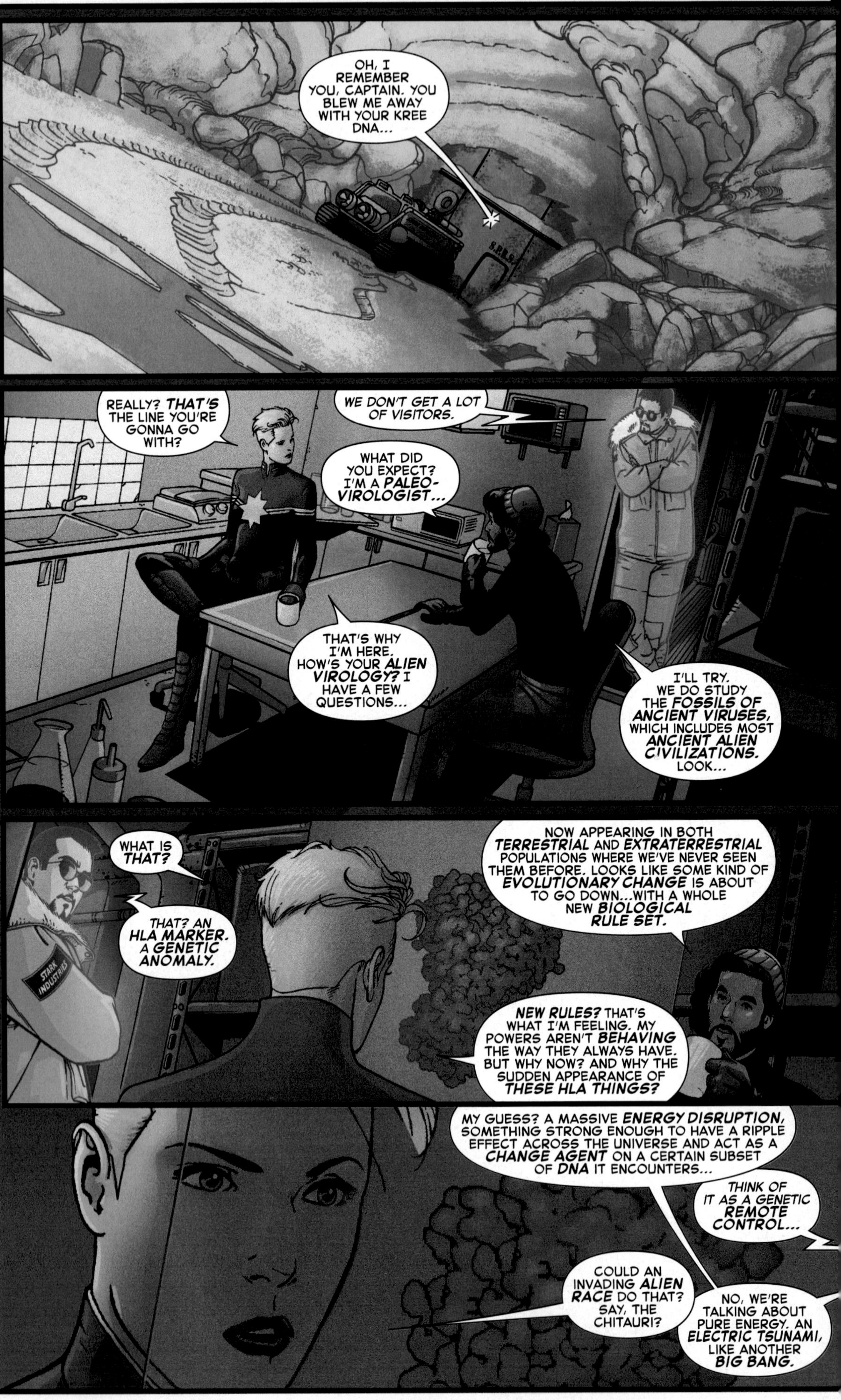
OH, I REMEMBER YOU, CAPTAIN. YOU BLEW ME AWAY WITH YOUR KREE DNA...
S.P.R.S.
REALLY? THAT'S THE LINE YOU'RE GONNA GO WITH?
WE DON'T GET A LOT OF VISITORS.
WHAT DID YOU EXPECT? I'M A PALEO-VIROLOGIST...
THAT'S WHY I'M HERE. HOW'S YOUR ALIEN VIROLOGY? I HAVE A FEW QUESTIONS...
I'LL TRY. WE DO STUDY THE FOSSILS OF ANCIENT VIRUSES, WHICH INCLUDES MOST ANCIENT ALIEN CIVILIZATIONS. LOOK...
WHAT IS THAT?
THAT? AN HLA MARKER. A GENETIC ANOMALY.
STARK INDUSTRIES
NOW APPEARING IN BOTH TERRESTRIAL AND EXTRATERRESTRIAL POPULATIONS WHERE WE'VE NEVER SEEN THEM BEFORE. LOOKS LIKE SOME KIND OF EVOLUTIONARY CHANGE IS ABOUT TO GO DOWN...WITH A WHOLE NEW BIOLOGICAL RULE SET.
NEW RULES? THAT'S WHAT I'M FEELING. MY POWERS AREN'T BEHAVING THE WAY THEY ALWAYS HAVE. BUT WHY NOW? AND WHY THE SUDDEN APPEARANCE OF THESE HLA THINGS?
MY GUESS? A MASSIVE ENERGY DISRUPTION, SOMETHING STRONG ENOUGH TO HAVE A RIPPLE EFFECT ACROSS THE UNIVERSE AND ACT AS A CHANGE AGENT ON A CERTAIN SUBSET OF DNA IT ENCOUNTERS...
THINK OF IT AS A GENETIC REMOTE CONTROL...
COULD AN INVADING ALIEN RACE DO THAT? SAY, THE CHITAURI?
NO, WE'RE TALKING ABOUT PURE ENERGY. AN ELECTRIC TSUNAMI, LIKE ANOTHER BIG BANG.

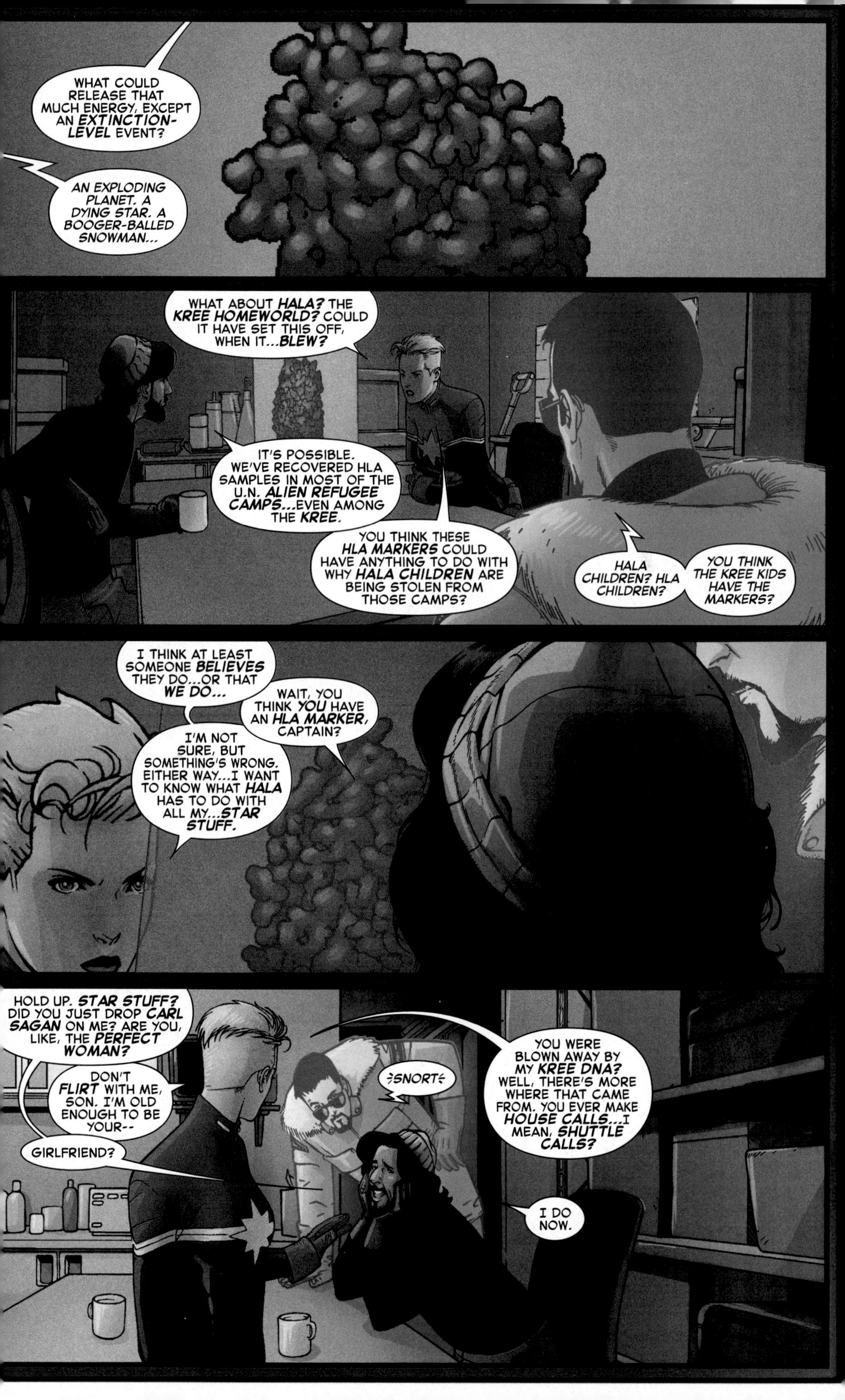
WHAT COULD RELEASE THAT MUCH ENERGY, EXCEPT AN EXTINCTION-LEVEL EVENT?
AN EXPLODING PLANET. A DYING STAR. A BOOGER-BALLED SNOWMAN...
WHAT ABOUT HALA? THE KREE HOMEWORLD? COULD IT HAVE SET THIS OFF, WHEN IT...BLEW?
IT'S POSSIBLE. WE'VE RECOVERED HLA SAMPLES IN MOST OF THE U.N. ALIEN REFUGEE CAMPS...EVEN AMONG THE KREE.
YOU THINK THESE HLA MARKERS COULD HAVE ANYTHING TO DO WITH WHY HALA CHILDREN ARE BEING STOLEN FROM THOSE CAMPS?
HALA CHILDREN? HLA CHILDREN?
YOU THINK THE KREE KIDS HAVE THE MARKERS?
I THINK AT LEAST SOMEONE BELIEVES THEY DO...OR THAT WE DO...
WAIT, YOU THINK YOU HAVE AN HLA MARKER, CAPTAIN?
I'M NOT SURE, BUT SOMETHING'S WRONG. EITHER WAY...I WANT TO KNOW WHAT HALA HAS TO DO WITH ALL MY...STAR STUFF.
HOLD UP. STAR STUFF? DID YOU JUST DROP CARL SAGAN ON ME? ARE YOU, LIKE, THE PERFECT WOMAN?
DON'T FLIRT WITH ME, SON. I'M OLD ENOUGH TO BE YOUR--
GIRLFRIEND?
SNORT
YOU WERE BLOWN AWAY BY MY KREE DNA? WELL, THERE'S MORE WHERE THAT CAME FROM. YOU EVER MAKE HOUSE CALLS...I MEAN, SHUTTLE CALLS?
I DO NOW.

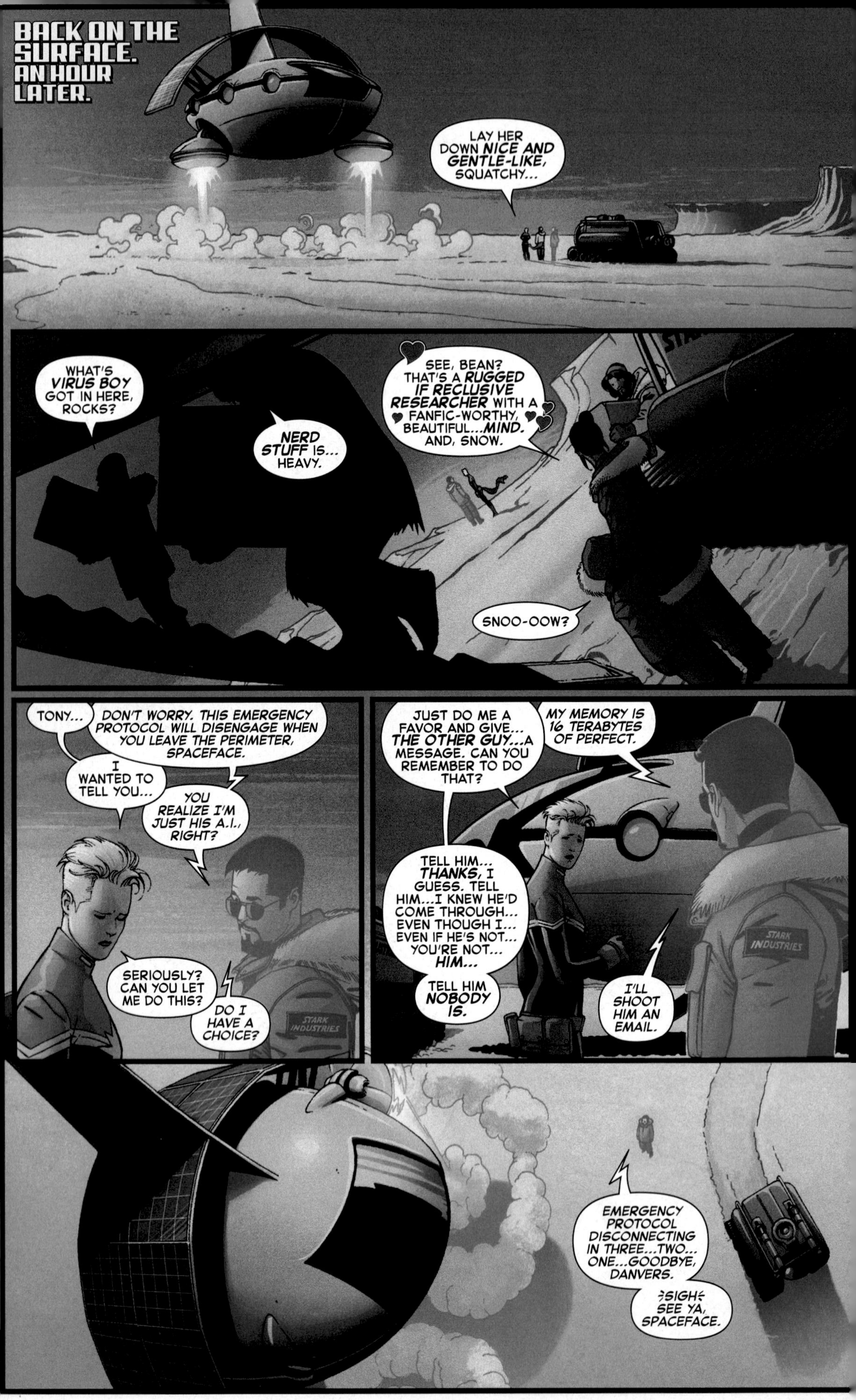
BACK ON THE SURFACE. AN HOUR LATER.
LAY HER DOWN NICE AND GENTLE-LIKE, SQUATCHY...
WHAT'S VIRUS BOY GOT IN HERE, ROCKS?
NERD STUFF IS... HEAVY.
SEE, BEAN? THAT'S A RUGGED IF RECLUSIVE RESEARCHER WITH A FANFIC-WORTHY, BEAUTIFUL...MIND. AND, SNOW.
SNOO-OOW?
TONY...
DON'T WORRY. THIS EMERGENCY PROTOCOL WILL DISENGAGE WHEN YOU LEAVE THE PERIMETER, SPACEFACE.
I WANTED TO TELL YOU...
YOU REALIZE I'M JUST HIS A.I., RIGHT?
SERIOUSLY? CAN YOU LET ME DO THIS?
DO I HAVE A CHOICE?
STARK INDUSTRIES
JUST DO ME A FAVOR AND GIVE... THE OTHER GUY...A MESSAGE. CAN YOU REMEMBER TO DO THAT?
MY MEMORY IS 16 TERABYTES OF PERFECT.
TELL HIM... THANKS, I GUESS. TELL HIM...I KNEW HE'D COME THROUGH... EVEN THOUGH I... EVEN IF HE'S NOT... YOU'RE NOT... HIM...
TELL HIM NOBODY IS.
I'LL SHOOT HIM AN EMAIL.
STARK INDUSTRIES
EMERGENCY PROTOCOL DISCONNECTING IN THREE...TWO... ONE...GOODBYE, DANVERS.
SIGH
SEE YA, SPACEFACE.

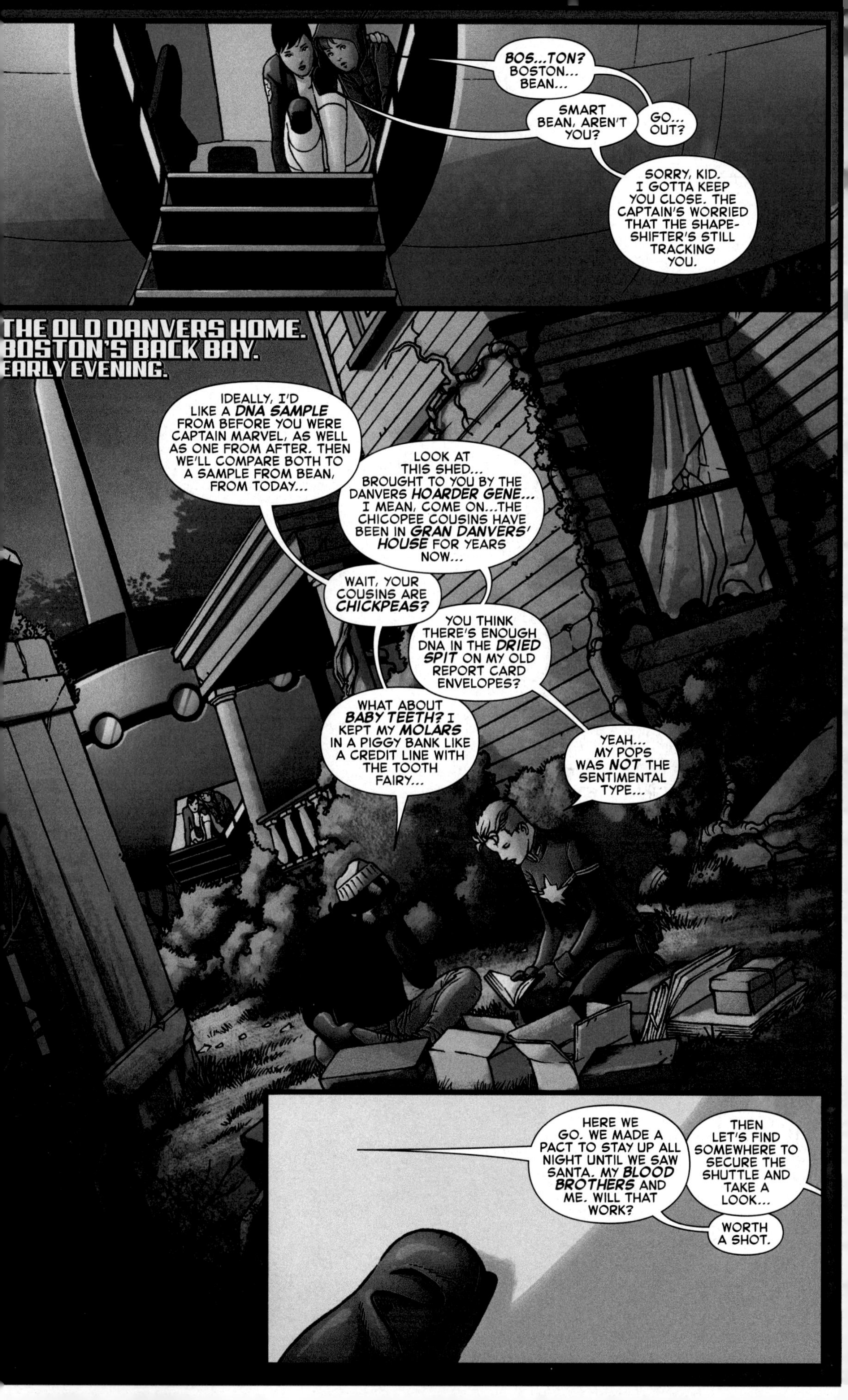
BOS...TON? BOSTON... BEAN...
SMART BEAN, AREN'T YOU?
GO... OUT?
SORRY, KID. I GOTTA KEEP YOU CLOSE. THE CAPTAIN'S WORRIED THAT THE SHAPE-SHIFTER'S STILL TRACKING YOU.
THE OLD DANVERS HOME. BOSTON'S BACK BAY. EARLY EVENING.
IDEALLY, I'D LIKE A DNA SAMPLE FROM BEFORE YOU WERE CAPTAIN MARVEL, AS WELL AS ONE FROM AFTER. THEN WE'LL COMPARE BOTH TO A SAMPLE FROM BEAN, FROM TODAY...
LOOK AT THIS SHED... BROUGHT TO YOU BY THE DANVERS HOARDER GENE... I MEAN, COME ON...THE CHICOPEE COUSINS HAVE BEEN IN GRAN DANVERS' HOUSE FOR YEARS NOW...
WAIT, YOUR COUSINS ARE CHICKPEAS?
YOU THINK THERE'S ENOUGH DNA IN THE DRIED SPIT ON MY OLD REPORT CARD ENVELOPES?
WHAT ABOUT BABY TEETH? I KEPT MY MOLARS IN A PIGGY BANK LIKE A CREDIT LINE WITH THE TOOTH FAIRY...
YEAH... MY POPS WAS NOT THE SENTIMENTAL TYPE...
HERE WE GO. WE MADE A PACT TO STAY UP ALL NIGHT UNTIL WE SAW SANTA. MY BLOOD BROTHERS AND ME. WILL THAT WORK?
THEN LET'S FIND SOMEWHERE TO SECURE THE SHUTTLE AND TAKE A LOOK...
WORTH A SHOT.

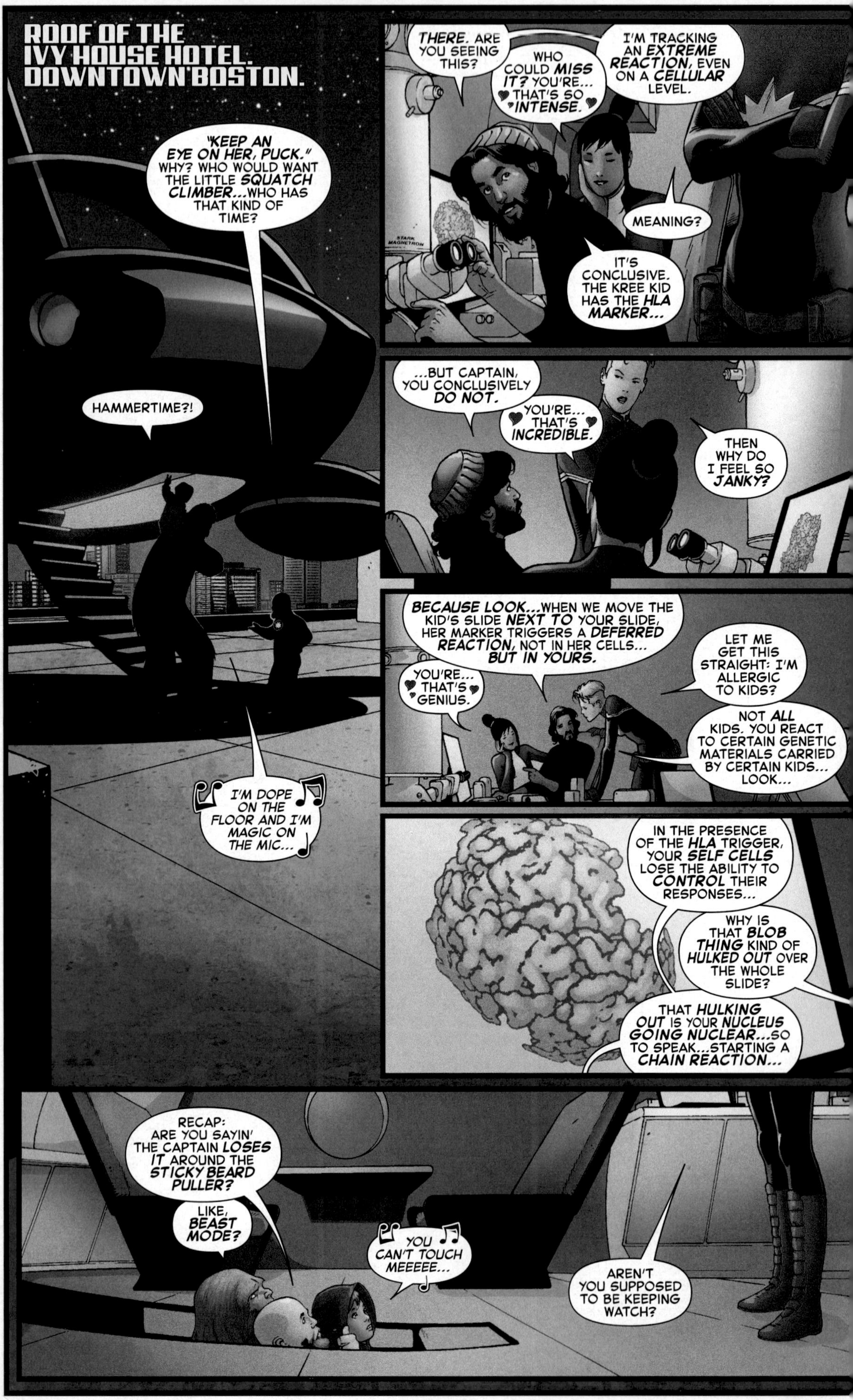
ROOF OF THE IVY HOUSE HOTEL. DOWNTOWN BOSTON.
"KEEP AN EYE ON HER, PUCK." WHY? WHO WOULD WANT THE LITTLE SQUATCH CLIMBER...WHO HAS THAT KIND OF TIME?
HAMMERTIME?!
I'M DOPE ON THE FLOOR AND I'M MAGIC ON THE MIC...
THERE. ARE YOU SEEING THIS?
WHO COULD MISS IT? YOU'RE... THAT'S SO INTENSE.
I'M TRACKING AN EXTREME REACTION, EVEN ON A CELLULAR LEVEL.
STARK MAGNETRON
MEANING?
IT'S CONCLUSIVE. THE KREE KID HAS THE HLA MARKER...
...BUT CAPTAIN, YOU CONCLUSIVELY DO NOT.
YOU'RE... THAT'S INCREDIBLE.
THEN WHY DO I FEEL SO JANKY?
BECAUSE LOOK...WHEN WE MOVE THE KID'S SLIDE NEXT TO YOUR SLIDE, HER MARKER TRIGGERS A DEFERRED REACTION, NOT IN HER CELLS... BUT IN YOURS.
YOU'RE... THAT'S GENIUS.
LET ME GET THIS STRAIGHT: I'M ALLERGIC TO KIDS?
NOT ALL KIDS. YOU REACT TO CERTAIN GENETIC MATERIALS CARRIED BY CERTAIN KIDS... LOOK...
IN THE PRESENCE OF THE HLA TRIGGER, YOUR SELF CELLS LOSE THE ABILITY TO CONTROL THEIR RESPONSES...
WHY IS THAT BLOB THING KIND OF HULKED OUT OVER THE WHOLE SLIDE?
THAT HULKING OUT IS YOUR NUCLEUS GOING NUCLEAR...SO TO SPEAK...STARTING A CHAIN REACTION...
RECAP: ARE YOU SAYIN' THE CAPTAIN LOSES IT AROUND THE STICKY BEARD PULLER?
LIKE, BEAST MODE?
YOU CAN'T TOUCH MEEEEE...
AREN'T YOU SUPPOSED TO BE KEEPING WATCH?

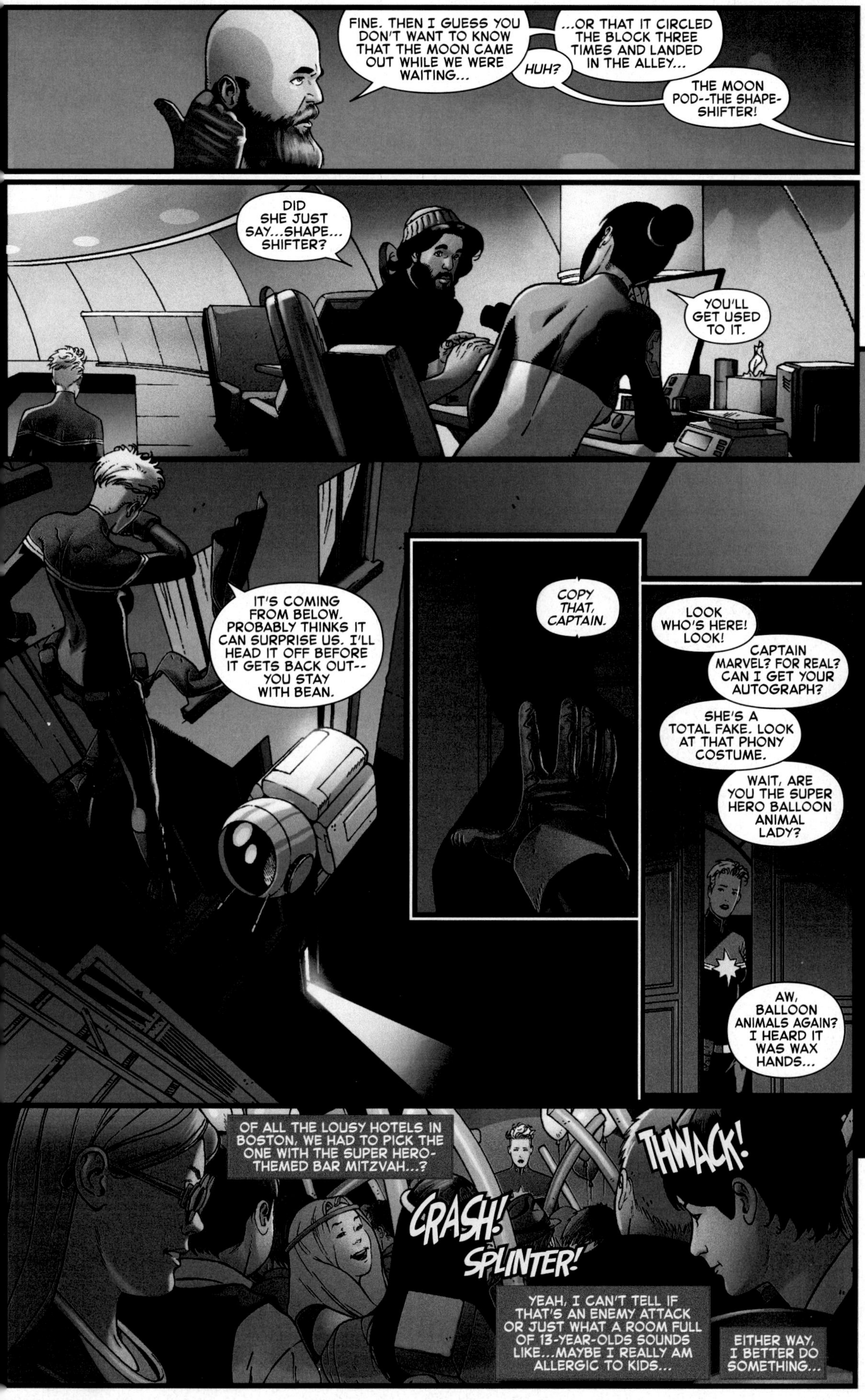

FINE. THEN I GUESS YOU DON'T WANT TO KNOW THAT THE MOON CAME OUT WHILE WE WERE WAITING...
HUH?
...OR THAT IT CIRCLED THE BLOCK THREE TIMES AND LANDED IN THE ALLEY...
THE MOON POD--THE SHAPE-SHIFTER!
DID SHE JUST SAY...SHAPE... SHIFTER?
YOU'LL GET USED TO IT.
IT'S COMING FROM BELOW. PROBABLY THINKS IT CAN SURPRISE US. I'LL HEAD IT OFF BEFORE IT GETS BACK OUT-- YOU STAY WITH BEAN.
COPY THAT, CAPTAIN.
LOOK WHO'S HERE! LOOK!
CAPTAIN MARVEL? FOR REAL? CAN I GET YOUR AUTOGRAPH?
SHE'S A TOTAL FAKE. LOOK AT THAT PHONY COSTUME.
WAIT, ARE YOU THE SUPER HERO BALLOON ANIMAL LADY?
AW, BALLOON ANIMALS AGAIN? I HEARD IT WAS WAX HANDS...
OF ALL THE LOUSY HOTELS IN BOSTON, WE HAD TO PICK THE ONE WITH THE SUPER HERO-THEMED BAR MITZVAH...?
THWACK!
CRASH!
SPLINTER!
YEAH, I CAN'T TELL IF THAT'S AN ENEMY ATTACK OR JUST WHAT A ROOM FULL OF 13-YEAR-OLDS SOUNDS LIKE...MAYBE I REALLY AM ALLERGIC TO KIDS...
EITHER WAY, I BETTER DO SOMETHING...

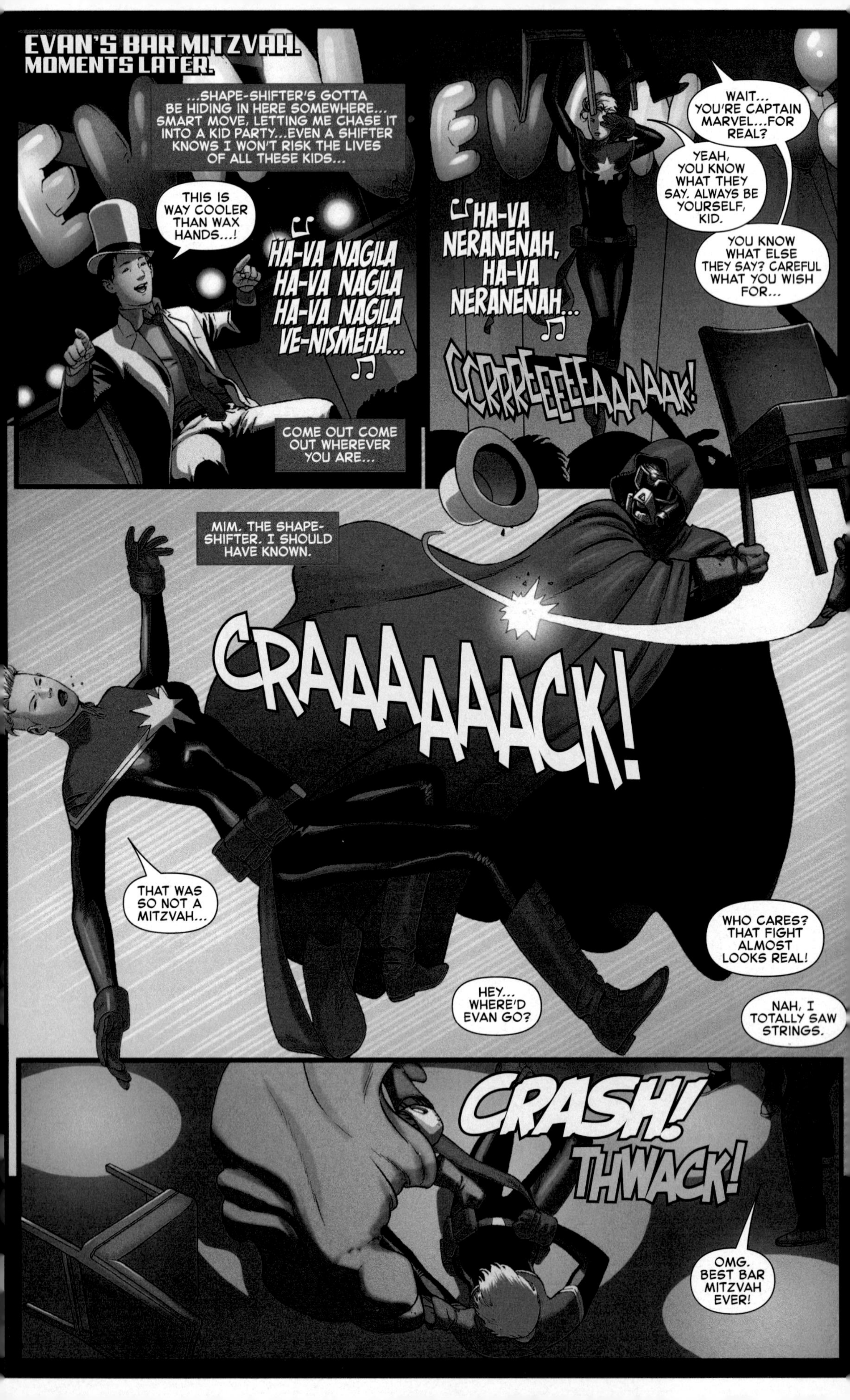
EVAN'S BAR MITZVAH. MOMENTS LATER.
...SHAPE-SHIFTER'S GOTTA BE HIDING IN HERE SOMEWHERE... SMART MOVE, LETTING ME CHASE IT INTO A KID PARTY...EVEN A SHIFTER KNOWS I WON'T RISK THE LIVES OF ALL THESE KIDS...
THIS IS WAY COOLER THAN WAX HANDS...!
HA-VA NAGILA HA-VA NAGILA HA-VA NAGILA VE-NISMEHA...
COME OUT COME OUT WHEREVER YOU ARE...
HA-VA NERANENAH, HA-VA NERANENAH...
WAIT... YOU'RE CAPTAIN MARVEL...FOR REAL?
YEAH, YOU KNOW WHAT THEY SAY. ALWAYS BE YOURSELF, KID.
YOU KNOW WHAT ELSE THEY SAY? CAREFUL WHAT YOU WISH FOR...
CCRRREEEEEAAAAAK!
MIM. THE SHAPE-SHIFTER. I SHOULD HAVE KNOWN.
CRAAAAAACK!
THAT WAS SO NOT A MITZVAH...
WHO CARES? THAT FIGHT ALMOST LOOKS REAL!
HEY... WHERE'D EVAN GO?
NAH, I TOTALLY SAW STRINGS.
CRASH!
THWACK!
OMG. BEST BAR MITZVAH EVER!

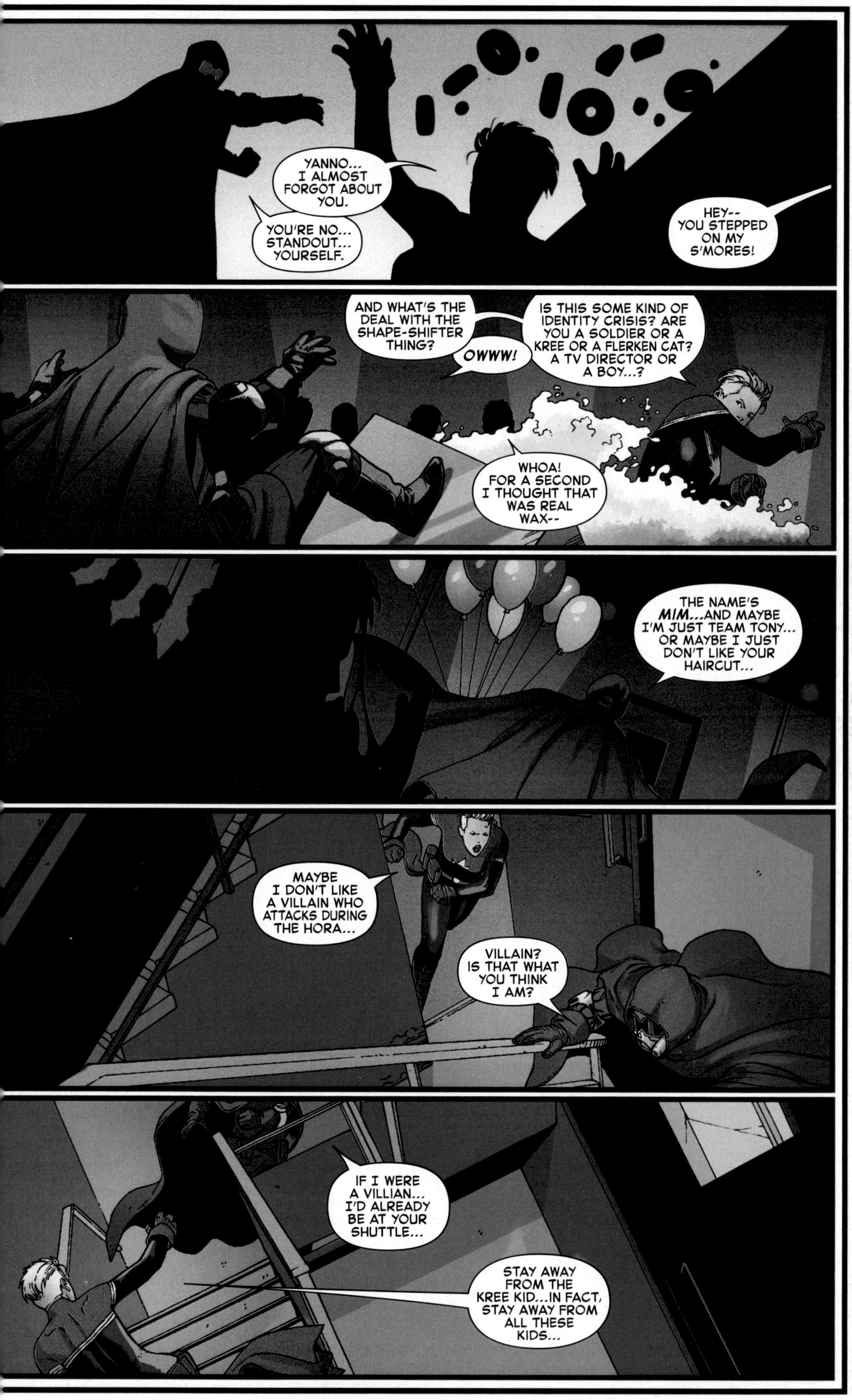

YANNO... I ALMOST FORGOT ABOUT YOU.
YOU'RE NO... STANDOUT... YOURSELF.
HEY-- YOU STEPPED ON MY S'MORES!
AND WHAT'S THE DEAL WITH THE SHAPE-SHIFTER THING?
IS THIS SOME KIND OF IDENTITY CRISIS? ARE YOU A SOLDIER OR A KREE OR A FLERKEN CAT? A TV DIRECTOR OR A BOY...?
OWWW!
WHOA! FOR A SECOND I THOUGHT THAT WAS REAL WAX--
THE NAME'S MIM...AND MAYBE I'M JUST TEAM TONY... OR MAYBE I JUST DON'T LIKE YOUR HAIRCUT...
MAYBE I DON'T LIKE A VILLAIN WHO ATTACKS DURING THE HORA...
VILLAIN? IS THAT WHAT YOU THINK I AM?
IF I WERE A VILLIAN... I'D ALREADY BE AT YOUR SHUTTLE...
STAY AWAY FROM THE KREE KID...IN FACT, STAY AWAY FROM ALL THESE KIDS...

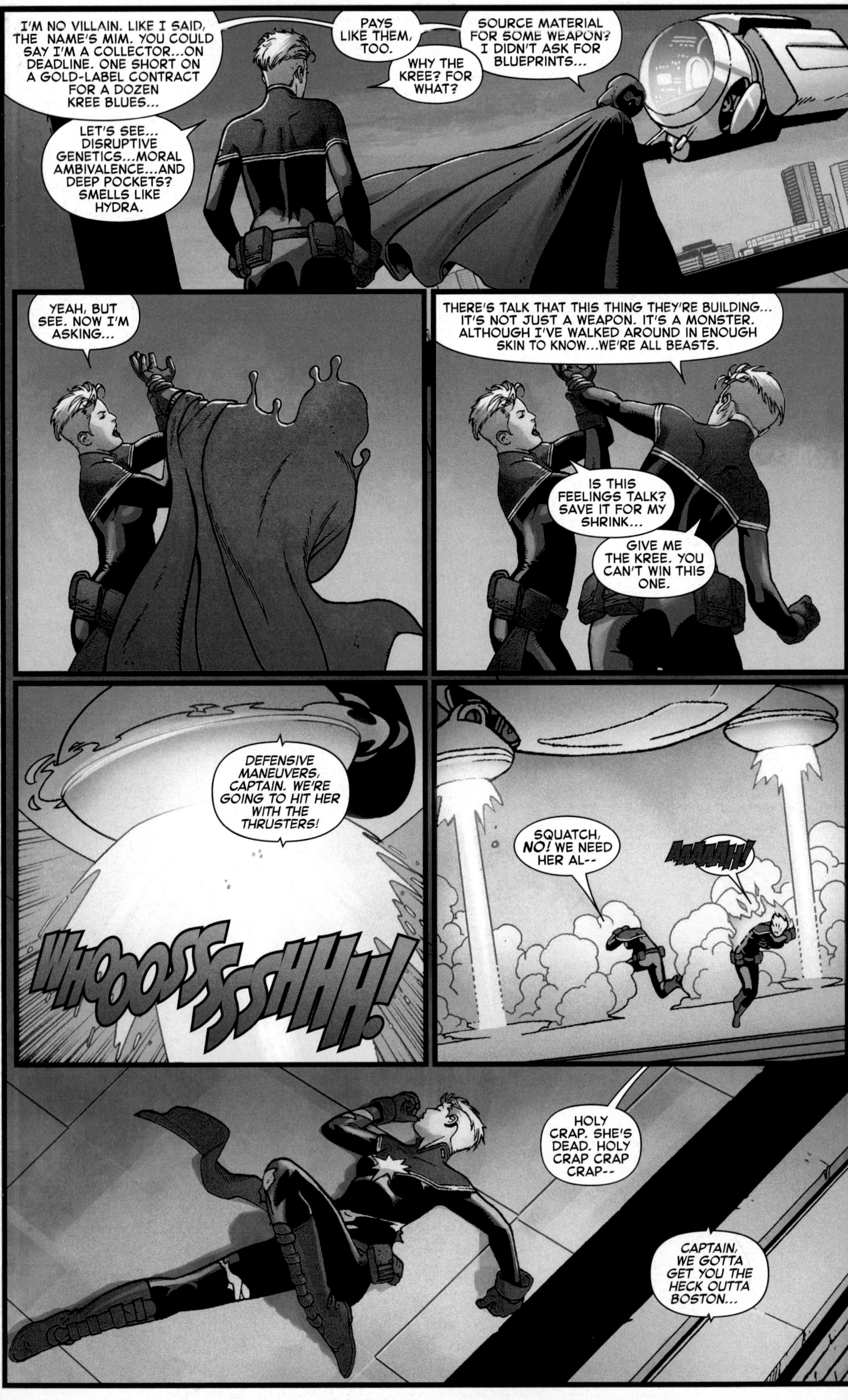
I'M NO VILLAIN. LIKE I SAID, THE NAME'S MIM. YOU COULD SAY I'M A COLLECTOR...ON DEADLINE. ONE SHORT ON A GOLD-LABEL CONTRACT FOR A DOZEN KREE BLUES...
PAYS LIKE THEM, TOO.
SOURCE MATERIAL FOR SOME WEAPON? I DIDN'T ASK FOR BLUEPRINTS...
WHY THE KREE? FOR WHAT?
LET'S SEE... DISRUPTIVE GENETICS...MORAL AMBIVALENCE...AND DEEP POCKETS? SMELLS LIKE HYDRA.
YEAH, BUT SEE. NOW I'M ASKING...
THERE'S TALK THAT THIS THING THEY'RE BUILDING... IT'S NOT JUST A WEAPON. IT'S A MONSTER. ALTHOUGH I'VE WALKED AROUND IN ENOUGH SKIN TO KNOW...WE'RE ALL BEASTS.
IS THIS FEELINGS TALK? SAVE IT FOR MY SHRINK...
GIVE ME THE KREE. YOU CAN'T WIN THIS ONE.
DEFENSIVE MANEUVERS, CAPTAIN. WE'RE GOING TO HIT HER WITH THE THRUSTERS!
WHOOOSSSSHHH!
SQUATCH, NO! WE NEED HER AL--
AAAAAH!
HOLY CRAP. SHE'S DEAD. HOLY CRAP CRAP CRAP--
CAPTAIN, WE GOTTA GET YOU THE HECK OUTTA BOSTON...

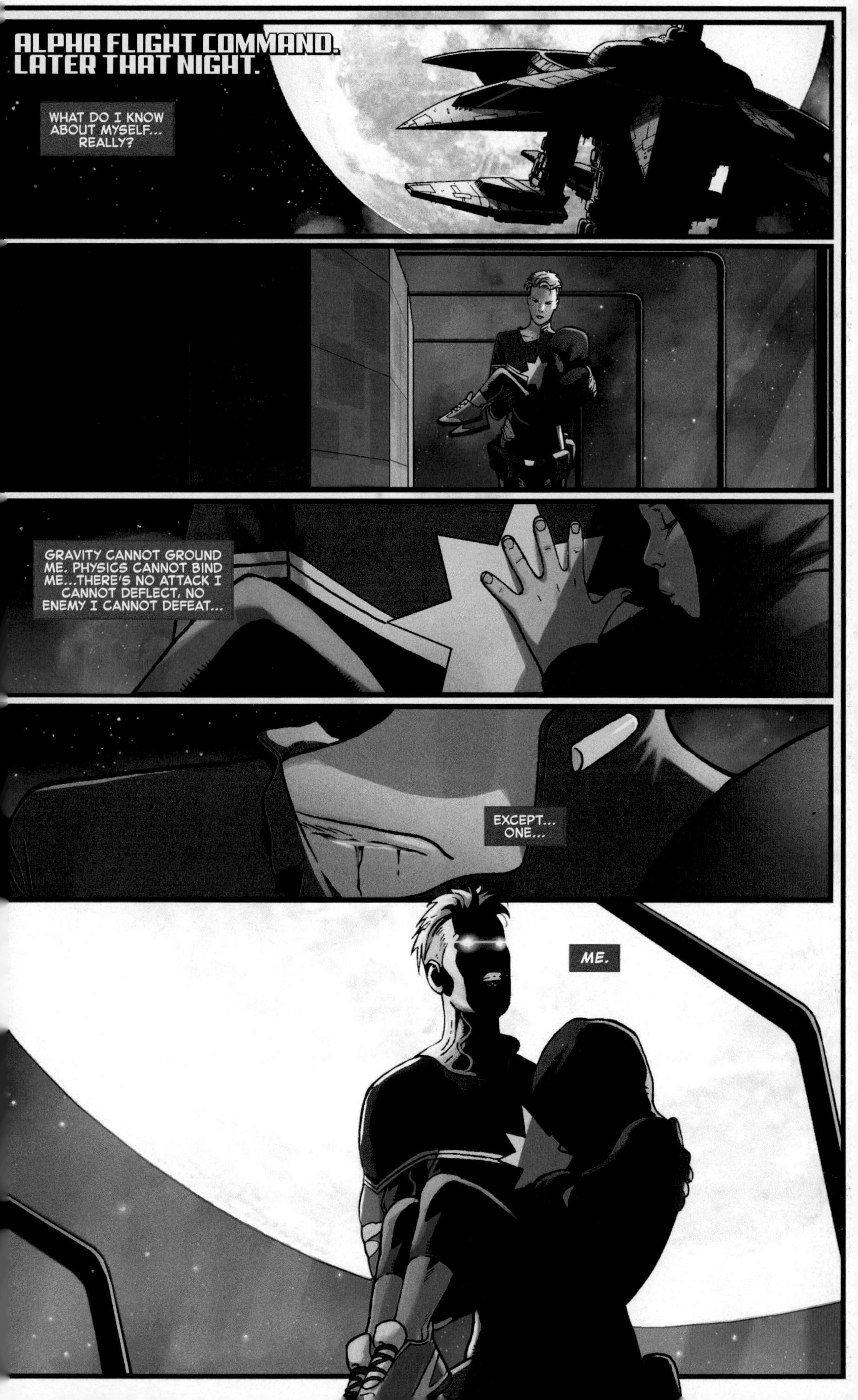
ALPHA FLIGHT COMMAND. LATER THAT NIGHT.
WHAT DO I KNOW ABOUT MYSELF... REALLY?
GRAVITY CANNOT GROUND ME. PHYSICS CANNOT BIND ME...THERE'S NO ATTACK I CANNOT DEFLECT, NO ENEMY I CANNOT DEFEAT...
EXCEPT... ONE...
ME.

4

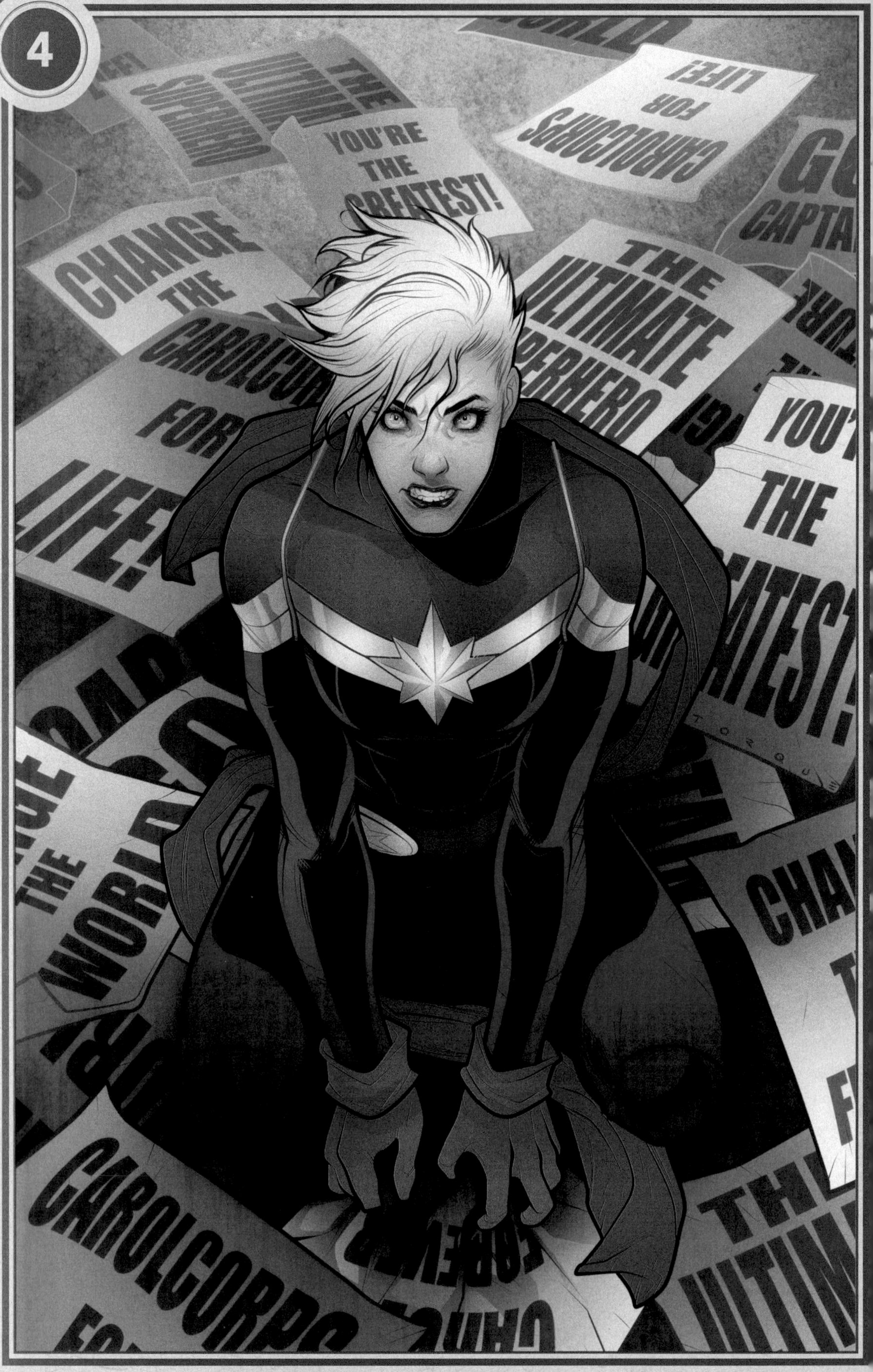
THE ULTIMATE SUPERHERO
YOU'RE THE GREATEST!
CAROLCORPS FOR LIFE!
CHANGE THE
FOR
LIFE!
THE ULTIMATE SUPERHERO
CAPTA
YOU'
THE
CAROLCORPS

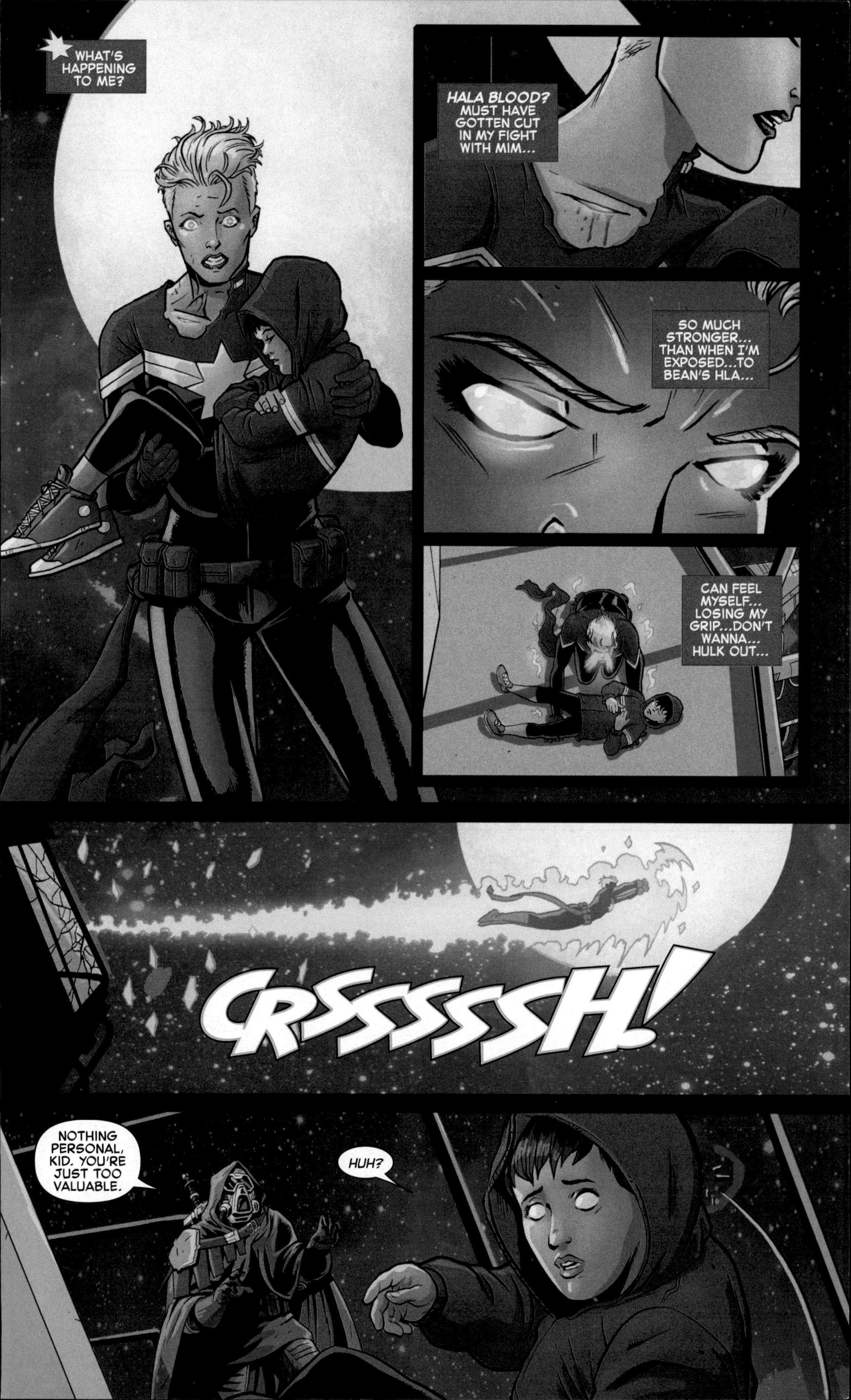
WHAT'S HAPPENING TO ME?
HALA BLOOD? MUST HAVE GOTTEN CUT IN MY FIGHT WITH MIM...
SO MUCH STRONGER... THAN WHEN I'M EXPOSED...TO BEAN'S HLA...
CAN FEEL MYSELF... LOSING MY GRIP...DON'T WANNA... HULK OUT...
CRSSSSSH!
NOTHING PERSONAL, KID. YOU'RE JUST TOO VALUABLE.
HUH?

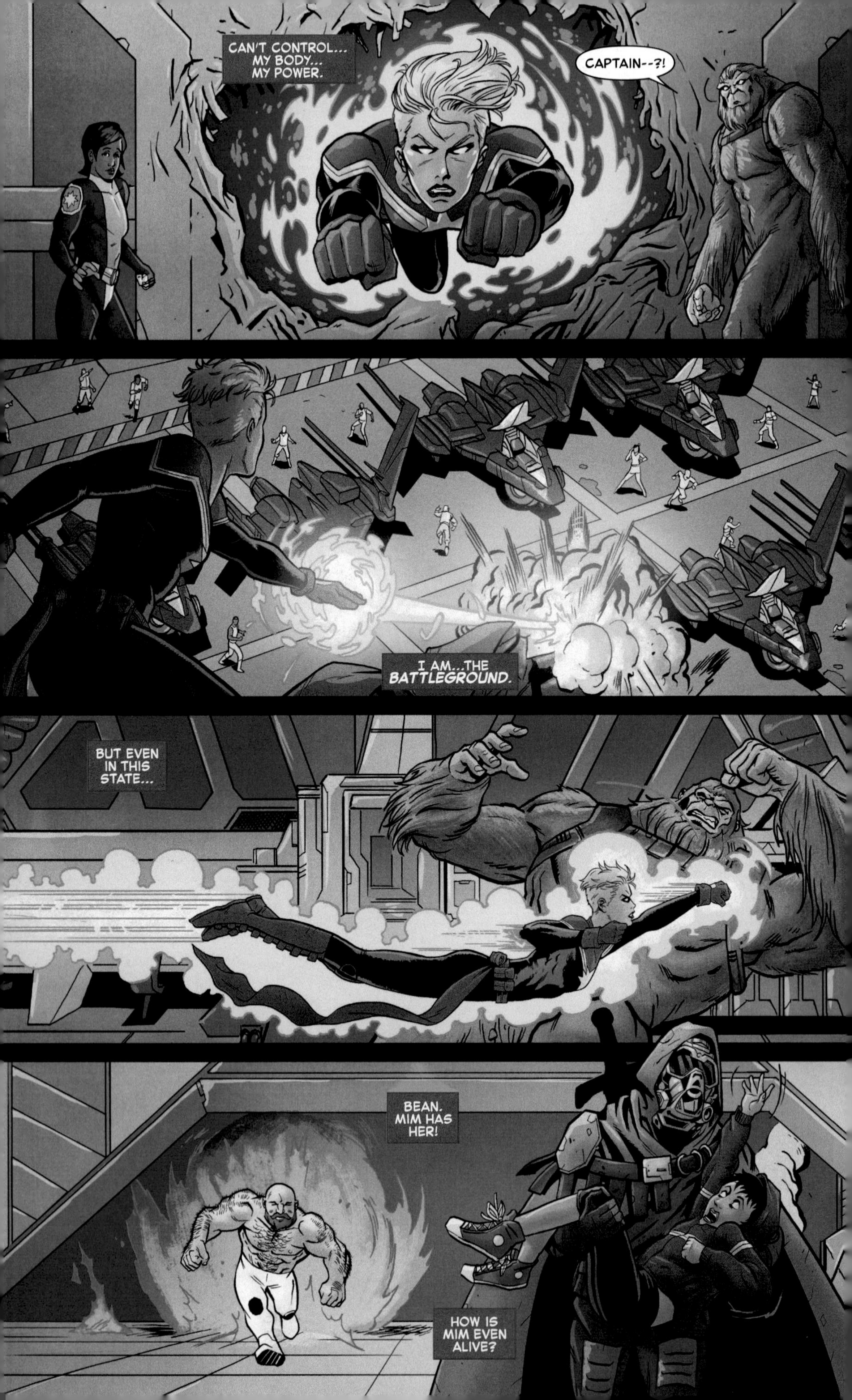
CAN'T CONTROL... MY BODY... MY POWER.
CAPTAIN--?!
I AM...THE BATTLEGROUND.
BUT EVEN IN THIS STATE...
BEAN. MIM HAS HER!
HOW IS MIM EVEN ALIVE?

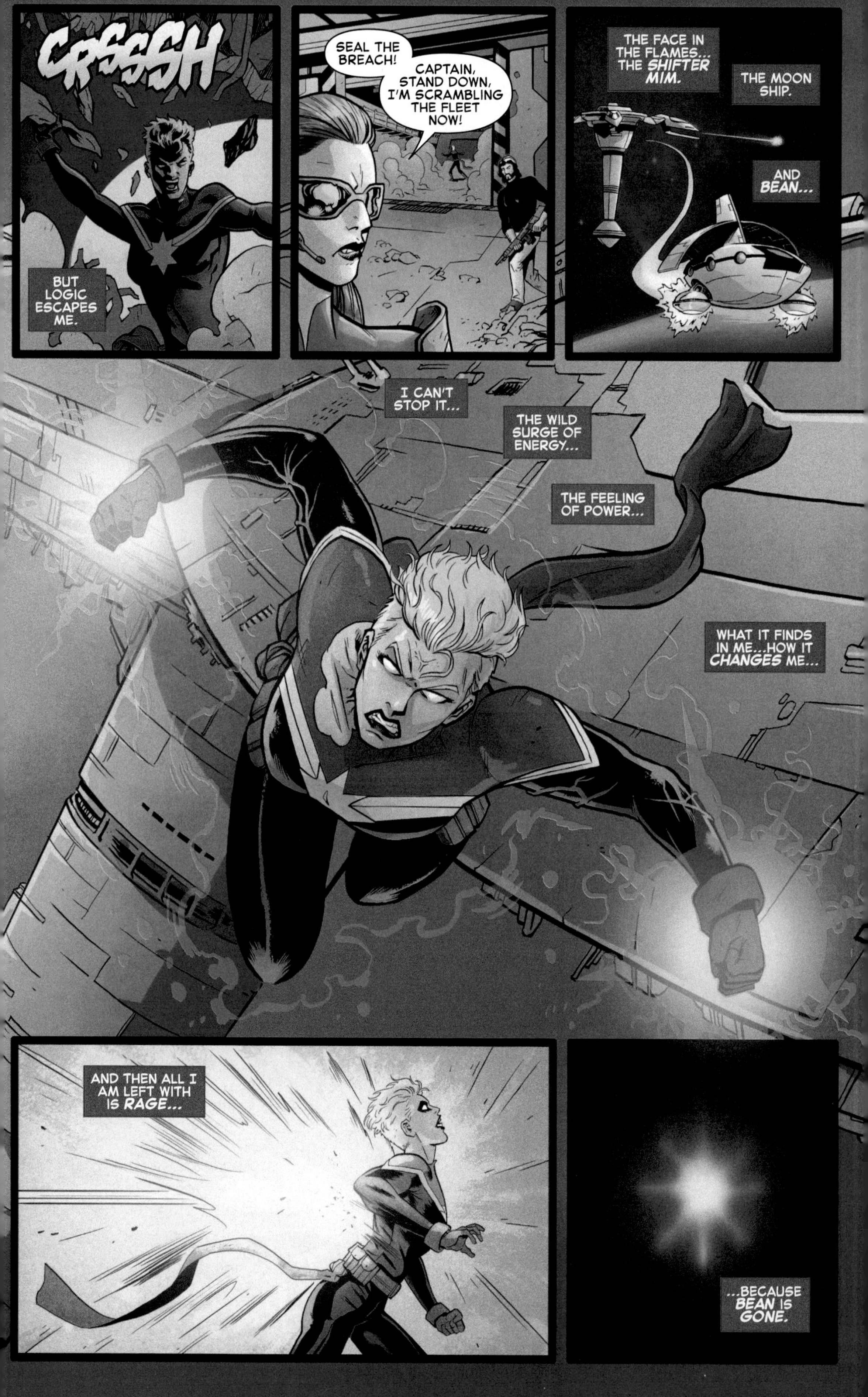
CRSSSH
BUT LOGIC ESCAPES ME.
SEAL THE BREACH!
CAPTAIN, STAND DOWN, I'M SCRAMBLING THE FLEET NOW!
THE FACE IN THE FLAMES... THE SHIFTER MIM.
THE MOON SHIP.
AND BEAN...
I CAN'T STOP IT...
THE WILD SURGE OF ENERGY...
THE FEELING OF POWER...
WHAT IT FINDS IN ME...HOW IT CHANGES ME...
AND THEN ALL I AM LEFT WITH IS RAGE...
...BECAUSE BEAN IS GONE.

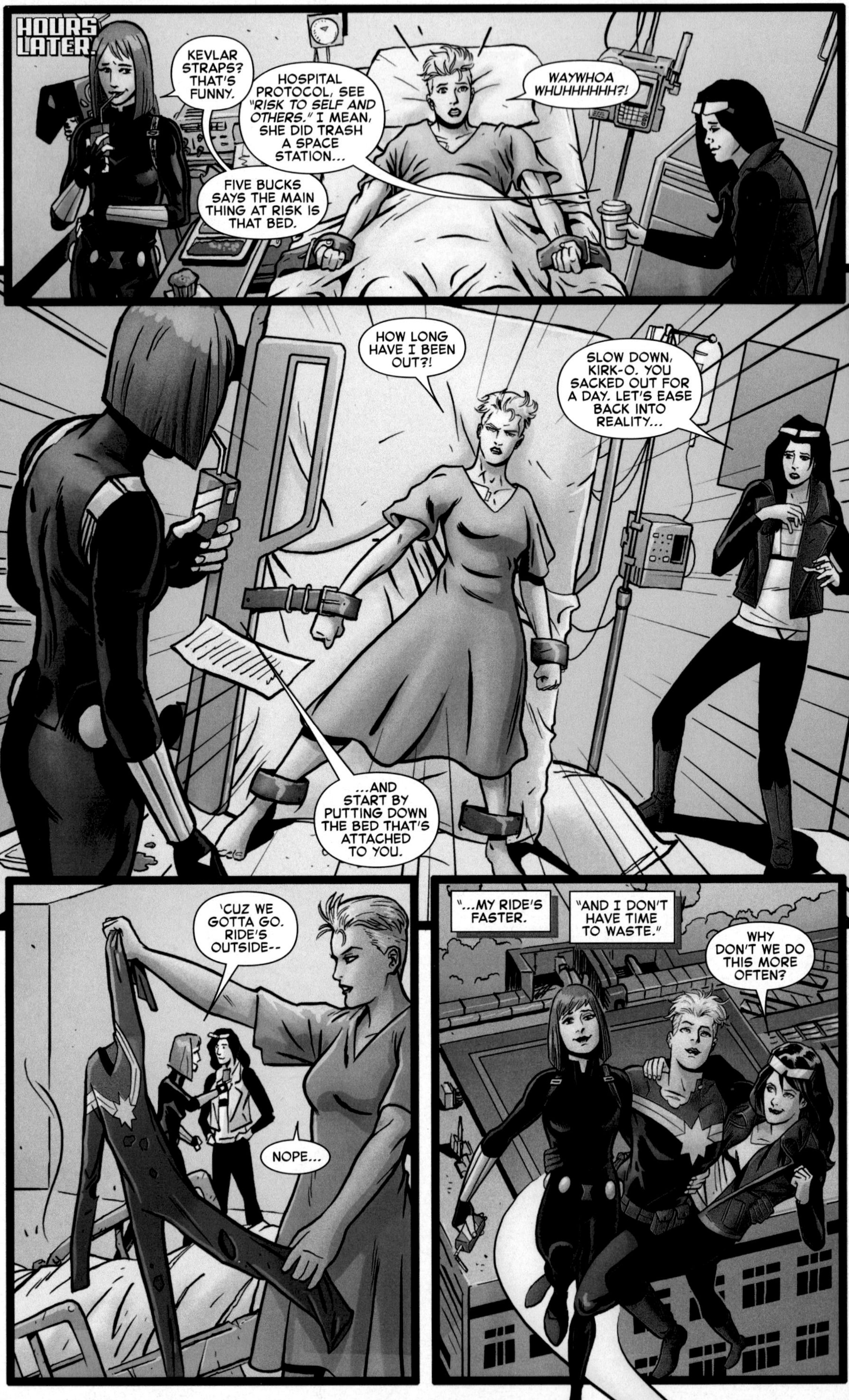
HOURS LATER...
KEVLAR STRAPS? THAT'S FUNNY.
HOSPITAL PROTOCOL, SEE "RISK TO SELF AND OTHERS." I MEAN, SHE DID TRASH A SPACE STATION...
FIVE BUCKS SAYS THE MAIN THING AT RISK IS THAT BED.
WAYWHOA WHUHHHHHH?!
HOW LONG HAVE I BEEN OUT?!
SLOW DOWN, KIRK-O. YOU SACKED OUT FOR A DAY. LET'S EASE BACK INTO REALITY...
...AND START BY PUTTING DOWN THE BED THAT'S ATTACHED TO YOU.
'CUZ WE GOTTA GO. RIDE'S OUTSIDE--
NOPE...
"...MY RIDE'S FASTER.
"AND I DON'T HAVE TIME TO WASTE."
WHY DON'T WE DO THIS MORE OFTEN?

"ALL I KNOW IS, I HAVE TO FIND BEAN."

"I DON'T KNOW WHAT'S HAPPENING... TO HER, OR TO ME."

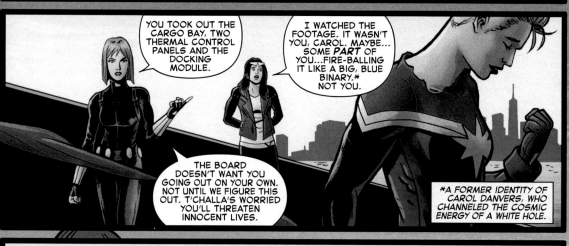

YOU TOOK OUT THE CARGO BAY, TWO THERMAL CONTROL PANELS AND THE DOCKING MODULE.

I WATCHED THE FOOTAGE. IT WASN'T YOU, CAROL. MAYBE... SOME *PART* OF YOU...FIRE-BALLING IT LIKE A BIG, BLUE BINARY.* NOT YOU.

THE BOARD DOESN'T WANT YOU GOING OUT ON YOUR OWN. NOT UNTIL WE FIGURE THIS OUT. T'CHALLA'S WORRIED YOU'LL THREATEN INNOCENT LIVES.

*A FORMER IDENTITY OF CAROL DANVERS, WHO CHANNELED THE COSMIC ENERGY OF A WHITE HOLE.

AND LET ME GUESS--THEY WANT YOU GUYS TO "KEEP ME CONTAINED."

FORGET THE BOARD. WE KNOW YOU. YOU GOTTA FIND BEAN.

THAT'S WHY WE BROUGHT YOU HERE. IF ANYONE ASKS, WE'RE KEEPING AN EYE ON YOU...IN A SECURE CONTAINMENT FACILITY. THAT'LL BUY YOU SOME TIME.

WENDY LOCATED THE KID'S HLA SIGNATURE A FEW HOURS AGO. YOUR NERDY SCI-GUY SAID THIS WILL HAVE EVERYTHING YOU NEED.

YOU MEAN HOPPER?

THE WEIRDO GEARDO WITH THE BEARDO.

YOU CAN LOAD BEAN'S COORDINATES RIGHT INTO YOUR FLIGHT HELMET.

BUT YOU'RE NOT GONNA BELIEVE WHERE THEY FOUND HER...

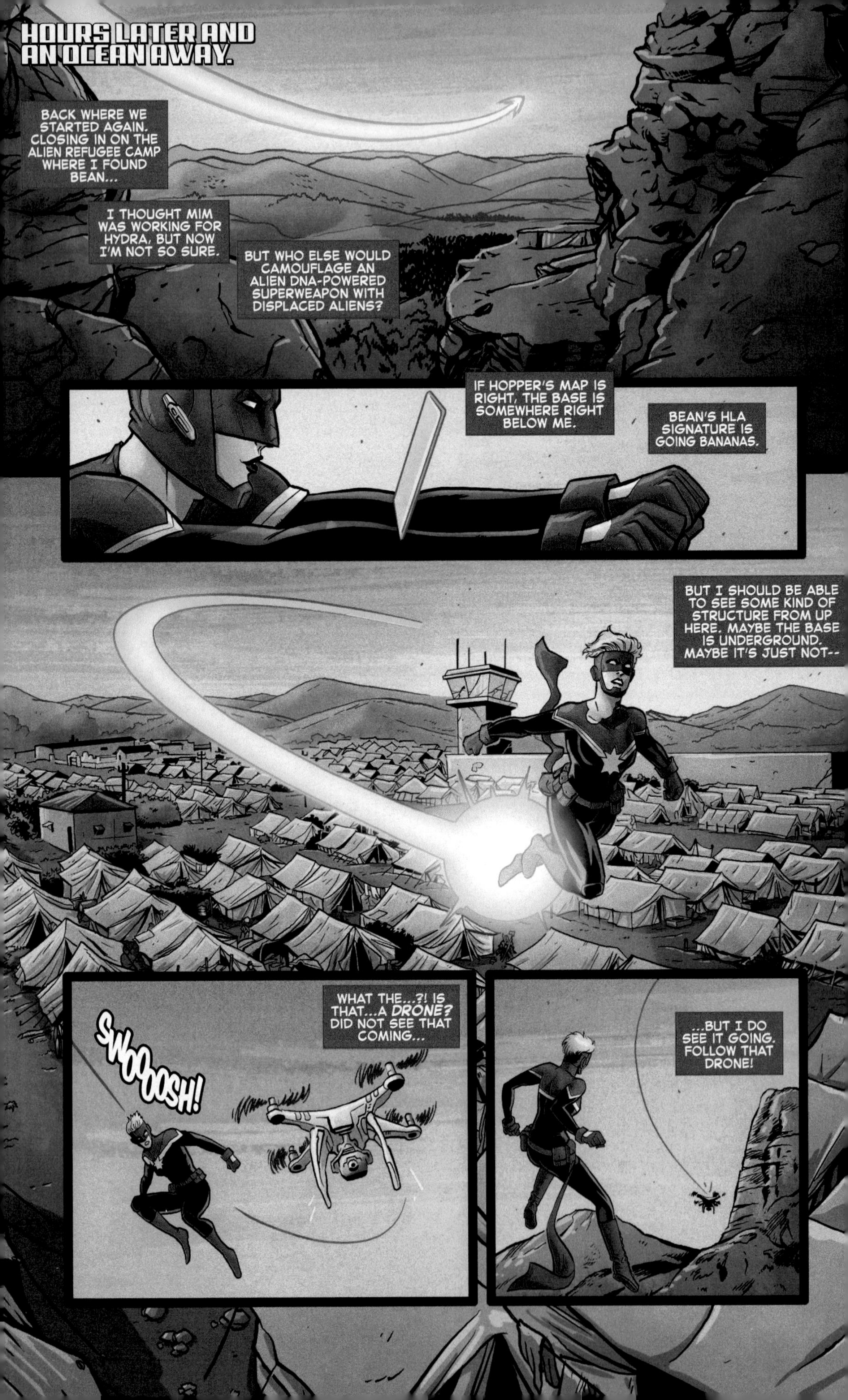
HOURS LATER AND AN OCEAN AWAY.
BACK WHERE WE STARTED AGAIN. CLOSING IN ON THE ALIEN REFUGEE CAMP WHERE I FOUND BEAN...
I THOUGHT MIM WAS WORKING FOR HYDRA, BUT NOW I'M NOT SO SURE.
BUT WHO ELSE WOULD CAMOUFLAGE AN ALIEN DNA-POWERED SUPERWEAPON WITH DISPLACED ALIENS?
IF HOPPER'S MAP IS RIGHT, THE BASE IS SOMEWHERE RIGHT BELOW ME.
BEAN'S HLA SIGNATURE IS GOING BANANAS.
BUT I SHOULD BE ABLE TO SEE SOME KIND OF STRUCTURE FROM UP HERE. MAYBE THE BASE IS UNDERGROUND. MAYBE IT'S JUST NOT--
SWOOOOSH!
WHAT THE...?! IS THAT...A *DRONE?* DID NOT SEE THAT COMING...
...BUT I DO SEE IT GOING. FOLLOW THAT DRONE!

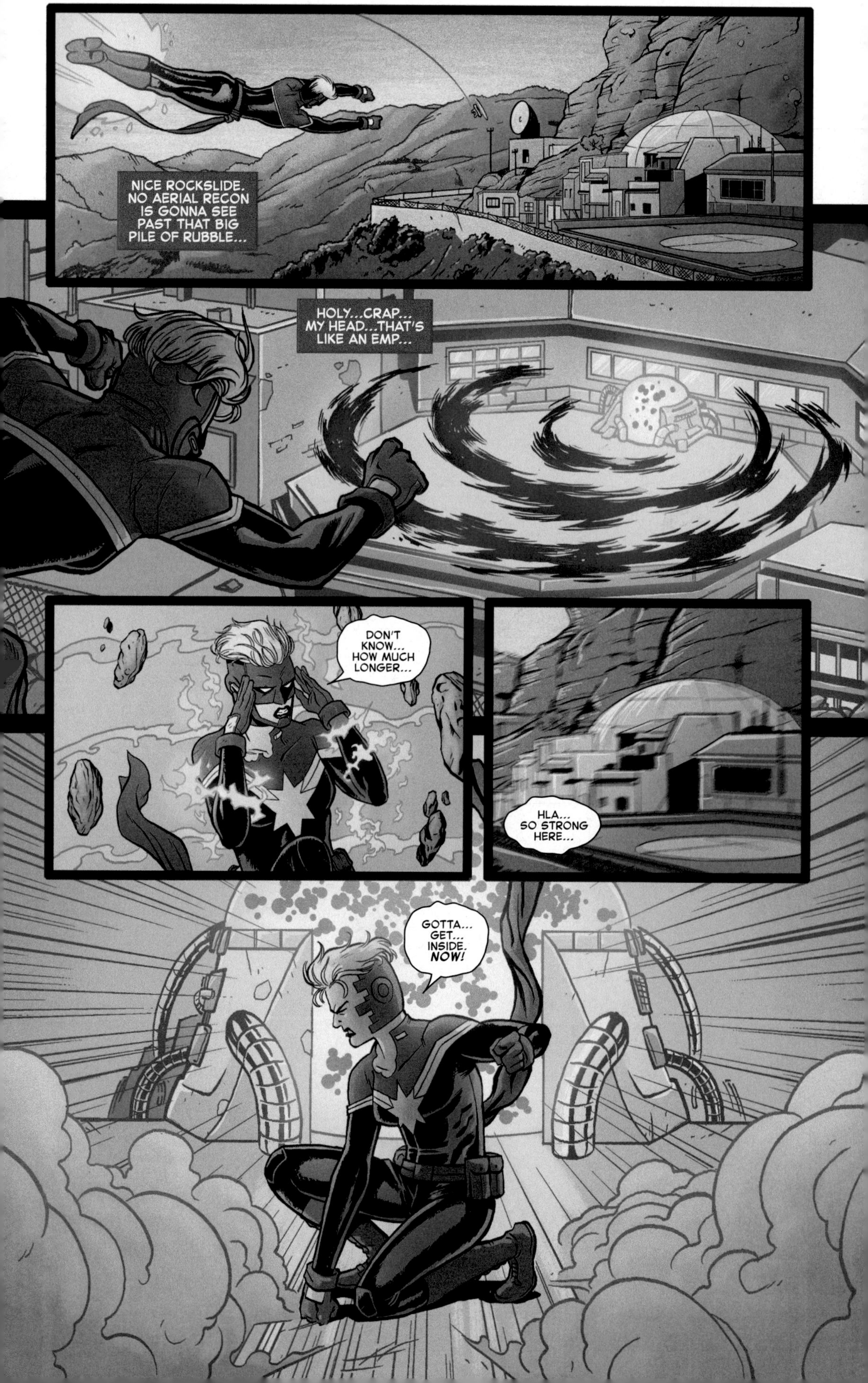
NICE ROCKSLIDE. NO AERIAL RECON IS GONNA SEE PAST THAT BIG PILE OF RUBBLE...
HOLY...CRAP... MY HEAD...THAT'S LIKE AN EMP...
DON'T KNOW... HOW MUCH LONGER...
HLA... SO STRONG HERE...
GOTTA... GET... INSIDE. NOW!

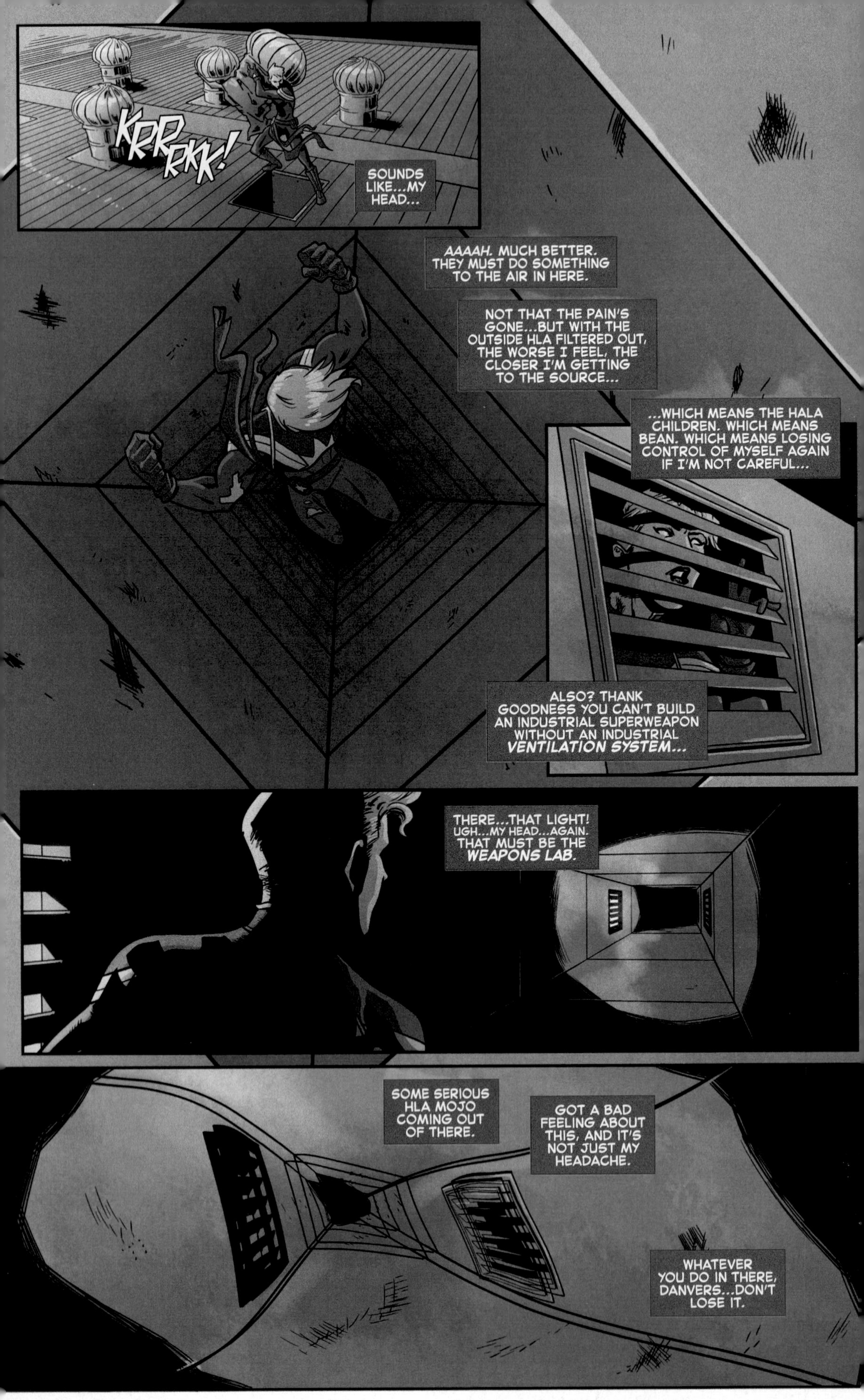
KRRRKK!
SOUNDS LIKE...MY HEAD...
AAAAH. MUCH BETTER. THEY MUST DO SOMETHING TO THE AIR IN HERE.
NOT THAT THE PAIN'S GONE...BUT WITH THE OUTSIDE HLA FILTERED OUT, THE WORSE I FEEL, THE CLOSER I'M GETTING TO THE SOURCE...
...WHICH MEANS THE HALA CHILDREN. WHICH MEANS BEAN. WHICH MEANS LOSING CONTROL OF MYSELF AGAIN IF I'M NOT CAREFUL...
ALSO? THANK GOODNESS YOU CAN'T BUILD AN INDUSTRIAL SUPERWEAPON WITHOUT AN INDUSTRIAL VENTILATION SYSTEM...
THERE...THAT LIGHT! UGH...MY HEAD...AGAIN. THAT MUST BE THE WEAPONS LAB.
SOME SERIOUS HLA MOJO COMING OUT OF THERE.
GOT A BAD FEELING ABOUT THIS, AND IT'S NOT JUST MY HEADACHE.
WHATEVER YOU DO IN THERE, DANVERS...DON'T LOSE IT.

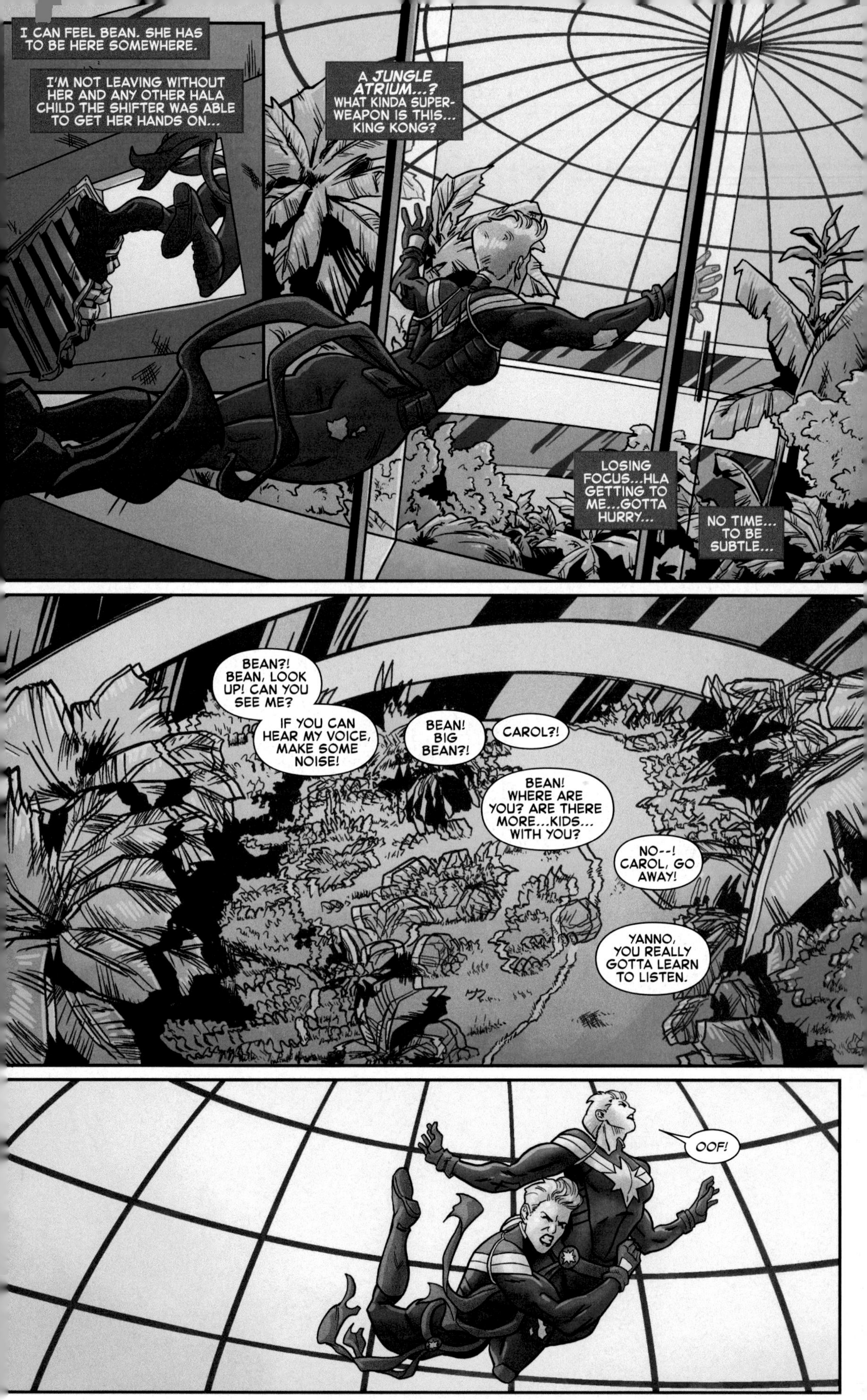
I CAN FEEL BEAN. SHE HAS TO BE HERE SOMEWHERE.
I'M NOT LEAVING WITHOUT HER AND ANY OTHER HALA CHILD THE SHIFTER WAS ABLE TO GET HER HANDS ON...
A JUNGLE ATRIUM...? WHAT KINDA SUPER-WEAPON IS THIS... KING KONG?
LOSING FOCUS...HLA GETTING TO ME...GOTTA HURRY...
NO TIME... TO BE SUBTLE...
BEAN?! BEAN, LOOK UP! CAN YOU SEE ME?
IF YOU CAN HEAR MY VOICE, MAKE SOME NOISE!
BEAN! BIG BEAN?!
CAROL?!
BEAN! WHERE ARE YOU? ARE THERE MORE...KIDS... WITH YOU?
NO--! CAROL, GO AWAY!
YANNO, YOU REALLY GOTTA LEARN TO LISTEN.
OOF!

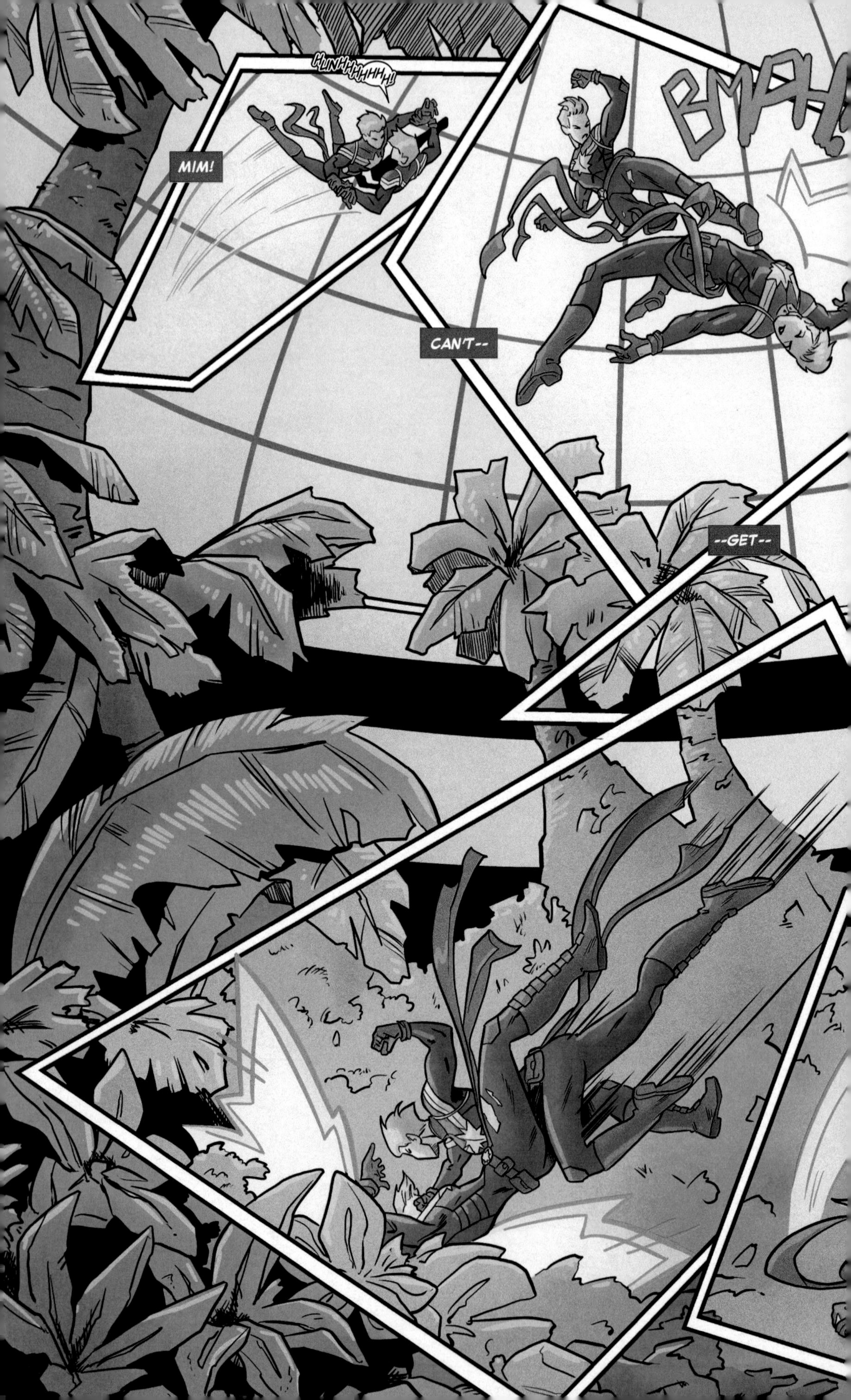
HUNHHHHHHH!
MIM!
BMAH!
CAN'T--
--GET--

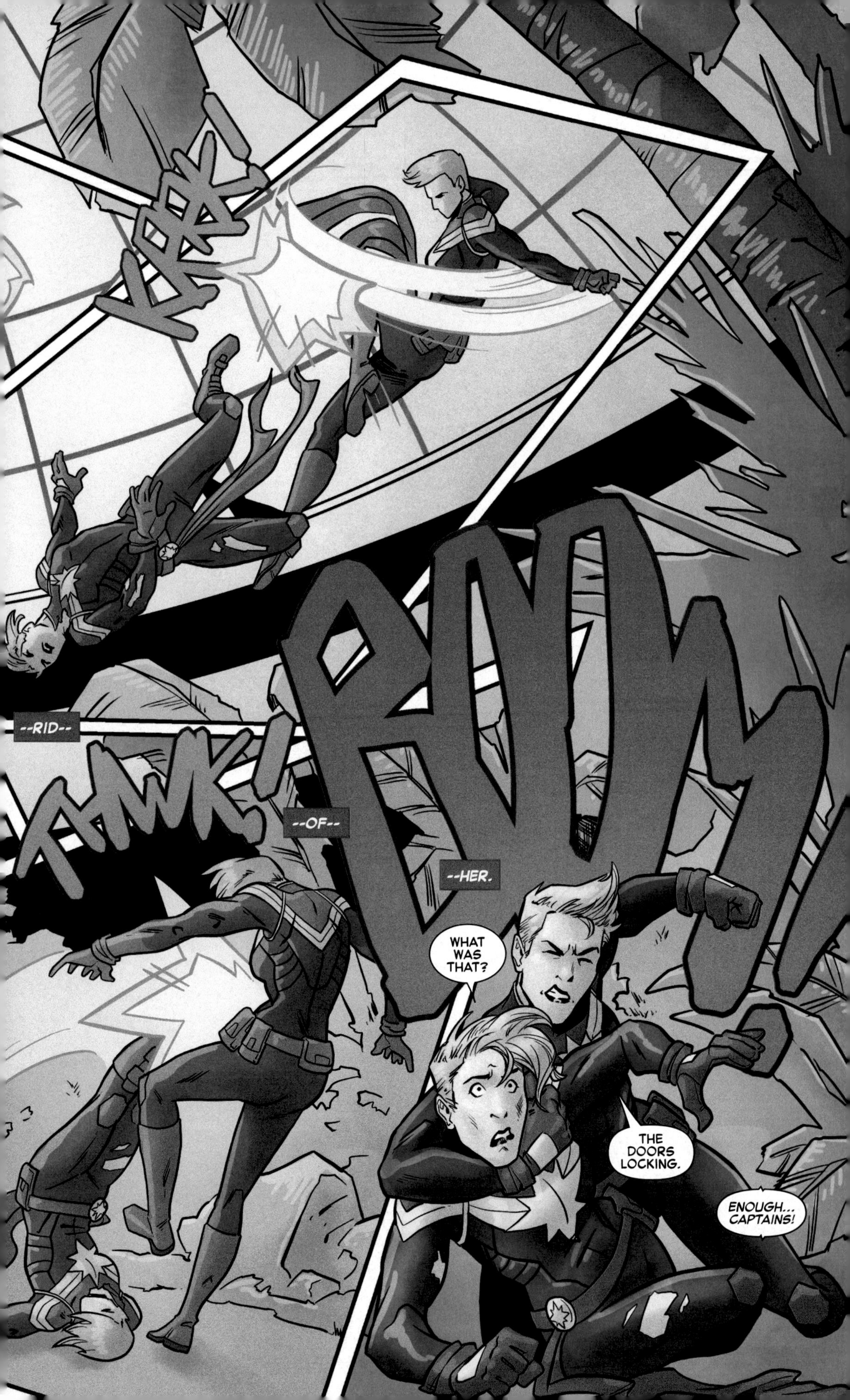
KRAK
--RID--
THWK!
--OF--
BOOM!
--HER.
WHAT WAS THAT?
THE DOORS LOCKING.
ENOUGH... CAPTAINS!

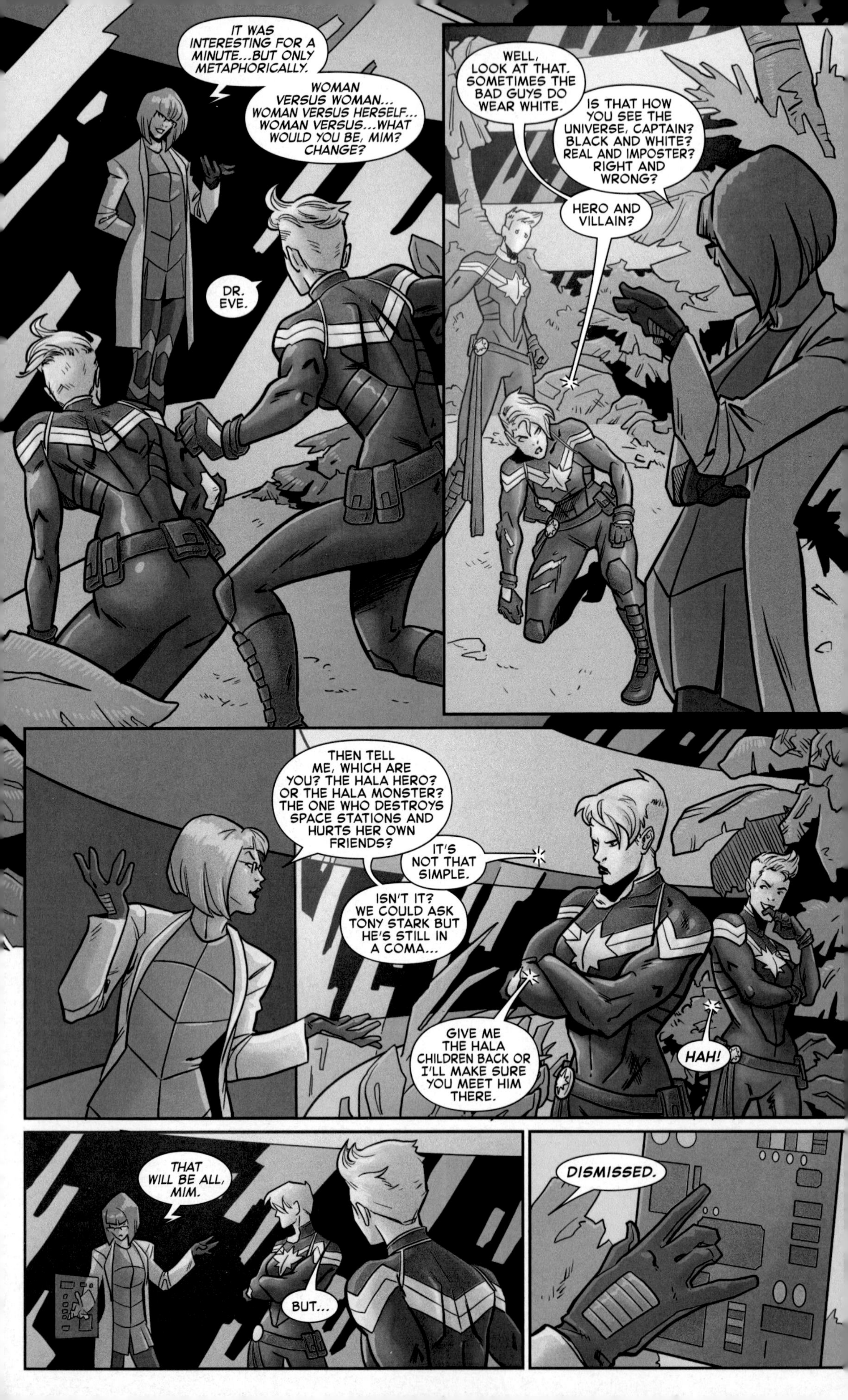
IT WAS INTERESTING FOR A MINUTE...BUT ONLY METAPHORICALLY.
WOMAN VERSUS WOMAN... WOMAN VERSUS HERSELF... WOMAN VERSUS...WHAT WOULD YOU BE, MIM? CHANGE?
DR. EVE.
WELL, LOOK AT THAT. SOMETIMES THE BAD GUYS DO WEAR WHITE.
IS THAT HOW YOU SEE THE UNIVERSE, CAPTAIN? BLACK AND WHITE? REAL AND IMPOSTER? RIGHT AND WRONG?
HERO AND VILLAIN?
THEN TELL ME, WHICH ARE YOU? THE HALA HERO? OR THE HALA MONSTER? THE ONE WHO DESTROYS SPACE STATIONS AND HURTS HER OWN FRIENDS?
IT'S NOT THAT SIMPLE.
ISN'T IT? WE COULD ASK TONY STARK BUT HE'S STILL IN A COMA...
GIVE ME THE HALA CHILDREN BACK OR I'LL MAKE SURE YOU MEET HIM THERE.
HAH!
THAT WILL BE ALL, MIM.
BUT...
DISMISSED.

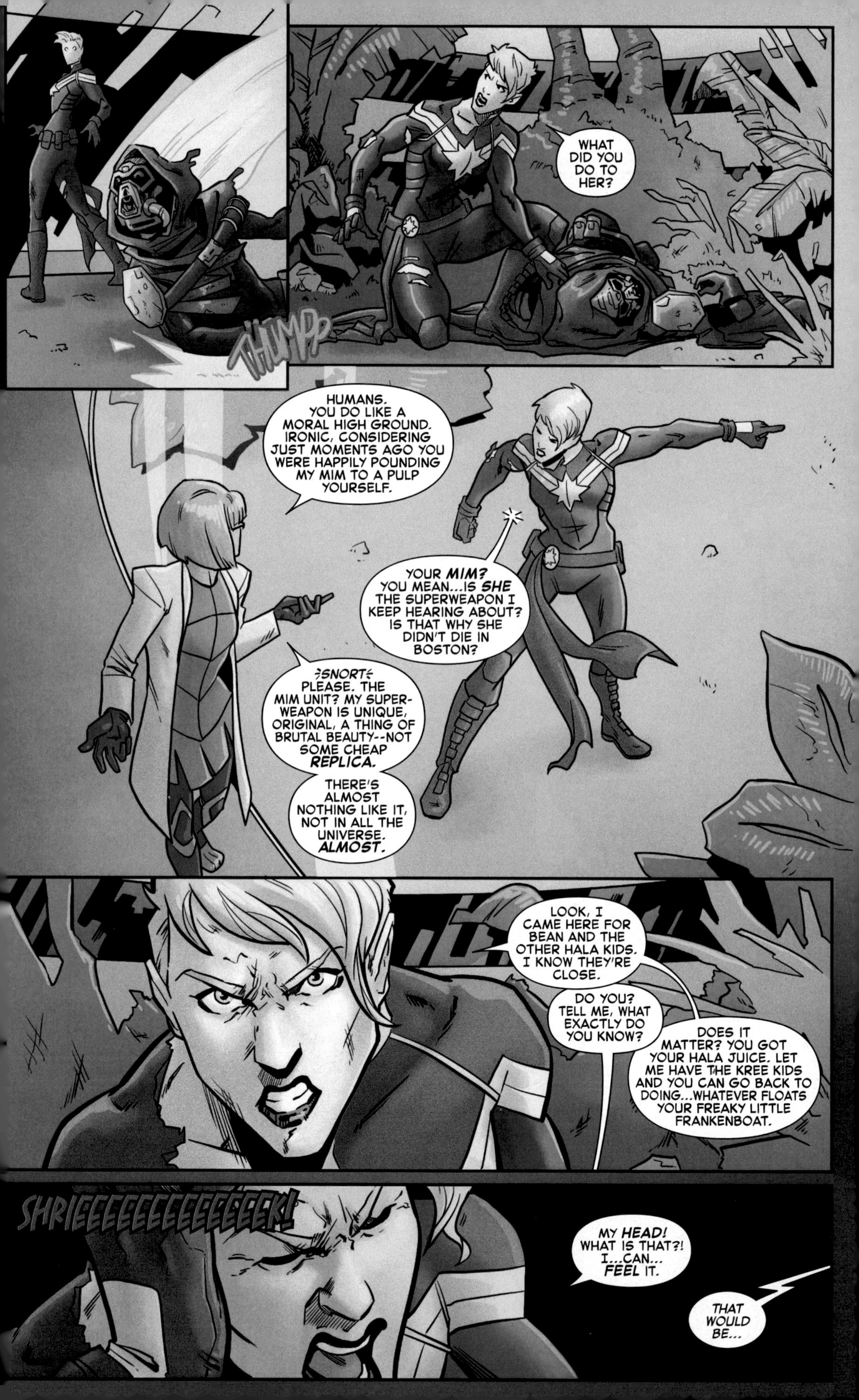
THUMP!
WHAT DID YOU DO TO HER?
HUMANS. YOU DO LIKE A MORAL HIGH GROUND. IRONIC, CONSIDERING JUST MOMENTS AGO YOU WERE HAPPILY POUNDING MY MIM TO A PULP YOURSELF.
YOUR MIM? YOU MEAN...IS SHE THE SUPERWEAPON I KEEP HEARING ABOUT? IS THAT WHY SHE DIDN'T DIE IN BOSTON?
SNORT PLEASE. THE MIM UNIT? MY SUPER-WEAPON IS UNIQUE, ORIGINAL, A THING OF BRUTAL BEAUTY--NOT SOME CHEAP REPLICA.
THERE'S ALMOST NOTHING LIKE IT, NOT IN ALL THE UNIVERSE. ALMOST.
LOOK, I CAME HERE FOR BEAN AND THE OTHER HALA KIDS. I KNOW THEY'RE CLOSE.
DO YOU? TELL ME, WHAT EXACTLY DO YOU KNOW?
DOES IT MATTER? YOU GOT YOUR HALA JUICE. LET ME HAVE THE KREE KIDS AND YOU CAN GO BACK TO DOING...WHATEVER FLOATS YOUR FREAKY LITTLE FRANKENBOAT.
SHRIEEEEEEEEEEEEEEEK!
MY HEAD! WHAT IS THAT?! I...CAN... FEEL IT.
THAT WOULD BE...

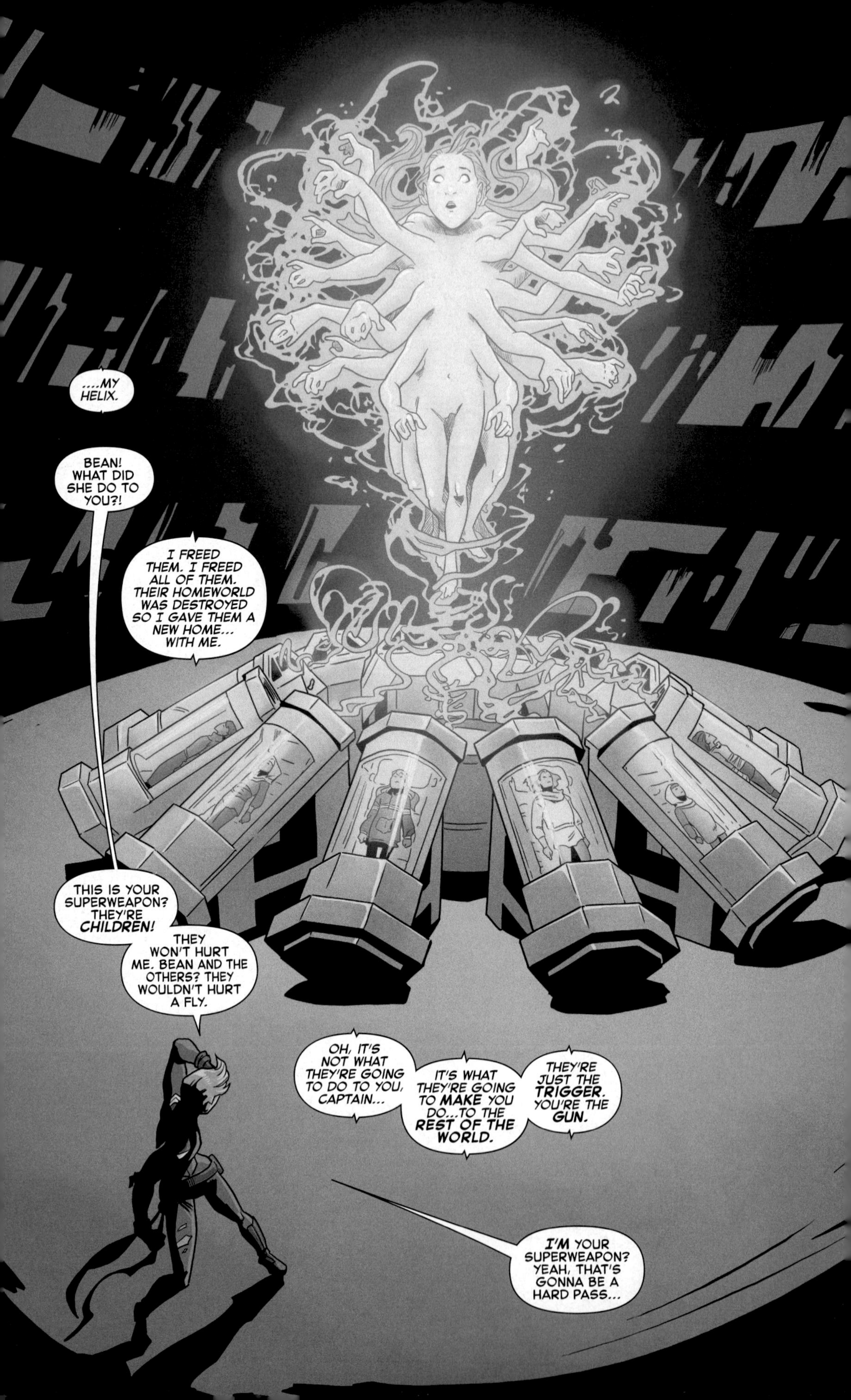
....MY HELIX.
BEAN! WHAT DID SHE DO TO YOU?!
I FREED THEM. I FREED ALL OF THEM. THEIR HOMEWORLD WAS DESTROYED SO I GAVE THEM A NEW HOME... WITH ME.
THIS IS YOUR SUPERWEAPON? THEY'RE CHILDREN!
THEY WON'T HURT ME. BEAN AND THE OTHERS? THEY WOULDN'T HURT A FLY.
OH, IT'S NOT WHAT THEY'RE GOING TO DO TO YOU, CAPTAIN...
IT'S WHAT THEY'RE GOING TO MAKE YOU DO...TO THE REST OF THE WORLD.
THEY'RE JUST THE TRIGGER. YOU'RE THE GUN.
I'M YOUR SUPERWEAPON? YEAH, THAT'S GONNA BE A HARD PASS...

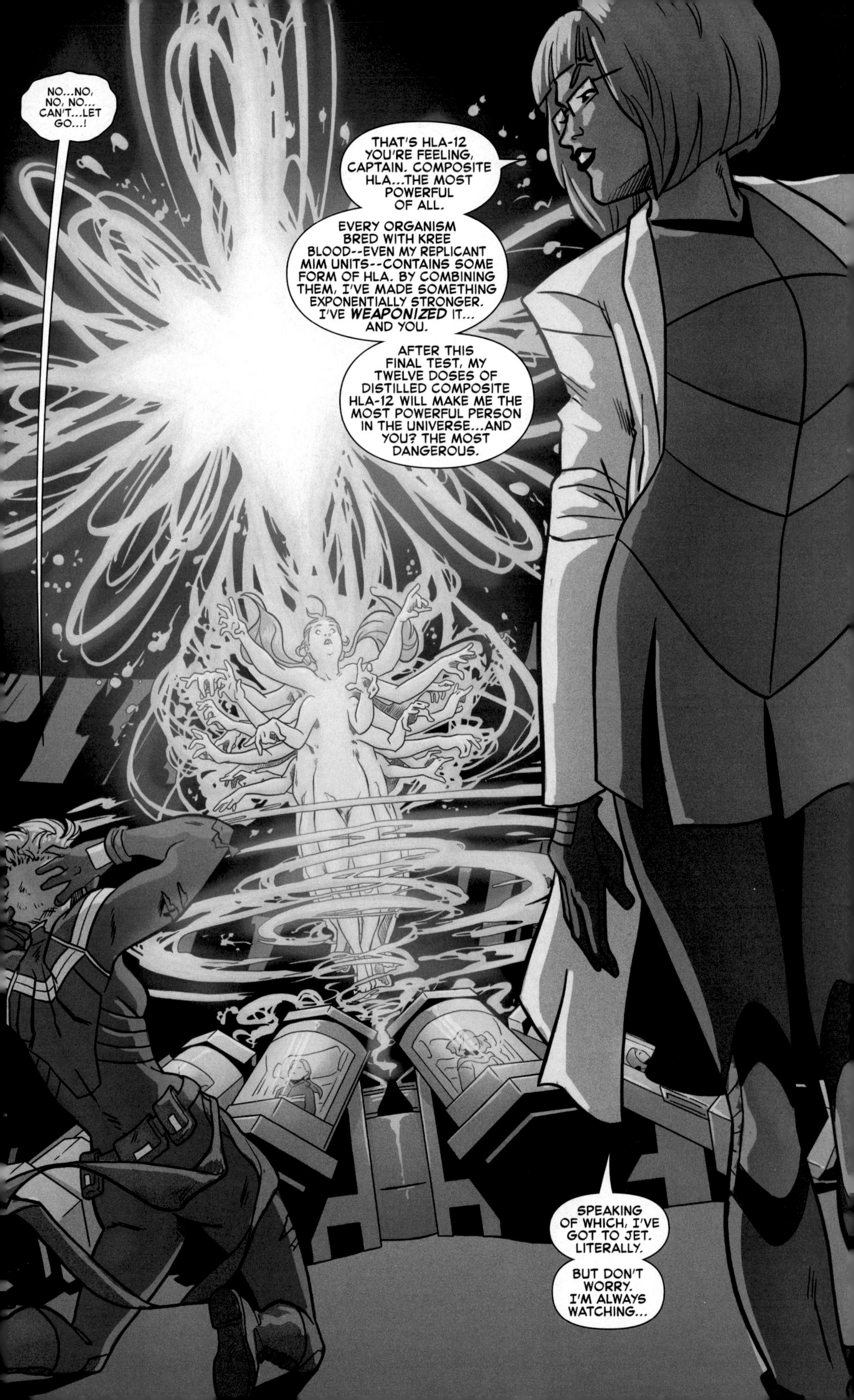
NO...NO, NO, NO... CAN'T...LET GO...!
THAT'S HLA-12 YOU'RE FEELING, CAPTAIN. COMPOSITE HLA...THE MOST POWERFUL OF ALL.
EVERY ORGANISM BRED WITH KREE BLOOD--EVEN MY REPLICANT MIM UNITS--CONTAINS SOME FORM OF HLA. BY COMBINING THEM, I'VE MADE SOMETHING EXPONENTIALLY STRONGER. I'VE WEAPONIZED IT... AND YOU.
AFTER THIS FINAL TEST, MY TWELVE DOSES OF DISTILLED COMPOSITE HLA-12 WILL MAKE ME THE MOST POWERFUL PERSON IN THE UNIVERSE...AND YOU? THE MOST DANGEROUS.
SPEAKING OF WHICH, I'VE GOT TO JET. LITERALLY.
BUT DON'T WORRY. I'M ALWAYS WATCHING...

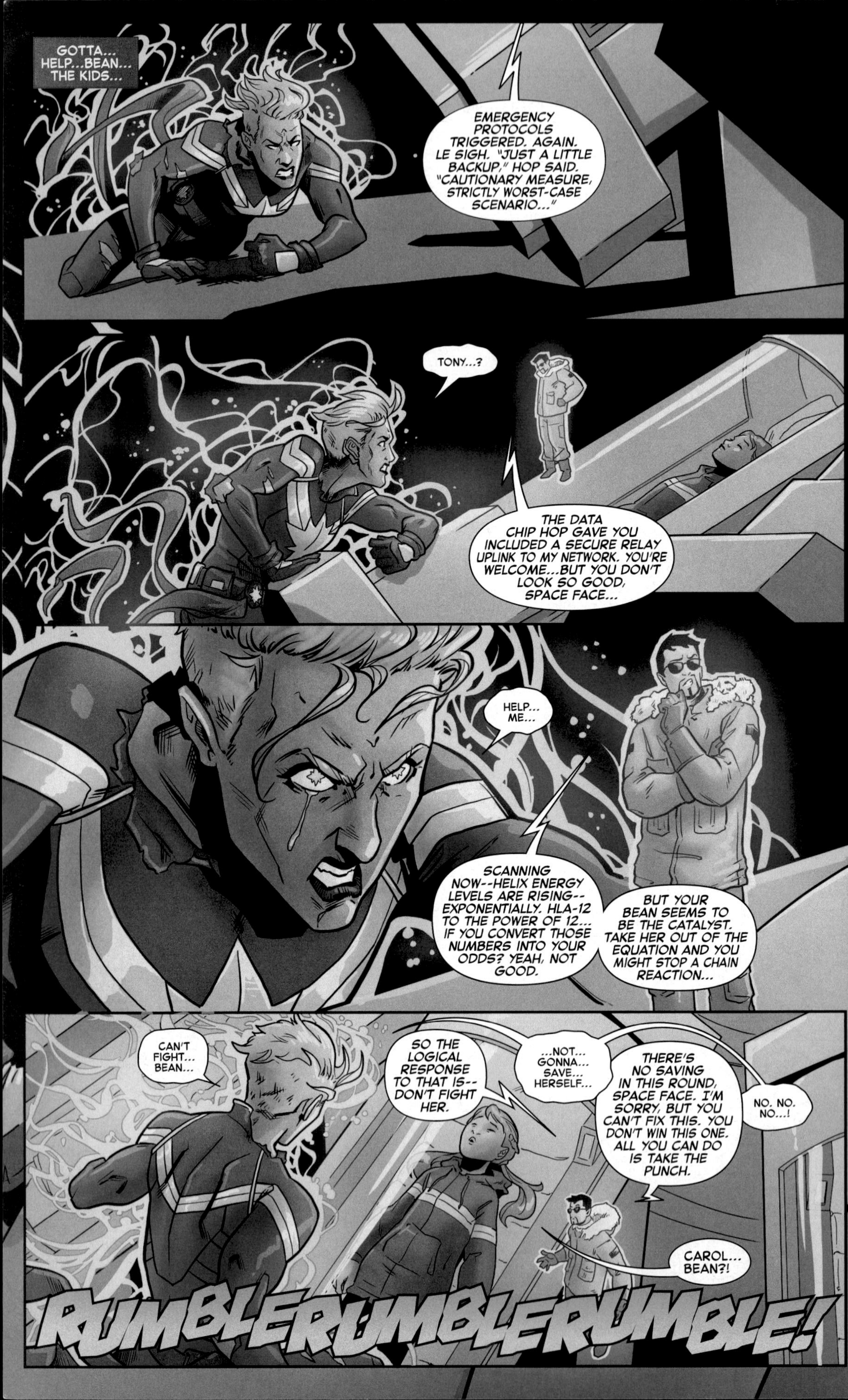

GOTTA... HELP...BEAN... THE KIDS...
EMERGENCY PROTOCOLS TRIGGERED. AGAIN. LE SIGH. "JUST A LITTLE BACKUP," HOP SAID. "CAUTIONARY MEASURE, STRICTLY WORST-CASE SCENARIO..."
TONY...?
THE DATA CHIP HOP GAVE YOU INCLUDED A SECURE RELAY UPLINK TO MY NETWORK. YOU'RE WELCOME...BUT YOU DON'T LOOK SO GOOD, SPACE FACE...
HELP... ME...
SCANNING NOW--HELIX ENERGY LEVELS ARE RISING--EXPONENTIALLY. HLA-12 TO THE POWER OF 12... IF YOU CONVERT THOSE NUMBERS INTO YOUR ODDS? YEAH, NOT GOOD.
BUT YOUR BEAN SEEMS TO BE THE CATALYST. TAKE HER OUT OF THE EQUATION AND YOU MIGHT STOP A CHAIN REACTION...
CAN'T FIGHT... BEAN...
SO THE LOGICAL RESPONSE TO THAT IS--DON'T FIGHT HER.
...NOT... GONNA... SAVE... HERSELF...
THERE'S NO SAVING IN THIS ROUND, SPACE FACE. I'M SORRY, BUT YOU CAN'T FIX THIS. YOU DON'T WIN THIS ONE. ALL YOU CAN DO IS TAKE THE PUNCH.
NO. NO. NO...!
CAROL... BEAN?!
RUMBLERUMBLERUMBLE!

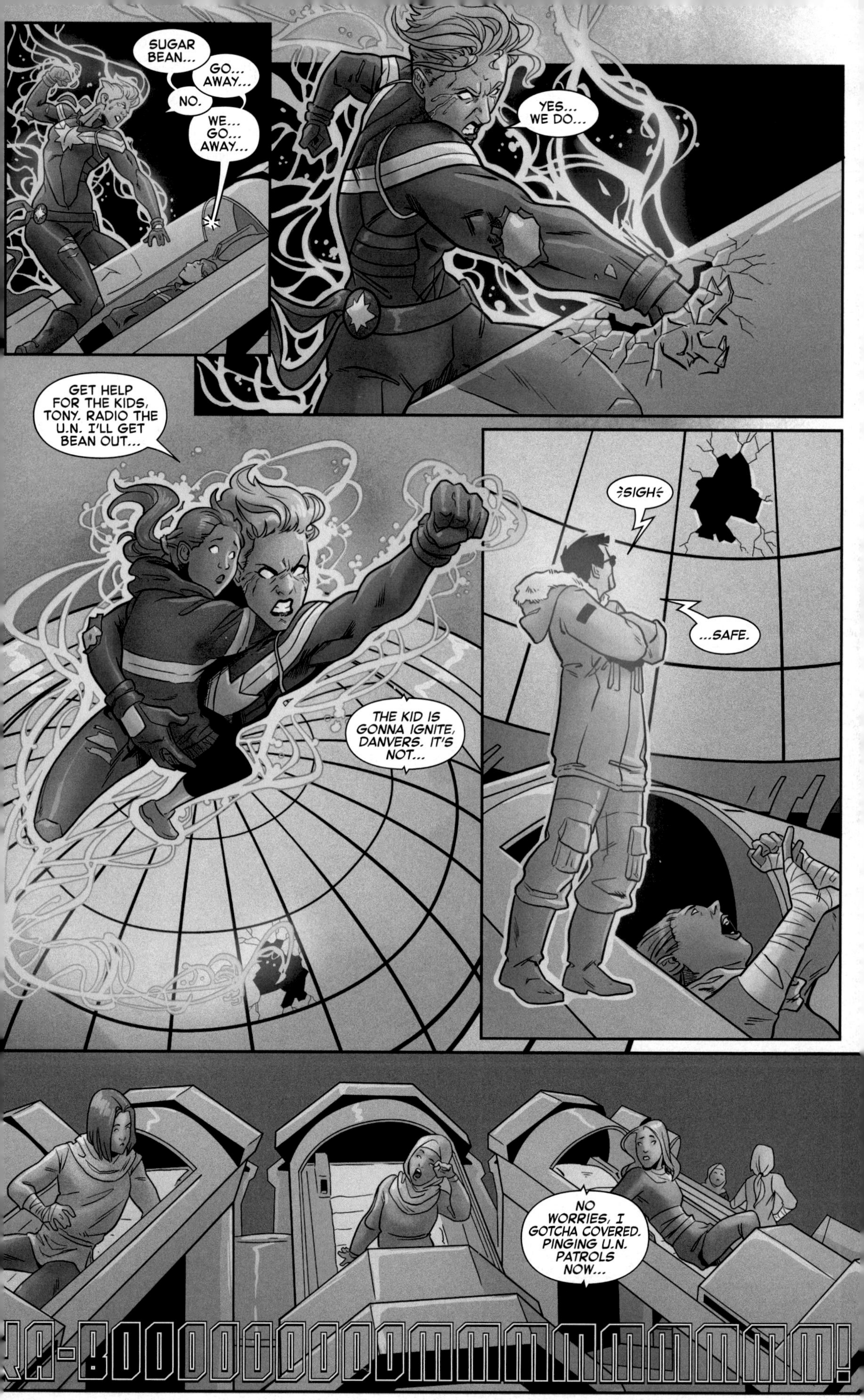
SUGAR BEAN...
GO... AWAY...
NO.
WE... GO... AWAY...
YES... WE DO...
GET HELP FOR THE KIDS, TONY. RADIO THE U.N. I'LL GET BEAN OUT...
THE KID IS GONNA IGNITE, DANVERS. IT'S NOT...
SIGH
...SAFE.
NO WORRIES, I GOTCHA COVERED. PINGING U.N. PATROLS NOW...
A-BOOOOOOOOOMMMMMMMMMMM!

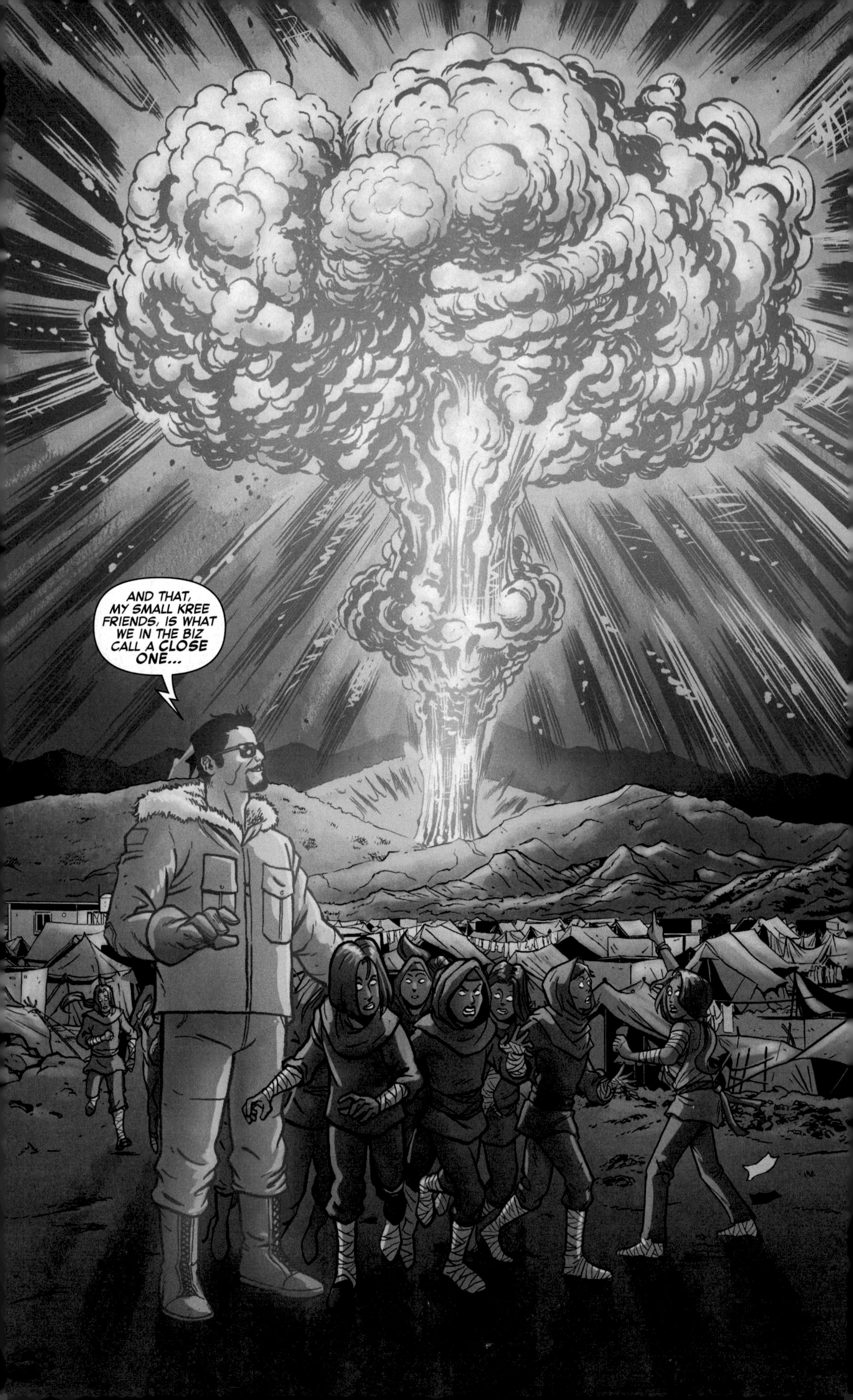
AND THAT, MY SMALL KREE FRIENDS, IS WHAT WE IN THE BIZ CALL A CLOSE ONE...

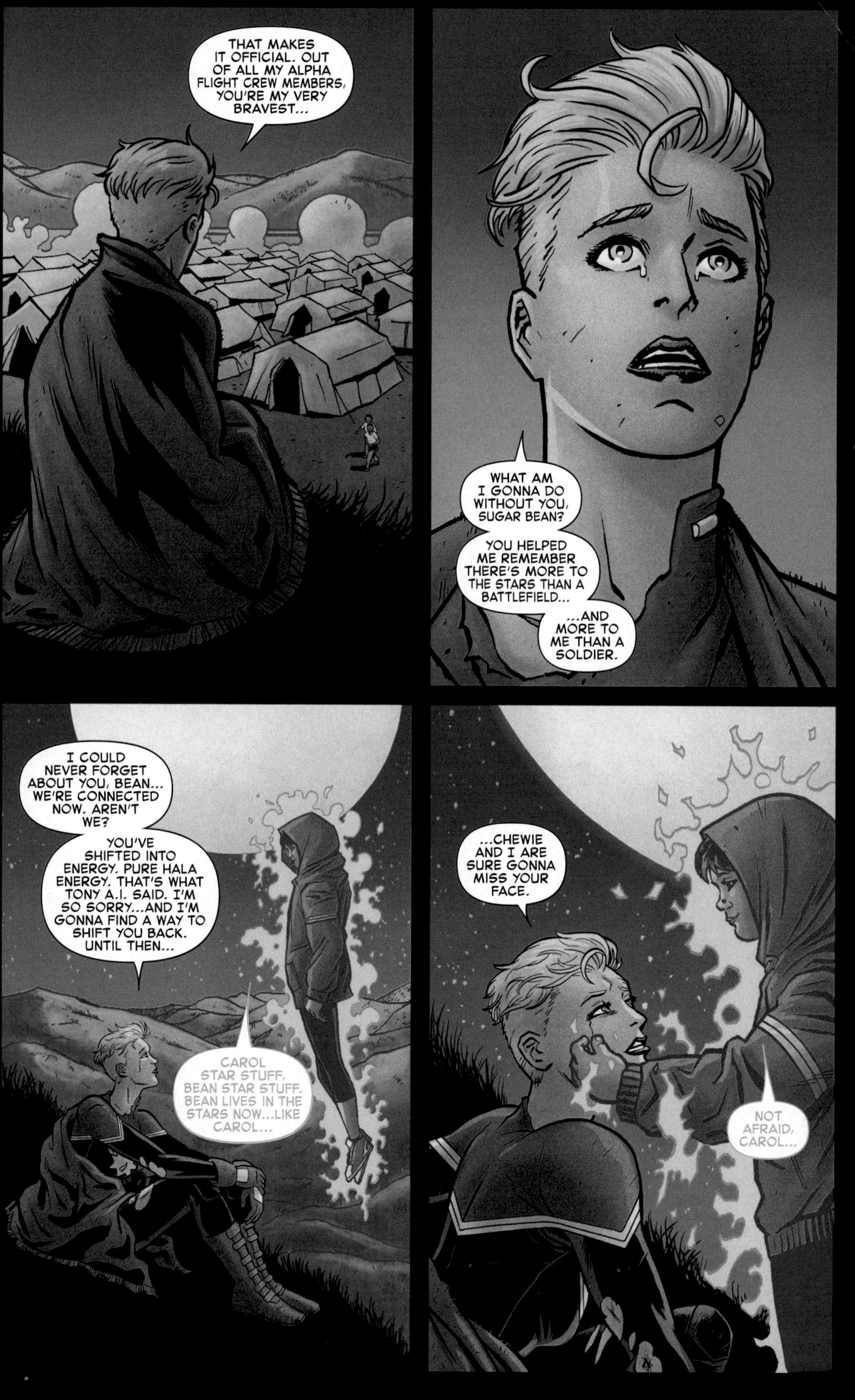
THAT MAKES IT OFFICIAL. OUT OF ALL MY ALPHA FLIGHT CREW MEMBERS, YOU'RE MY VERY BRAVEST...
WHAT AM I GONNA DO WITHOUT YOU, SUGAR BEAN?
YOU HELPED ME REMEMBER THERE'S MORE TO THE STARS THAN A BATTLEFIELD...
...AND MORE TO ME THAN A SOLDIER.
I COULD NEVER FORGET ABOUT YOU, BEAN... WE'RE CONNECTED NOW. AREN'T WE?
YOU'VE SHIFTED INTO ENERGY. PURE HALA ENERGY. THAT'S WHAT TONY A.I. SAID. I'M SO SORRY...AND I'M GONNA FIND A WAY TO SHIFT YOU BACK. UNTIL THEN...
CAROL STAR STUFF, BEAN STAR STUFF. BEAN LIVES IN THE STARS NOW...LIKE CAROL...
...CHEWIE AND I ARE SURE GONNA MISS YOUR FACE.
NOT AFRAID, CAROL...

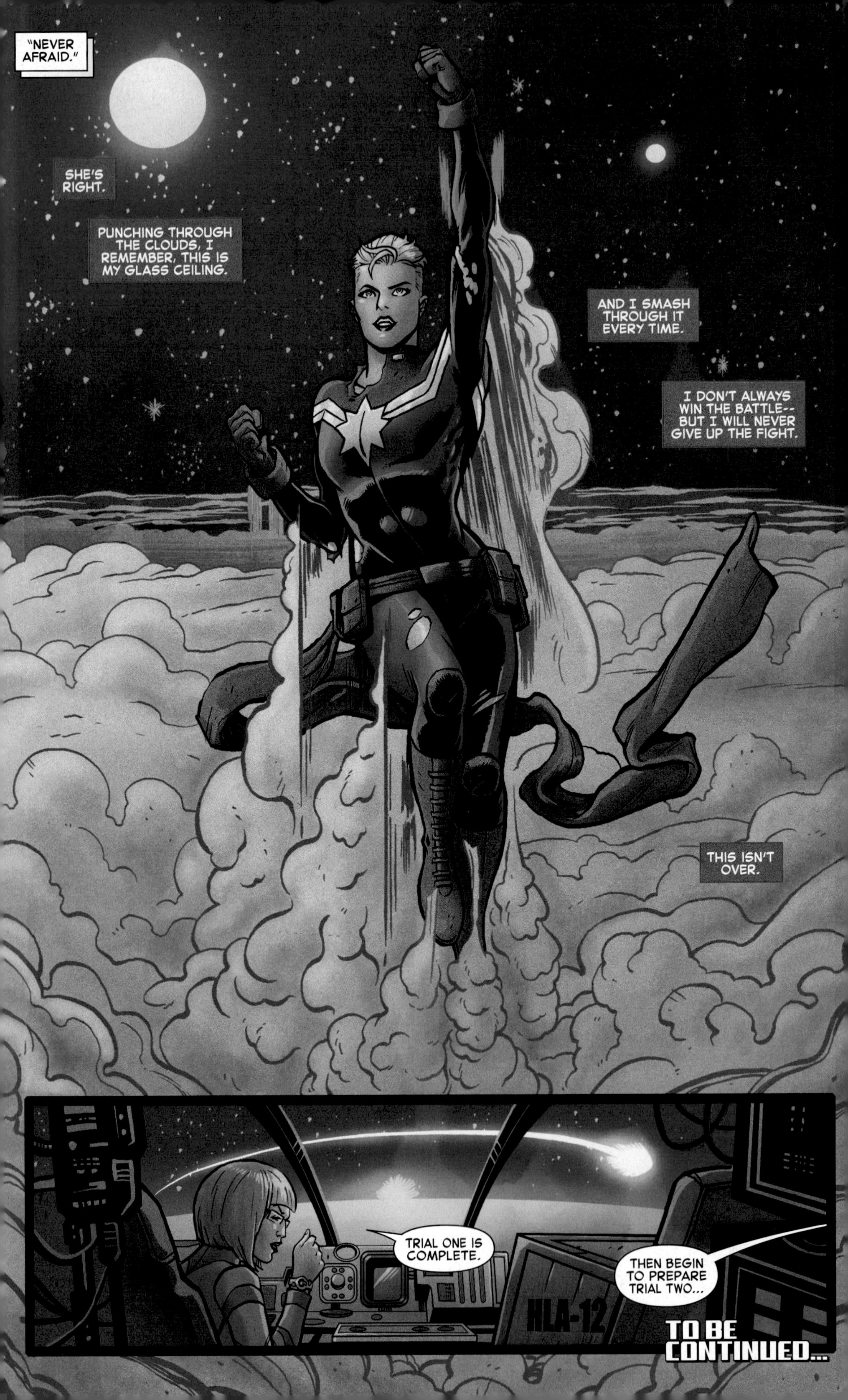
"NEVER AFRAID."
SHE'S RIGHT.
PUNCHING THROUGH THE CLOUDS, I REMEMBER, THIS IS MY GLASS CEILING.
AND I SMASH THROUGH IT EVERY TIME.
I DON'T ALWAYS WIN THE BATTLE-- BUT I WILL NEVER GIVE UP THE FIGHT.
THIS ISN'T OVER.
TRIAL ONE IS COMPLETE.
THEN BEGIN TO PREPARE TRIAL TWO...
HLA-12
TO BE CONTINUED...

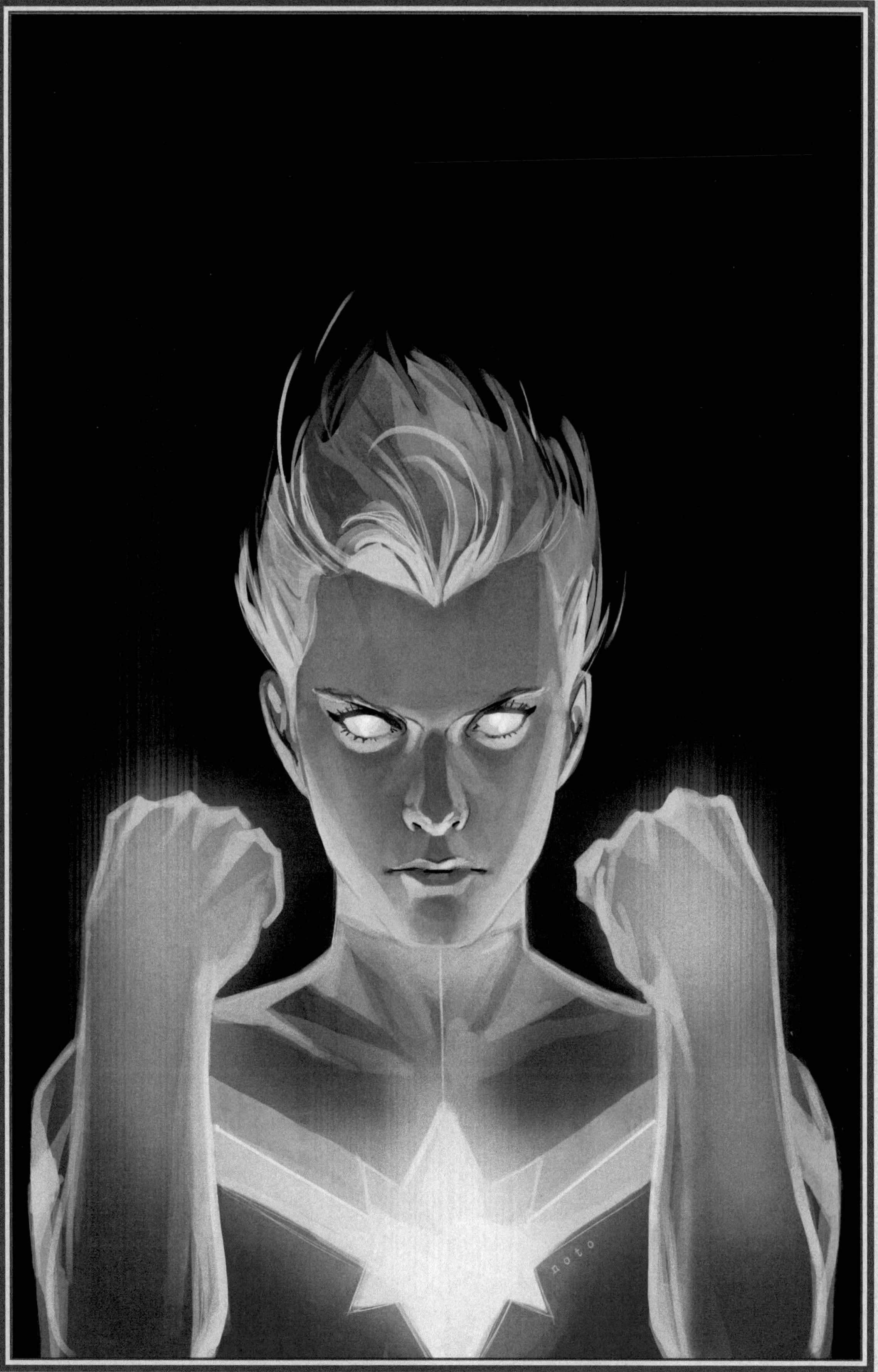
noto

#0 VARIANT BY
PHIL NOTO

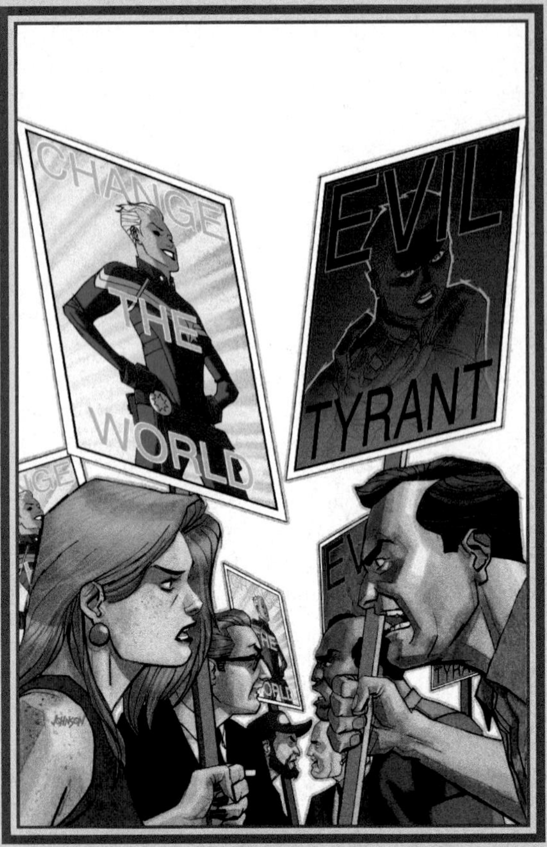
CHANGE
THE
WORLD
EVIL
TYRANT

#0 VARIANT BY
DAVE JOHNSON

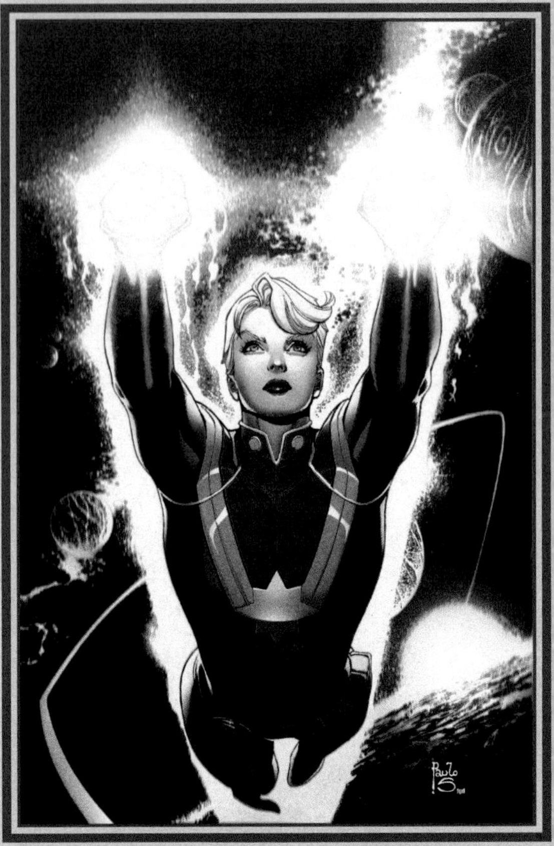

#1 VARIANT BY
PAULO SIQUEIRA

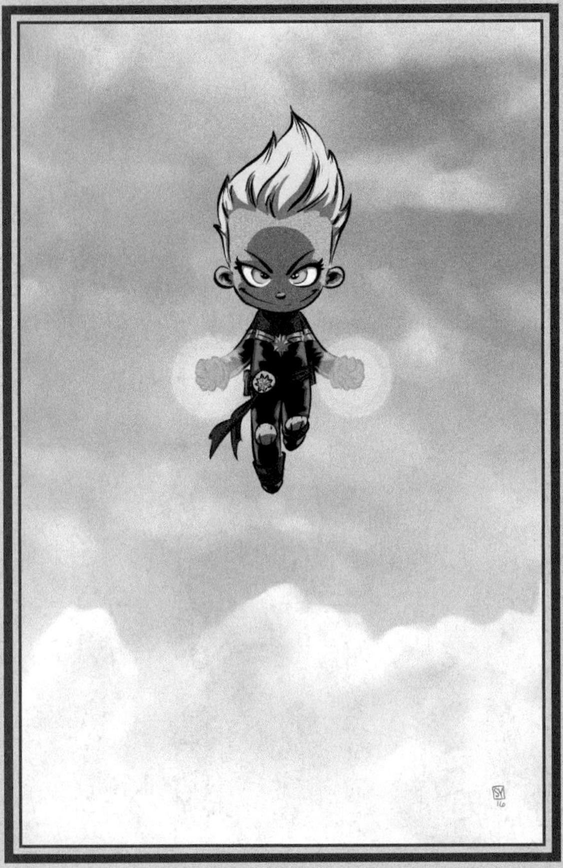

#1 VARIANT BY
SKOTTIE YOUNG

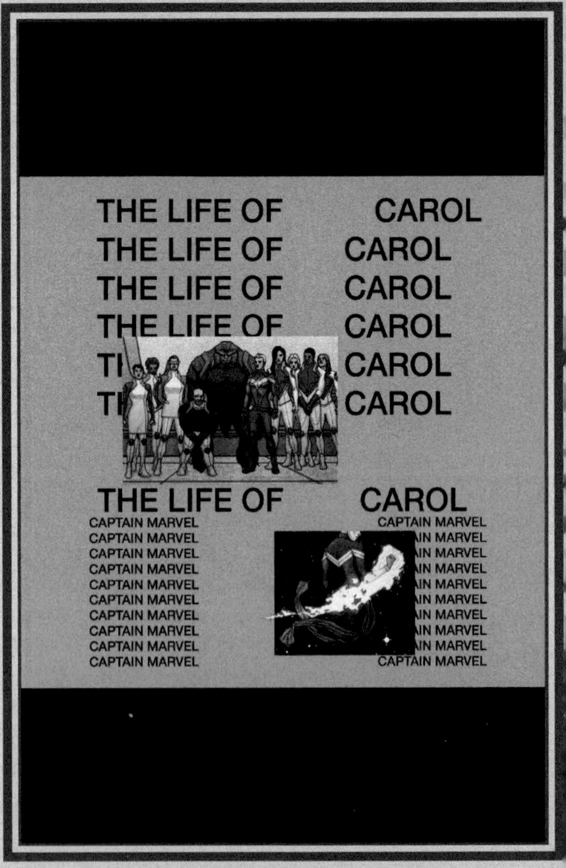
THE LIFE OF CAROL
THE LIFE OF CAROL
THE LIFE OF CAROL
THE LIFE OF CAROL
CAROL
CAROL
THE LIFE OF CAROL
CAPTAIN MARVEL
CAPTAIN MARVEL
CAPTAIN MARVEL
CAPTAIN MARVEL
CAPTAIN MARVEL
CAPTAIN MARVEL
CAPTAIN MARVEL
CAPTAIN MARVEL
CAPTAIN MARVEL
CAPTAIN MARVEL
CAPTAIN MARVEL
CAPTAIN MARVEL

#1 HIP-HOP VARIANT BY
JENNY FRISSON

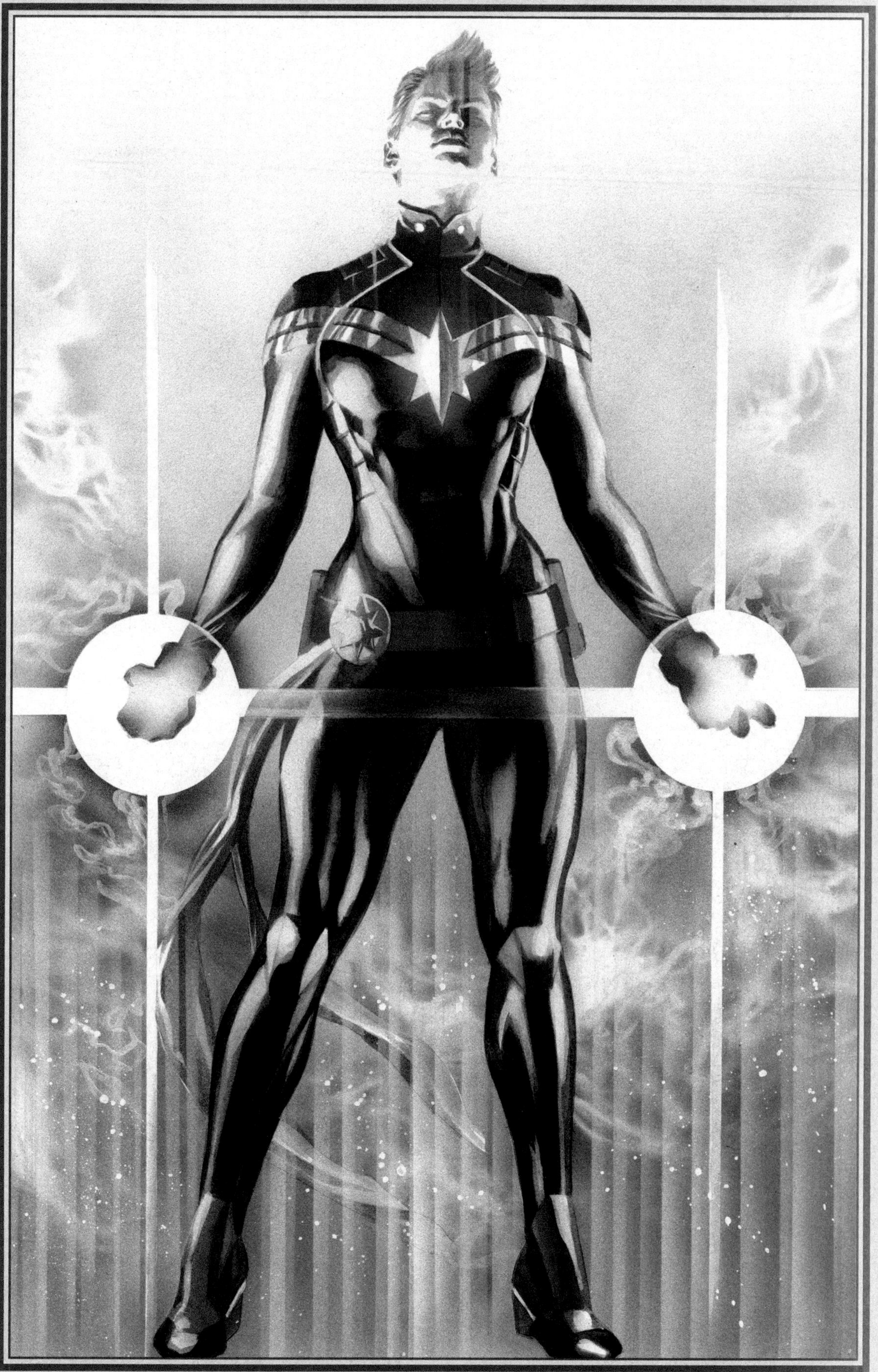

#0 VARIANT BY
ALEX ROSS

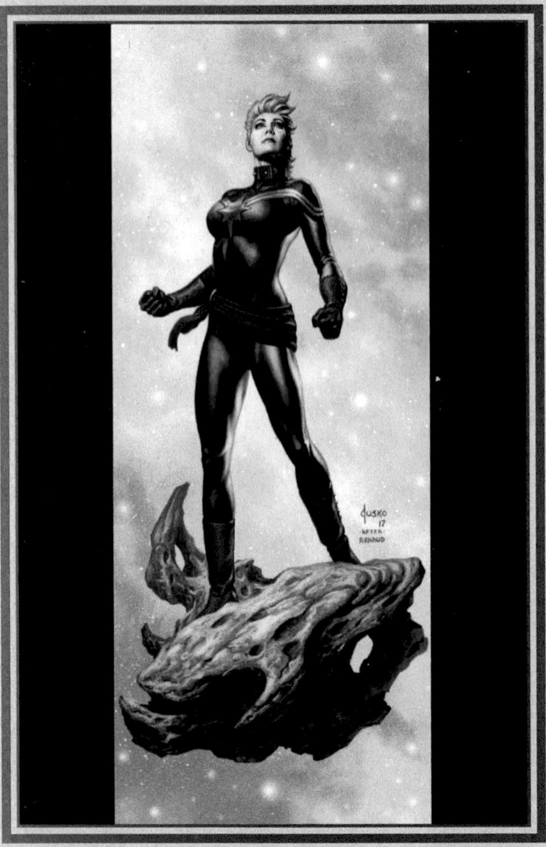

#2 CORNER BOX VARIANT BY
JOE JUSKO

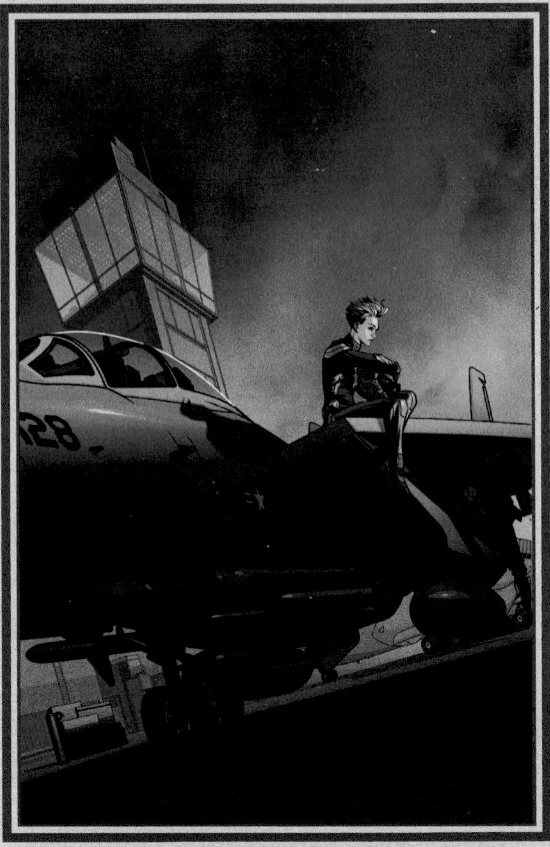

#2 VARIANT BY
MIKE McKONE & DAVE McCAIG

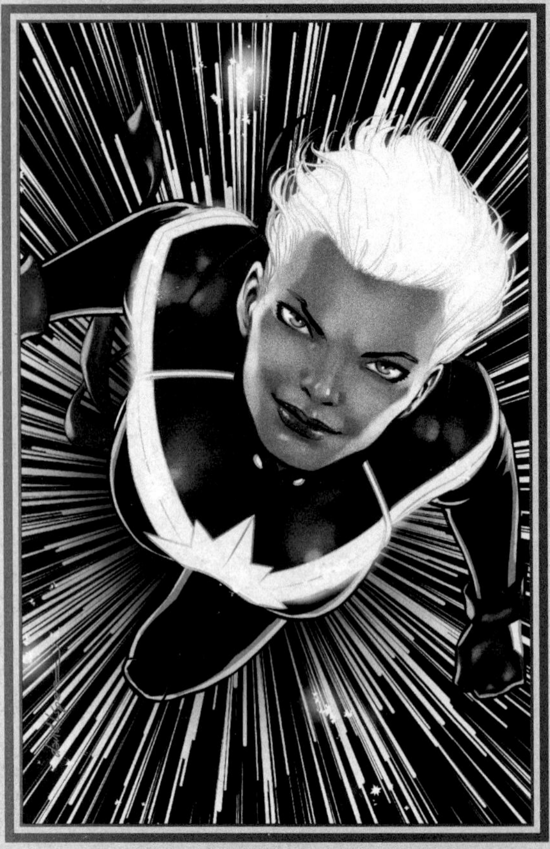

#3 VARIANT BY
DAVID LOPEZ

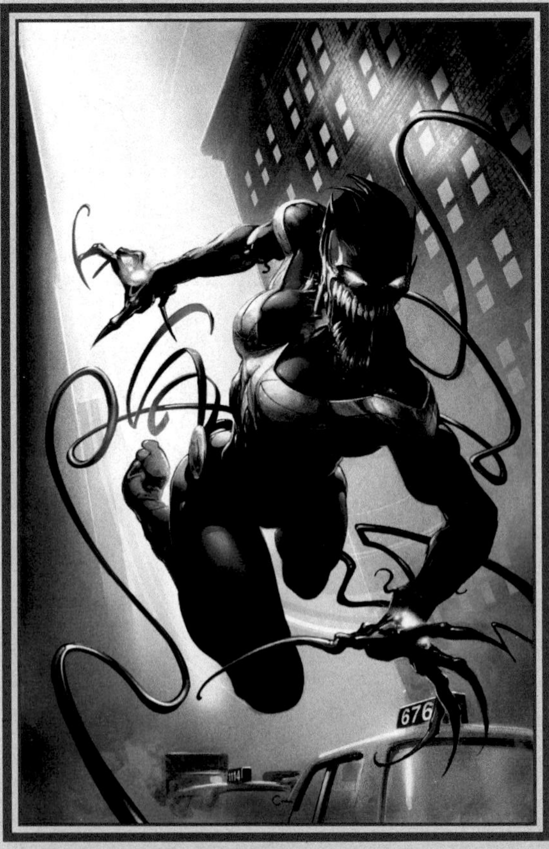
676

#3 VENOMIZED VARIANT BY
CLAYTON CRAIN